MAY THE CIRCLE BE UNBROKEN

MAY THE CIRCLE
BE UNBROKEN

AN INTIMATE JOURNEY
INTO THE HEART OF ADOPTION

LYNN C. FRANKLIN
WITH ELIZABETH FERBER

Harmony Books • *New York*

AUTHOR'S NOTE: Actual names have been retained for adoption professionals and public figures in the adoption community. When requested, names of other individuals and situations have been changed to protect their privacy and identity.
I refer throughout the book to "birth parents" in two words except when quoting other sources that refer to "birthparents" in one word. Both versions are in common usage.

Permissions for reprinting copy of already published material appear at the back of the book.

Published by Harmony Books, a division of Crown Publishers, Inc., 201 East 50th Street, New York, New York 10022. Member of the Crown Publishing Group.

Random House, Inc. New York, Toronto, London, Sydney, Auckland
www.randomhouse.com

HARMONY and colophon are trademark of Crown Publishers, Inc.

Printed in the United States of America

Design by Cynthia Dunne

Library of Congress Cataloguing-in-Publication Data

Franklin, Lynn C.
May the circle be unbroken : an intimate journey into the heart of adoption / by Lynn C. Franklin with Elizabeth Ferber. — 1st ed.
p.   cm.
Includes index.
1. Adoption—United States—Case studies. 2. Parent and child—United States—Case studies. 3. Adoptees—United States—Psychology—Case studies. 4. Birthparents—United States—Psychology—Case studies. I. Ferber, Elizabeth, 1967– . II. Title.
HV875.55.F7   1998
362.73'4'0973—dc21   98-7418
                                                         CIP

ISBN 0-517-70755-1
10   9   8   7   6   5   4   3   2   1

First Edition

In memory of my father, Joseph B. Franklin

Come outside the sun is shining
And the sky is endless blue
The leaves will sigh the wind's reminding
That this life was lent to you

Lyrics by Beth Nielsen Chapman

CONTENTS

PART TWO
Let Us Live in as Small a Circle as We Will (J. von Goethe)

PART THREE
The Wheel Is Come Full Circle (William Shakespeare)

ACKNOWLEDGMENTS

First and foremost, I would like to thank all members of my family for their support and participation. I especially thank my son and his parents for their trust in me and for their generous contribution to this book, which has served as a catalyst for us and has helped us gain understanding for each other. I would also like to thank my daughter-in-law for her loving spirit that nurtures and encourages us all. I hope this book will one day help the children understand more about their daddy and his parents and birth family and how the pieces of our lives fit together and the ties of love extend in many directions.

I thank my mother, Terry Franklin, and sister, Laurie Callahan, for their willingness to revisit the past and share their memories. In opening our hearts to each other, we have cleansed our souls of the secrets of so many years and have brought new light into our lives. A special thanks to my niece Erin, who at age ten read my proposal and urged me to write more about my feelings.

My sincere thanks also go to: Heather Schroder, my agent, who inspired—even pushed me—to write this book and whose confidence in my endeavor I have relied on. Elizabeth Ferber, whose steadfast efforts sustained me throughout our reading, interviewing, researching and writing. I am especially grateful for her dedication to learning the ins and outs of adoption and for helping me to write this book. Thanks go, too, to her agent and my friend Janis Vallely, whose insight and wisdom guided us throughout our collaboration. My editor, Shaye Areheart, whose early enthusiasm for the book never wavered and whose insightful editorial guidance inspired my best effort. Laura Orsini for transcribing volumes of interviews and for her expert research assistance. Her comments were always thoughtful and thought provoking. Candace Rondeaux for her unfailing willingness to read and reread innumerable versions of each chapter. She has been without doubt my most loyal reader and helpful critic, urging me on whenever she sensed my stamina waning. The many members of the

Spence-Chapin staff who lent their voices and their personal and professional support to me and to this project and those who read and fact-checked the manuscript. Special thanks to Katharine S. Legg, Joanne Remy, Gretchen Viederman, Judy Greene, Ronny Diamond, and Sandra Ripberger. Warm thanks are also extended to Judy Link for her sensitive personal understanding and to Eleanor Oakley for our much cherished Shelter Island conversations. All those birth mothers, adoptees, and adoptive parents who graciously contributed their stories that provide the emotional underpinning for the issues presented in this book.

Sincere gratitude is extended to Annette Baran, who took me under her wing and made sure I was meeting all the right people; Marcy Wineman Axness, who embraced my effort and gave generously of her time and experience and gave me extraordinarily detailed fact-checking and editorial notes; Carol Schaefer, whose book *The Other Mother* resonated deeply for me and who helped me stretch myself emotionally; Sharon Kaplan Roszia, who provided warm and wise counsel; and Lois Melina for her sensible and sound comments on portions of the manuscript.

Thanks as well to Madelyn Freundlich, executive director of the Evan B. Donaldson Adoption Institute, for reading and providing factual clarification, as well as to Debbie Martin, director of information management and research resources, for providing countless articles and the latest in adoption information.

Warm appreciation goes to trustees of Spence-Chapin's board of directors as well as the trustees of the Evan B. Donaldson Adoption Institute, who have been enthusiastic about this book and who have followed with interest its progress.

I am deeply indebted to my business partner, Todd R. Siegal, and our staff and publishing clients, and especially my author clients for their tolerance and encouraging support for this literary scout and agent who dared to see life from "the other side."

Special thanks go to friends Iara Rodrigues and Maria del Mar Ravassa, who were brave enough to read the earliest drafts of my manuscript and gave me the courage to believe in my work.

Finally, I thank all my friends who have stood by me even when that meant I had to excuse myself from many of our usual activities and gatherings.

Elizabeth Ferber gratefully acknowledges for their support and wisdom Jane S. Ferber, Josh and Gideon Lebowitz, and Janis Vallely.

PROLOGUE

There are moments in life that heighten our awareness about what it truly means to be alive. They bring us closer to our inner selves in a profound yet often inexplicable way. Death of a loved one can strip our souls bare; so can the renewal of ties with family separated by difficult circumstances. In his poem *The Waste Land,* T. S. Eliot says "April is the cruelest month." In April of 1993, I lost my father and was reunited with the son I had placed for adoption in 1966. I certainly felt the truth of Eliot's words, but that April also brought with it the promise of healing and regeneration. I found myself experiencing intermittent mind-numbing sadness along with utter joy and excitement. I was compelled to confront and find new meaning in the dramas of my earlier life, and to move toward the possibility of a brighter outlook for the future.

It began when I stepped out of a New York City cab in front of my apartment building into the tentative spring night air that tries to find a place for itself among the stone buildings and concrete sidewalks of Manhattan. I was exhausted the evening of April 4, not only from the long flight from Los Angeles, but also from the emotionally draining visit I had just had with my father, who was going through the final stages of prostate cancer. The lobby was quiet, shutting out the busy traffic outside, and I was fortifying myself, shifting gears, in order to greet a Russian friend waiting in my apartment upstairs. I headed for my mailbox, expecting nothing more than perhaps some catalogs and a few bills. What I was to discover in the narrow, steel box, one that rarely held any surprises for me, would inexorably change my life from that moment forward.

Inside was a letter from Spence-Chapin Services to Families and Children, the adoption agency where I had placed my newborn son twenty-seven years earlier. I kept looking from the agency's name in the upper left-hand corner of the envelope to my own name and address, trying to get a handle on time and space. Since 1966, I had been in touch only once (in 1990) to update my address and to inquire how I might file papers with the state so that my son would be able to find me if he was searching. I suppose it could have been some general informational letter, but I knew instinctively that it was not. My hands shook as I walked to the elevator. The doors parted; I stepped inside and carefully opened the envelope.

My premonition was correct. Spence-Chapin was informing me that my grown son had recently registered with the state, and he was seeking identifying information about me, in adoption lingo, his birth mother. My intense excitement was kept in check, tempered by the knowledge that I had just come from seeing my father for the last time. My feelings about these extraordinary events collided, and I would spend the next weeks, and indeed years, sorting through the beginning and ending of two of the most important relationships in my life. I couldn't take it all in at once. I had to compartmentalize my feelings in order to function.

I entered my apartment to find my gregarious Russian friend Vlad ready for his visit with me to begin. We began to talk as I clutched the letter in my hand. I have no idea what we said to each other. My mind was racing with the steps I needed to take next. At some point, I put up my hand, shook my head, apologized, and said that I had to call my parents. "You see," I said to my perplexed friend as I headed toward the bedroom to make my call, "I just read a letter in the elevator that's changing my life. I'll tell you about it in a minute."

"Mom," I began when my mother answered the phone, my voice just barely masking the emotion and tears that were welling up inside me. I quickly told her about the letter, and after a stunned pause, she said, "Darling, I'll tell Daddy," and hung up. A few minutes later they called me back, and they were both crying. My father, a retired career military officer and World War II veteran, a man who knew how to compose himself in the face of adversity, now allowed his emotions free rein. My mother said they were both crying from joy, that they had never forgotten the small boy handed over to the arms of others nearly three decades before.

My father was definitely getting his house in order those last weeks, sorting out his will and finances. Knowing that the end was near, he was determined to make everything as smooth as he could for my mother, as well as for me and my sister, Laurie, and niece Erin, then only eight years old. In the midst of this frantic effort, he was completely overjoyed at the news, despite his weak voice. He asked me if I was happy, and even though I could not process all that was happening, I answered him that yes, I was very happy, ecstatic really. My family was never good at discussing emotions, so it felt strange to share with my father these new overwhelming feelings. Still, everything about this time was strange. My dad was dying, and that was excruciating for me. It was important for every minute to count. This was our chance to lift off the layers of restraint and checked emotions, and I truly feel that my news brought him some final peace.

Like my mother and father, my sister, Laurie, offered unconditional love and acceptance regarding a possible reunion with my son. Her daughter, Erin, was until now the only child of the next generation in our family, and she carried with her all of our hopes and dreams for the family's future. During my father's final weeks, Laurie and Erin spent time with my parents. Erin sat with my father each day, held his hand, read to him, sang to him, and without emotional hindrances from the past, gave selflessly to her grandfather as he gained acceptance that the end was nearing. On the horizon, meanwhile, was a young man we had never known who brought with him the promise of new life, and who without them ever meeting also lifted my father's spirit in his last days.

During the next days, as my father was dying, going as gently as he could "into that good night," I turned my attention to the details of the letter. It told me that my son had the full support of his adoptive parents in seeking me out, and that he wanted more than just cursory information. The words in the letter initiated a litany of questions in my mind: "What is his name?" "Will he be like me?" and "Will he want to build a relationship?" I felt from the moment I received the letter that my life had changed. My perception that I was ultimately alone in the world was gone in a flash, replaced by a subtle sense that my universe was expanding. It was now me and "another," a son. I felt like I had slipped into a new skin.

I called the social worker who had written to me and met with her as soon as we could arrange a time. In our meeting, she gave me information about my son, including his name, Andrew, his family background and current occupation, and the fact that he was recently married. I in turn also provided details of my life to be shared with him. He had indicated that he was eager for us to talk before exchanging letters or pictures, and I readily agreed. But who would make the call? The answer was clear to me immediately. Andrew had waited all these years to know me and had had the courage to search for me. The least I could do was take the first step now. I left the agency full of new information about a grown man I had last seen as a five-day-old infant. The sensations swirling in my head were at once profound and surreal.

I related my new knowledge about my son to my parents, and as we pieced together the missing years, I sensed they were beginning to comprehend more fully what it had meant for me to relinquish my baby in 1966. My father had been very emotionally involved in the process but had left most of the work to my mother. As I recounted the details I had been given, painful memories, flashes from the past, disturbed my thoughts. It was as if by trying to move into the future and rid myself of decades of hiding my feelings and the truth, I was suddenly pulled back to the past, to relive the shame and to experience, at long last, the full depth of the loss. There is no canon of socially accepted rules on how to deal with the crater in a person's life that adoption creates. This principle certainly held true for me. For Andrew, I could not say how the loss of his birth mother affected him throughout his life. I would try to uncover and reconcile some of those hidden feelings in the years to come, but during that April of 1993, I could only speculate. My imagination, meanwhile, had often run wild through the years, as I wondered how he was doing, what he was feeling, and if I would ever see him alive. Now, I would know the truth and could let go of the fantasies.

As my world shifted, and I struggled to accommodate my new sense of self, my work kept me solidly grounded, as it always has. Nevertheless, the emotions were building as the story I had lived with in relative isolation for all these years began to unfold. I drew on inner resources I did not know I had, and relied on faith and my daily meditations as I prayed simultaneously for my father's gentle passing and for a joyful reunion with my son.

As I waited at my Shelter Island weekend refuge for the appointed time to call Andrew, I found myself as nervous as if I were waiting for word from a lover. My family had comforted me, and told me that they loved me. I needed to hear it. Tears were close at hand as I made the call and heard his voice for the first time. I was transported somewhere else, to a state of mind that I had never before experienced. I was talking to my child. I was immediately struck by his enthusiasm for life, his energy, and his love for his wife, Chloe. He assured me from the start that he had wonderful parents and was happy with the life he had with them. We talked for forty-five minutes, and I was floating by the time we ended the conversation. For me, this was truly a dream come true, and I felt blessed beyond measure for the simple details that Andrew shared about his life. We ended by setting a date to meet on April 28.

The end of the month neared, and my father slipped in and out of consciousness. My mother said she noticed an immediate decline in his health directly after my sister and niece departed. He was no longer able to speak, but my mother reported that he smiled when he heard my voice. I would have liked to have given Dad a picture of Andrew, but that never happened. On the eve of April 21, my mother told me to prepare myself, and I already began to miss him. I felt my father's love for me and was so glad that we had shared such momentous and joyful news before the end. On April 22, at six-thirty in the morning, I wrote a simple sentence in my journal: "He's gone." His funeral at Arlington National Cemetery was set for April 28— the same day that Andrew and I were first scheduled to meet.

On the day of the funeral, Andrew left a message for me on my home answering machine. He said he was thinking about me and the family, and he hoped I was doing all right. Another week would pass before we would meet.

INTRODUCTION

Until Andrew and I met, I had had almost no contact with other birth parents and had never known any adoptive families intimately. That all changed soon after the reunion when I was invited to join a birth parent advisory committee at Spence-Chapin. As I came face-to-face with other birth mothers, I discovered how adoption practices have changed since the 1960s and 1970s. I also attended workshops where I met adoptees and adoptive parents. A whole new world opened up for me as I learned how families are created through adoption. I quickly realized that although I had direct insight into how birth parents perceive their experience, I knew nothing about the life of adoptive families. Like most people, I had based my opinions on what I read in the papers or saw on television, and I now know how limited a view that is.

Adoption can be a wonderful way of creating a family. The woman who is not able or ready to parent can offer her child a life she could not otherwise provide, and she can go on to lead a productive fulfilling life. The child can grow in a family that is prepared to love him as their own and can have the same fun of childhood and the growing pains of adolescence as his non-adopted peers. The adoptive parents who are given the gift of that child to love can have the same joy of raising a family as any of their friends and relatives. No life, however, is lived free of pain, and people involved with adoption have their share of sadness and loss. Their true feelings are often hidden or overlooked, and the general public has the barest notion of the underlying issues inherent in adoption. I learned firsthand that even members of the adoption triad of birth parents, adoptees, and adoptive parents may know little of one another's experience.

While there is no lack of love in adoptive families, the issues at the heart of adoption are not a consideration for families that are biologically related. There are feelings and experiences that are unique to adoption. It begins with one set of parents deciding to surrender their child, and the effect of relinquishment on their lives is lifelong. The adopted child grows up knowing he was relinquished, and as he grows and establishes his individuality he has to assimilate the different parts of who he is. That includes reconciling what he has inherited genetically and what he takes from his adoptive upbringing. Most people adopt because they are unable to have their own biological children. They live with the memory of lost dreams and raise children who were born to other parents.

Each of us in the adoption triad is challenged to come to terms with our experience. It is often difficult and lonely. Feelings are not always easily communicated, and we do not always listen to one another. We naturally shy away from emotional discomfort or uncertainty. When we cut ourselves off from one another's feelings we are vulnerable to misunderstanding and misinterpretation, and we limit our opportunity for growth and true intimacy. Yet, the reality of people's experience is the basis of any mutual understanding. While it may be difficult to open ourselves to one another, it provides us an opportunity for greater clarity and understanding. This in turn allows us to deepen our connections with the people we love. The therapeutic process is based on this principle.

In writing this book, I have sought clarity for myself by exploring the inner reaches of the adoption experience. I have read extensively and have had the privilege of interviewing scores of people who reveal themselves in these pages. In the process, I have had to examine feelings of my own that had long been buried, and at times have had to overcome my own fear of looking too deeply into the recesses of my heart. I have needed to draw on strength I did not know I had and have looked to others for guidance and counsel. Through it all, as I give voice to birth parents, adoptees, and adoptive parents, I have been propelled forward in my desire to break through our stereotypical judgments and to provide a fully three-dimensional perspective of everyone affected by adoption.

I have structured this book as a written conversation with space allotted for each member of the triad. I follow the chronology of adoption, beginning with the birth parents' decision to relinquish and the adoptive parents' decision to adopt. I look closely at how birth parents move on in their lives and how children grow up in their adoptive homes, and I end with families in search and reunion. Each section explores the experiences of birth parents, adoptees, and adoptive parents respectively, and each chapter opens with a personal account of our family's adoption story. Andrew and his adoptive parents have generously contributed their memories and thoughts about their lives, individually and as a family, and together our voices serve as a springboard into the larger picture of how adoption shapes people's reality.

It is my hope that fellow members of the triad who read this book will find their experience validated and will feel a deeper kinship with other members of the triad. It is my hope that our extended families, neighbors, friends, and acquaintances will also gain new insight into this special world. For those who come thinking about adopting, it is my hope you will be better prepared to assume your role as parents and to embark on the wonderful journey of raising your children. And for readers with no connection to adoption, I hope you will find resonance in your own life with the stories and experiences shared in these pages. For although I am writing specifically about adoption, I am also writing more broadly about childhood and parenting and how we can all grow up and stretch beyond our fears when faced with personal adversity. Although the roots of our experiences may be different, many of the feelings are common to us all, and there are parallels we can draw with other situations that life presents to us. As we expand our own awareness of one another's reality, we can be agents for change in our families and in our community.

My inner inquiry has led me to explore new approaches to old dilemmas, broaden the definition of family, and truly examine what we are all capable of in our relationships with others. It has taught me that change is possible when we want it, and that it opens doors to a different future. I believe that when we listen carefully, trust in ourselves, take a chance, step out and seize the moment, we all have an opportunity to stretch our boundaries and experience a new and richer dimension of life.

PART ONE

WEAVE A CIRCLE
ROUND HIM

SAMUEL TAYLOR COLERIDGE

ONE

CONSUME MY HEART AWAY

The Birth Parents' Farewell

Lullabye Goodbye

> One memory sweet
> I'll always keep
> Though it will make me cry
> The day I gave
> You life and sang
> This lullabye goodbye
>
> Lyrics by Beth Nielsen Chapman

THERE IS A mythology surrounding the first time one makes love. It is an act that holds all the potential and awe of adulthood, the loss of childhood and innocence, and it is the ultimate act of independence from one's family. When I first had sex, it was also considered a sin for a young, unmarried woman to have "carnal relations," a transgression for which she should be ashamed and perhaps pay a price. What I knew and felt during the time I was dating Tom in 1965 was that I was taking part in the great American culture of romance, that I was like most of my peers. I had spent so many childhood years feeling like the outsider, the skinny, self-conscious, shy "army brat" who was somehow not a part of my own American society. We had been stationed in France during my early teen years, and I attended the French *lycée*. Coming back for my senior year of high school had been tough, and I had been eager to get to college.

My father was often away on military assignments during my early life. While home, he was loving and affectionate but also strict and controlling. This was true when I was a child and continued on through my adolescent and young adult years. We have never talked easily as a family, and we have tended to act out rather than discuss our feelings, allowing them to build up until they spill over. Tom represented a break from the confining discipline, and being with him gave me an opportunity to experiment with a blossoming, but not terribly experienced, side of myself. There was also, I suppose, an element of rebellion to my attraction to him. He was a German national serving in the American Army. My father had served in World War II and was in one of the first groups to enter Dachau when the war ended. We are also Jewish by birth, and although he tried, it was especially hard for my father to extend himself to Tom's German military father. Mostly, however, I think I was drawn to him because of his good looks, and because he was foreign and reminded me of my friends in Europe.

Tom and I were together for over a year, and I spent time visiting him at the base. During the summer of 1965, he was sent to Europe. I had no idea that I was pregnant, and it did not occur to me that anything was wrong until August, when I had the first symptoms of morning sickness. My family was on vacation in Puerto Rico when I started feeling nauseated and had trouble eating. I could barely get through a day's sight-seeing. My mother has a picture on her bureau of me taken during that trip, and every time I look at it I think back on how sick I was. Somehow, in some part of my brain, I managed to push back the truth and to keep anyone from knowing how I was feeling. It was the beginning of my secret life.

I was very thin then, and the fact that I gained little weight—and hid my growing bulge with a girdle—allowed me to hide the truth from everyone for six months. The death of my grandfather in my fourth month stalled my plan to tell my mother. I know that I just wanted this problem to go away, that I wanted to miscarry and pretend that nothing had ever happened. The stress I was feeling must have affected the nascent life growing inside me, but I was not yet thinking about the pregnancy as a baby that might some-day be born. When I finally told my mother, she was furious at herself for not catching on earlier. "To say it was a shock is putting it mildly," she says. My father was devastated, and my mother also tells me he could not get over what was happening to his "bright and beautiful" daughter. He did not actually tell me how deeply shattered he felt, but I immediately felt a sense of shame and disappointment from him that I spent much of my adult life trying to overcome.

Events continued to unfold without my having much control over them, but I followed, trying to be the dutiful daughter making her way back into the family's heart. I wrote to Tom in Europe, and to the surprise of those around me, he came back on emergency leave, prepared to marry me. I remember feeling pleased by his response and excited that we would get married. Nobody in my family wanted the marriage, although this was what society expected of middle- and upper-middle-class white girls circa 1965 who stepped over the line of acceptable behavior and found themselves in my situation. My father never really liked Tom and wanted nothing to do with him when he came back. My mother says, "He thought he was a very cocky young man, and he felt that the relationship was based on a physical attraction, that it wasn't a real love." She reluctantly went along with plans for a private wedding, which Dad refused to attend. Everything was happening so fast, that I did not know what to do exactly. I was as much afraid my parents would reject me if I married Tom, as if I did not. He was a good guy, but I had never really thought about marriage, and when I did, I realized we had very different dreams and aspirations.

Our family friend Presbyterian minister Henry Baumann and our wonderful next-door neighbor Jane Elliot begged me to think through what I was doing. This was the first time in my life I knew my actions had real consequences. At the time, however, we were only focused on whether or not to marry. It had not yet registered that not marrying meant giving up the baby. One evening, Tom and I went to a party organized by friends of his. When I grew tired and wanted to leave, Tom resisted and remarked sarcastically, "So this is the way it's going to be." He did not seem to care that I was pregnant and only wanted to stay with his friends. I had an epiphany of sorts and somehow knew that the marriage would result in an even greater disaster than the one I was already in. I know he had returned to the States to do what he thought was right, but ultimately, I think he also knew it would be a mistake. I realize now how difficult it must have been for him to handle what was happening, and that he must have been terrified of a marriage with someone he was not sure he loved. He was also trying to cope in a clearly hostile environment, and in a sense it is no wonder he needed to party with his friends.

Tom did not seem bitter when my family and I saw him off at the military airport. He even seemed cheerful. Later when I was alone at the maternity home, I wondered about that and was upset that he was able to get on a plane without any indication he was thinking about the baby. I know now that birth fathers do not readily connect to their unborn child, and his reaction makes more sense to me. He was off the hook, and more than anything, he must have been relieved. I also think my family gave him permission to drop out, as we preferred to take matters into our own hands.

I spoke to Tom once more, a month after Andrew was born, and he seemed surprised about the adoption. I was surprised too by his response, because I was certain I had told him that is what I would do. It obviously had not registered. Now I sometimes wonder what in fact I had told him. In Europe, it is not as common as here for people to relinquish a child for adoption, and I can appreciate that it might not have been clear to him under the stressful circumstances. In any case, it was the last time we spoke.

After Tom left we moved quickly to finalize our plans. With the baby due in March, there was little time. I felt that so much was out of my control; my parents discussed options and exchanged information without consulting me. I found out many years later, for example, that when Tom's parents learned I had relinquished the baby, they were outraged, for they had expected me to keep Andrew. They sent my parents a telegram, which I never saw.

To this day I sometimes ask myself if we had talked more openly as a family whether we might have decided to raise Andrew ourselves. I do not remember much about my conversations with my family, but my mother says, "We talked about how we felt that the child would be better off having a father and a mother to bring him up." She adds, "But the separation was traumatic for everybody. None of us ever got over it, especially you, my dear, but none of us did." In retrospect, I see that we had no place to turn, no support group to attend, no books to read that would guide us through this lonely journey that at any other time in life, and under other circumstances, would be such a joyous experience. My mother has told me recently about how she and my father deliberated and considered the various options. They were especially concerned about my education, because my mother had not been able to go to college, and my father had left after only one year:

> You were nineteen and we wanted you to go back to school and get
> your degree. If we kept him, I would have brought him up and we
> didn't think that was a good idea. He would have been pulled this way

and that, and there would have been times when we disagreed about how he was to be raised, and you could have taken him away at any moment. Your father felt that I would have been brokenhearted and that since we had raised our family, it would be better if the child were with someone younger, someone who couldn't have children of their own, who could give the child a good home.

My sister, Laurie, who was fourteen at the time, knew I was pregnant, but true to family form, we did not talk much about it. "I was not part of the decision-making process," she says. "It was pretty much all up to my parents."

In the midst of everything, I was trying to finish the semester at college, and I still hid the pregnancy from everyone I could by wearing large coats and oversize shirts. I do not know who I really fooled. Our next-door neighbor Jane, herself the mother of seven, was a great comfort to me. I was able to discuss with her many of the fears and concerns I had that I could not or would not talk to my parents about. In my mind, I longed for the problem to go away, for the situation to be resolved. I wanted to get on with my young life.

First, I needed to have the baby. Shortly after Tom left, I went to New York for the last weeks of my pregnancy. The doctor at the army clinic in Virginia where I was examined told my parents about a maternity residence in the city, and from the residence, we learned of Spence-Chapin, an adoption agency that would find suitable parents for my child.

My memories of this time are vague. I wrapped myself in a tight cocoon and got through each day. I had the support of my parents, but I knew that they too wanted the bad dream to end and for their innocent Lynn to return to her "virginal" state. Somehow, I walled off my feelings to prepare for what lay ahead.

The maternity residence did nothing to foster my or anyone else's maternal senses, but they did try to engage us in activities suited to "proper" young women, like sewing (I made two skirts), and trips to museums. It all seemed rather beside the point considering "our condition," but it did pass the time. My sense is that none of us, at least none of us where I was staying, wanted to create any more trouble. We wanted to make right our wrongs and go home. I do not remember talking to anyone about whether or not they wanted to keep their babies, but I am sure some of us were thinking about it.

In her book *The Other Mother,* Carol Schaefer describes how she and the

other women at Seton House maternity residence had to confess regularly
their "mortal sin." Although the nuns and priest of Seton House, and society in general, considered Carol and the other women at her residence sin-
ners, she knew she desperately wanted to keep her baby, and unlike me and
the teens and women I knew in my maternity home, tried to find a way. She
tells of meeting with one of the nuns to try to persuade her to help her:

> The last time I had sat opposite her I had been a naive teenager accom-
> panied by my mother. Now I felt I had matured almost to the point of
> becoming an old woman. Boldly I leaned forward and rested my folded
> hands on the edge of the desk. "I can't go through with this," I stated,
> looking her square in the eyes. Since I had lived such a sheltered life, I
> didn't know exactly what to ask for in the way of assistance. I had
> known no one who was raising a baby as a single mother.

There was no guidance for Carol on how to keep her baby, nor was there
any for many others who hoped and prayed in silent darkness for someone
to show them a place where they and their babies could live together.

Cynthia Beals also spent time in a Catholic maternity residence while she
was pregnant, but for her it was a safe haven away from the turmoil of her
family life:

> I was protected from society's and my family's judgments, and I was
> able to continue my senior year of high school. The nuns were very
> non-judgmental and gave me a completely new perspective on Catholic
> nuns. I felt more love there than anywhere else and support for the
> schoolwork I wanted to do. They also told me while I was there, that it
> was my choice whether I wanted to keep the baby or not. I think that's
> what got me through the six months I was there, the love that I had for
> my child and that I would be able to take her home.

Cynthia ultimately surrendered her baby, but the intensity with which
she connected to her infant during pregnancy left a lifelong impression on
both mother and child.

The stories of these women impress me because they have clear memories
of their experiences and had strong feelings about wanting to keep their
babies. I, on the other hand, was still basically operating on automatic, following only semiconsciously the program set by my parents, and I remember very little from my time at the residence. I was numb to what was
happening to me, as if it were someone else's life. I do know that we were

not prepared in any way for the experience of labor and delivery. My labor began on a weekend when my parents happened to be visiting from Washington, D.C. The twenty-seven-hour ordeal was complete with water breaking, vomiting, moaning, and pain like I had never known before. My mother and father staggered their time with me in the labor room, and I remember Dad staying with me as I threw up and tried to keep breathing. We did not say much to each other. I was terrified and yearned for someone to care for me. Without ever being able to say anything directly, I think he sensed that. I know he needed to be sure his daughter was all right. We were perhaps closest that day in the tacit understanding of our needs.

The pain became too excruciating to bear, and the anesthesiologist began giving me Demerol. I was completely knocked out for the birth. When I came to, I remember being told it was a boy. I asked if he was okay, and then I looked at the clock to check the time of birth. Later, one of the first things the doctor said to me was how lucky I was to have a father who would come to the hospital with me. Most parents would have nothing to do with their daughter's hospital stay, but I was too traumatized at the time to appreciate that my mother and father were the exception.

Andrew was taken to the nursery, and my father left the hospital, unable to bring himself to see the grandson he would never know. I think he just expected I would have a girl, since we did not have a boy in our family, and he was overcome. My mother stayed with me and remained a constant presence. I only recently realized how painful it was for her to bear both my pain and the loss of her first grandchild.

Hospital staff have never been overly sensitive with birth mothers, or 'out-of-wedlock' mothers, as they referred to us back then. Doctors and nurses lacked, and still do in many cases, training with adoption issues and are generally prone to the same misconceptions regarding birth parents as the rest of society. My experience with the staff at New York Hospital, however, was not overtly negative. Nor was anyone particularly hostile to me. I was on a ward, and I can recall the doctors on rounds going by my bed commenting that I was "o/w" (out-of-wedlock), but I was allowed to see and care for my baby boy.

When I first saw him, feelings poured over me that I never could have anticipated while I was pregnant, never truly believing that a perfect person in miniature would miraculously appear from inside my womb. There was another teen in the bed next to me, and she and I sat together in our beds, holding the infants that would soon go home with someone else. We talked about their toes, their eyelashes, and their button mouths hollering for food. My mother and I both thought Andrew looked like my father.

When the nurses brought the babies back each morning, I continued to marvel at this new life. I held him close, I talked to him and told him how much I loved him. I tried to memorize his features and looked for distinguishing marks that I might recognize later. In the course of the five days I spent with Andrew, I did make one decision that made me, even for the briefest of moments, indisputably his mother. It was routine in the hospital to ask parents if they wanted their sons circumcised, and when I made this decision for Andrew, I began to realize the enormity of the loss that lay ahead for me.

Andrew was nestled in my arms one afternoon when my ward mate pulled a camera out of her bag and took a picture of us. I still wonder what became of that photograph, that single memento of a time that has long been etched in my memory. I would give a great deal to have that snapshot of the two of us, child and mother together, before time put so many years between us. With that picture went my youthful spark and some of my trust and hope for the future.

Our Final Days Together

Only what I have lost is what I possess forever.

Rachel

I had five days in the hospital to shower upon my baby all the maternal love I would be allowed for the next twenty-seven years. I knew that we would soon be parted, and I was shattered. Perhaps it was then that I began to draw on my experience as a military child, one who was always having to let go, never able to hold on to anyone for too long before saying good-bye. Already conditioned to these feelings, I summoned my strength to bid Andrew farewell.

My mother and I left the hospital with Andrew and took a taxi to the agency's door. I was conscious as we drove through the city streets of looking out at people involved in their everyday lives. As we arrived in front of the agency, I struggled to get out of the taxi, holding the baby in one arm and formula in the other. A casual passerby would not have noticed anything out of the ordinary, whereas I have never forgotten that image of myself as a nineteen-year-old teenager at the doors of the adoption agency, where within the hour I would say good-bye to my baby.

We were escorted into the agency and shown to a small room where we were given a few minutes to be with Andrew. I felt rushed and pressed by the social worker who took charge of us. I clearly remember my anger and thinking that I was in enemy territory. Gretchen Viederman, the current director of domestic adoptions, remembers, "We had two elevators, one carried the birth mothers, and the other the adoptive parents. We stopped that practice of keeping things hidden and apart long ago."

As my mother held my free hand, I signed the papers that officially terminated my parental rights to Andrew. My mother says, "I don't think the terrible sadness about what we were doing actually came about until you had the child and you were signing those papers." When it was over, and we had said good-bye to the tiny, swaddled bundle, we walked down Fifth Avenue back to the maternity home. I could not fully absorb then everything I was feeling. I liken it to looking out over the Grand Canyon. Being overpowered by its vastness, I was able to experience very little. A feeling of nothingness hung over me. Apparently this sensation is not unusual, because I have since heard many birth mothers speak of how they shut down to cope with the trauma of relinquishment.

After a few more days in New York City, my mother and I traveled back to Virginia to begin life over again, each of us accompanied by the ghosts we had both helped to create. Adoptee and author Betty Jean Lifton talks extensively of the spirits that inhabit the "Ghost Kingdom" of people touched by adoption. In her book, *Journey of the Adopted Self,* she says the birth mother "is accompanied by a retinue of ghosts. The ghost of the baby she gave up. The ghost of her lost lover, whom she connects with the baby. The ghost of the mother she might have been. And the ghosts of the baby's adoptive parents." These ghosts accompany us for a lifetime.

I was encouraged to put the past behind me by the few people who knew what had happened. I was expected to get my life back on track. I worked for several months before returning to school, moving forward in a daze of supposed normalcy, while on the inside I cried out to hold the infant who was no longer in my arms. I longed to embrace a baby, feel the tiny, precious weight of a new body, and nuzzle my face in the smooth down that rests atop an infant's head. Whenever I could, I would visit my neighbor Jane and spend time with her six-month-old baby boy. That is how I connected with my own pain and managed to feel during those stolen moments the deep well of grief I held within me. I held that baby much as Andrew must have been held by his adoptive mother, and I whispered to him about my baby boy. Margaret Moorman, birth mother and author of *Waiting to Forget,* writes of a similar experience after baby-sitting one night: "How was this night different from all other nights? It was the only time I had thought of the child I had relinquished as 'my baby.' It was the only moment when simple grief broke through my protective shell."

I had to be with and hold a baby even if it could not be my own. That was the only way I could keep going and begin to heal. Instinctively I knew, as Lao-tzu says, "A journey of a thousand miles starts from beneath one's feet." My feet, while bruised and battered from months of trauma, would move haltingly toward the redemptive power of healing in the decades before me.

How Society Set the Stage

Adoption forces people to embrace a certain set of
beliefs.... Without those beliefs, adoption would
probably not take place.

Marlou Russell

In the 1960s in the United States, society looked upon few things with such shaming judgment as a woman with an unwanted pregnancy. The message from the prevailing culture was quite clear, as plainly as is written in Corinthians 5:4—"Ye are fallen from Grace." The threat of the fall did not, nor will it ever, prevent a pregnancy. When actually faced with one, most family members, religious advisors, medical practitioners, and educational professionals put their collective heads together and tried to determine the swiftest and most clandestine cure for the condition. Prior to World War II, a child born out-of-wedlock was usually considered a child of sin, the fruit of an obviously mentally deranged woman. After the war, the tainted mother was offered a redemptive option by society: adoption. Until 1972, however, school officials could legally expel her from an educational institution.

In 1957, the official number of children born to mothers who were not married rose for the first time above 200,000, and many considered it an undercount of gross proportions. Abortions were not legal until *Roe v.*

Wade in 1973, but doctors did perform the procedure if you knew where to find them and if you had enough money to pay their fees. Even if money was available, doctors very often insisted on sterilizing the woman. Bonnie Bis, who is currently the national president of Concerned United Birthparents (CUB), remembers what it was like when abortion was not legal. "I was typically naive for those days," she says, "and I certainly didn't know any abortionists or anyone who had had an abortion. I feel strongly pro-choice now, but at the time, I don't know what I would have done if I had had the chance to have an abortion."

An unwed pregnant woman was always a fertile subject for gossip. In *The Other Mother,* Carol Schaefer says, "out-of-wedlock pregnancies were an intriguing topic of conversation, but never discussed except in whispers and innuendoes. To the whole community, as well as my parents, secrecy was easier. I did not feel 'unwed' or 'out of wedlock.' I felt pregnant with a baby for whom I already had a great deal of love. But I accepted the situation. This was how it was done."

The climate of the 1960s was such that women like me felt we had no choice. The social stigma of our situation was considered untenable, and our parents assumed authority over us. We were for the most part quite young and often emotionally immature, and without financial resources we acquiesced and did what we were told. Even today, many young women find themselves in similar situations. Whether it be the 1960s or the 1990s, the decision to relinquish is traumatic. It is made when women are extremely vulnerable, during a crisis pregnancy or after the birth of a baby when hormones are fluctuating wildly. It is made within the frame of a set of circumstances that cause them to feel they cannot, or are simply not ready to, parent their child. When the decision to relinquish is made with the benefit of good counseling, it may in fact be the best decision for mother —and child—given the circumstances of that woman at that time. Those of us who have relinquished might say with hindsight that we would not sur-render our children again even if faced with the same difficulties, but we do not know that.

Youth certainly played a large role in my relinquishment of Andrew. My parents' concern about my education and the difficulties they foresaw if they took on the responsibility for the baby caused them to opt for adop-tion. The decision was made in isolation, because there were no support networks or role models to help us more fully consider all our options. Had there been, I might still have made the decision to relinquish, but I believe I would have done so feeling I had made a conscious positive choice for me and my child.

The Difference Was Race

It is striking how the black community organized itself to accommodate mother and child while the white community was totally unwilling and unable to do so.

Rickie Solinger, *Wake Up Little Susie*

In researching this book, I have learned that what was happening in white middle-class America was not duplicated in the black and ethnic communities. Is this coincidence, or is it because the societal divisions between black and white during the tumultuous 1960s spread far enough to reach the issues surrounding the relinquishment of children? Even now, adoption in the African-American community is not as accepted as it is in the white population. In their book *Birth Bond,* Judith S. Gediman and Linda P. Brown say that "Babies born to black women unable to raise them are more likely to be 'informally' adopted—that is, raised by relatives, friends, neighbors—than placed for formal adoption with strangers." Recently, the margins have narrowed, largely because of fewer placements overall. Between 1982 and 1988 only 3 percent of pregnant unmarried white women placed at least one child compared to 1 percent of unmarried black women.

How were the extended families of young black American women able to embrace and accept children born out of wedlock, while largely middle- and upper-middle-class white girls were ferried off to maternity residences before they showed enough to draw attention to themselves and their families? According to Rickie Solinger, "The good and protective intentions of parents notwithstanding, society and complicit mothers and fathers insisted that pregnant, broadly middle-class white girls be institutionalized and rendered invisible." By making their daughters disappear (many of whom were sent away from home for the first time), parents hoped that their own precarious status in post–World War II America would remain untarnished.

Another factor in the predominance of white placements versus black was the business of baby brokering. Certain agencies and institutions abused their power and fostered illegal and lucrative adoption practices. But it was individual baby brokers—generally lawyers, doctors, and other unaffiliated intermediaries—who committed the worst abuses. Vulnerable and needy women were easy prey, and marketeers offered them money and support in order to ensure that they would relinquish their babies. White babies were, and still are, a premium in the adoption market. As Solinger points out, "Some proponents of the adoption of white illegitimate babies promoted, wittingly or not, a basic disregard for the individual unwed girl or woman. While many agency workers did serve the mothers well, enthusiasm about the baby sometimes eclipsed focus on the mother's human predicament." The large numbers of available white infants during the 1950s and 1960s extended the leverage and power of adoptive parents, and simultaneously increased the disregard for the birth mother.

A Scared and Lonely State

> I said some words to the close and holy darkness, and
> then I slept.
>
> Dylan Thomas

We know how society viewed birth mothers during the 1960s, but how did it feel to be on the receiving end of this perception? How did it feel to be so harshly judged and then punished by being hidden away? How, quite honestly, did women cope in such a scared and lonely state at a time before society allowed them to make choices about their bodies and their pregnancies? For many of us our truth was whispered in the dark hours of the night. During the light of day, keeping our secret was paramount, and pretending not to remember exacted a heavy toll. I never felt free to talk of my loss, and I have since been told that there was always a sense of hidden sadness about me.

While I anesthetized myself emotionally before and after the relinquishment, others vividly recall how desperate they felt. Jane Leeds, divorced and embroiled in a custody battle for her two children when she became pregnant, knew she could not ask her family for help. She was struggling to survive, and the man she was dating did not want to support the child she was carrying. He had recently lost his wife in childbirth and had one son, whom he was raising by himself. Jane and her son's father eventually married and had another child, but not before they relinquished this baby in 1961. Neither the father nor Jane wanted an abortion, and Jane says, "I didn't think there was any other option other than to place Michael." She found her way to Spence-Chapin and after the fourth month of her pregnancy lived in a residency hotel courtesy of the agency in a county north of New York City. At the age of twenty-six, she sent her two children to live with her parents while she "traveled" on business for a few months. Jane remembers feeling mortified about anyone discovering her condition and says there was an air of secrecy around the whole thing:

> As I walked along the street toward the agency, I had such an awful, awful feeling. I was afraid of being caught, afraid of having the baby alone, afraid of being in this big city by myself. I was truly intimidated by the whole process, and yet I was very strong in knowing what I needed to do and that I was going to do it so I could take care of my other children. I had to sacrifice one for the others. I never questioned while I was pregnant what I was going to do because I had made my decision that the adoption was the best thing for him and the rest of us. It was an unfortunate and very sad thing for me to have to do.

Two great myths surround adoption: birth mothers do not care about their babies so they give them away, and they (and the birth fathers, if they are involved) will forget about their children. Neither Jane nor I stopped caring for our children, and we certainly did not forget about them. Jane believed, as did many other birth mothers who were counseled by family members, clergy, and social workers, that relinquishing her child was best for his welfare. At the same time she was also accused of abandoning her child. These "caretakers" of ours somehow expected us to reconcile this paradox when neither they nor we could even acknowledge it.

Jane left the hospital after twenty-four hours, never having seen her baby:

> I was afraid to even consider holding him because I knew I could never give him up if I did. I decided not to see him; that was the only way I could see dealing with it. I left the hospital by myself and I was scared to death. Was I doing the right thing? How could I face other people? I had a terrible sadness, but at least the fear that someone would find out was over. I went back home and saw my children. It turns out my mother was in the hospital, one of my good friends had just died of cancer, and my sister had just had a baby, all at the same time. I tried not to think about Michael. I tried to just let it be in the past. It's hard to even think of how I felt then. I swallowed it for so long.

It is difficult now to imagine how I and other birth parents, and by extension our families, managed to keep silent, swallowing our grief for so many years. We had to postpone our mourning for decades, by which time the unexpressed grief had wreaked havoc on our lives. Historically, the reported incidence of birth mothers suffering depression after relinquishment has been low. This, however, is primarily due to their silence surrounding the subject, not their lack of pain and loss. I also suspect that until recently there was little interest in research about the birth mother's state of mind.

Bonnie Bis became pregnant with her first child in 1962 when she was sixteen years old, and another pregnancy followed just a few years later. Her Catholic upbringing dictated the tenor of her parents' reactions, and she feels that in getting pregnant twice she was continuing the pattern of her "shame-based" childhood. In both cases, like me, she shut down emotionally and "got through" the pregnancies and relinquishment of her children. She does, however, remember the terror of going through labor and delivery alone, cursorily attended to by a staff that understood nothing about a birth mother's situation:

> I was isolated with my first delivery, kept alone, in pain, and bleeding all over the place. The staff was doing the most despicable acts to me, poking and prodding without one kind word. There was no such thing as modesty and I couldn't wait for it to be over. It was just like torture. Looking back now, I don't think I allowed myself to think that I had given birth to a human being, a baby, because that would have been more than I could have handled. It was all I could do to get through the delivery. All I wanted to do was get out of there. When it was over, I remember a sense of feeling completely alone.

The only way Bonnie could cope was to dissociate herself from the pain —and more importantly from her baby. In more extreme cases of denial, we see young women today throwing their babies in Dumpsters, killing them, because they cannot be allowed to exist. This is the psychology that infects the minds of young women when they are desperate and feel they have nowhere to go. Somehow we have to reach them and their families to help them understand that there are options, that they do not have to be isolated in their crisis.

Cynthia Beals was seventeen when she had her daughter. She says the day she went into labor, all she wanted to do was go into the chapel at the maternity home and pray that she would find a way to keep her baby. She felt that as long as she was carrying the baby, no one could take it away:

> But it had become a reality, I was truly in labor, and I held off as long as I could before I told anyone because I didn't want to go to the hospital. And all I could remember at the time was God speaking to my heart because I was in so much emotional pain. And God said to me, "You know, Cynthia, it's not your child. It's mine, and I will take care of it." I had a sense of what I had to do and a sense of acceptance, but I did not like it. I didn't want to let go. The baby arrived two weeks early, when my parents happened to be at a funeral and out of contact. Here I was, giving birth for the first time, scared out of my mind and no one was there. Thankfully, I had a very easy delivery. She was such a beautiful girl, and I'm so thankful that I was able to hold her and see her because that memory is etched in my mind for the rest of my life. That's all I had to hold on to, the memory.

After Cynthia relinquished her daughter, she was told to just get on with her life. No one told her that it was natural for her arms to ache for her lost baby and that by facing her pain, she would be better able to move forward. Jim Gritter, the child welfare supervisor for Community, Family and Children's Services in Traverse City, Michigan, says, "Pain and goodness, or pain and health are not always antithetical notions. Sometimes they are very real companions. The pain is there, whether we are going to recognize it or not."

Feelings of emptiness and depression are familiar companions to women who relinquish their babies. Women of my generation especially were made to feel, whether explicit or not, that our maternal instincts were misplaced and that because we had not intended to become pregnant, we could not be mothers. In *Primary Maternal Preoccupation,* published in 1956, D. W. Winnicott offers a thesis that validates all the women who ached for their babies during their pregnancies and after delivery. "I suggest," he begins, "that sufficient tribute has not yet been paid in our literature, or perhaps anywhere, to a very special psychiatric condition of the mother, of which I would say the following things:

> It gradually develops and becomes a state of heightened sensitivity during, and especially towards the end of, pregnancy. It lasts for a few weeks after the birth of the child. It is not easily remembered by mother

once they have recovered from it. I would go further and say that the memory mothers have of this state tends to become repressed.

Can a woman ever truly recover from her "heightened preoccupation" if she is never allowed to nurture the child she gave birth to? The answer is yes, but the feelings accompanying her loss will not find resolution until she first faces what happened to her. Polarity therapist and body worker John Beaulieu also contends that the energetic connection to the baby is never lost. He says the body remembers and lies in wait even when the feelings are repressed. Over time, those "stored" feelings affect our physical health.

For years, I regarded the agency that arranged my son's adoption as the enemy. Over time my image of Spence-Chapin has changed, but for many birth mothers of my era it does not matter how we viewed the agency. Adoption agencies seemingly offered us the only path out of our predicament. Jane says she thought of the agency as providing the help she needed, but she never considered that they may have been able to help her consider parenting her child. She says, "I don't think they offered any kind of counseling at the time, and I never dreamed of asking for it."

Another of the great myths of adoption was that secrecy is necessary to protect all members of the triad. Agency workers and state laws placed enormous barriers in the way of birth parents and their children from ever contacting one another by making identifying information inaccessible. When birth mothers signed consenting papers that officially terminated their parental rights, most were made to understand that they would never see their children again, and that this was best for everyone. This "promise" of anonymity may have been intended to reassure adoptive parents that there would be no intrusion on their lives. It may have also consoled birth grandparents concerned with society's perception of them and their wayward daughters. And it may have originally protected adoptees from the shame of illegitimacy. But despite arguments to the contrary from parties interested in maintaining the closed system, there was little interest in or concern for birth mothers, and it was rarely a guarantee wished for or requested by us. The adoptee's birth certificate was, and still is in most cases, sealed by the state. An amended version is made that identifies the adoptive parents as the only parents. It is *as if* the adoptee is born to them, and the birth mother, once again, is rendered invisible.

What Role Did They Play?

> Birth fathers are perhaps the most forgotten part of
> the adoption triad. Some birth fathers were never
> told of the pregnancy. Other birth fathers are told
> that they cannot take part in the planning of the
> future of their child. Some birth fathers leave of their
> own accord because they don't want to deal with the
> situation.
>
> Marlou Russell, *Adoption Wisdom*

If birth mothers were once rendered invisible by their families, community, and society in general, birth fathers, now numbering over six million in the United States alone, were truly nonexistent. Casual liaisons that resulted in pregnancy were easier for men to forget than for women. There is no such thing as a brief affair or a quick one-night stand for a woman when a child results. Often by the time a birth mother delivered her child, the birth father was no longer involved in her life and in fact was often unaware of the pregnancy. Some birth fathers tried to do "the right thing," as Tom did, making vague and half-hearted plans to marry the women they had "gotten in trouble." Others attacked their pregnant lovers, claiming that the child was not theirs, thereby abandoning them in the crisis.

Perhaps one of the most traumatic situations that birth mothers face is rape, where a woman not only has to reconcile being violated and abused, but also has tangible evidence that the incident actually occurred. Cynthia Beals conceived her child as a result of a date rape. She says, "My parents tried to make the boy 'do the right thing,' but his father was a policeman, and he turned the entire incident into my fault. My father just got very upset and left. I think the boy admitted that the baby was his, because he wanted to hurt his father. He was almost proud of it. I, being the victim, took the natural victim's response and blamed myself for the whole thing. I realize now that the boy was very troubled and that the entire incident was about power and control."

It was only in the mid-1970s that birth fathers began to have an impact on how adoption is practiced. Fathers' rights are now a serious legal consideration, and with proper counseling more women and men are deciding their children's fates together. "As time has passed," notes Judy Greene of

Spence-Chapin, "we've gone back and looked at it statistically, and on average over the years 55 percent of our birth fathers are not named by the birth mothers. Of the remaining 45 percent, 20 to 25 percent are very involved, very concerned, and very responsible. The rest have been named by the birth mother, but for the most part are not involved in the women's life or the welfare of the baby."

Not all birth fathers disappear from the scene, but that is the prevailing stereotype of them. In *Dear Birthfather,* Randolph W. Severson says, "Once, when leafing through an 'adoption calendar,' I ran across a picture labeled 'Birthfather,' which showed a doorway through which a man had just run out, obviously sprinting as fast as he could, so that the only thing visible was the flash of his disappearing foot and ankle. To many in the adoption world, the birthfather truly has been the Magic Man with an incredible disappearing act."

Birth father Paul Adams knew that the woman he had been having a "fiery" affair with was pregnant and that she planned to relinquish the child, and he can barely remember the events surrounding the conception of his daughter. When told of the pregnancy, Adams, a true product of the sexually promiscuous 1960s, said, "Fine." He says, "She just wanted to let me know that I would have a kid running around in the world. Then I went my way and she went hers." Nineteen years old at the time of his daughter's birth and certainly not ready to parent, Adams had no concept of how he would feel years later when he finally met the child who had been "running around in the world." He says, "When I first spoke to her, I didn't feel great. I felt more ashamed than anything else. I apologized for my sexual irresponsibility and told her I had thought about her over the years." If the birth mothers of the 1960s were forced by their families to take some responsibility and blame for their sin of an unwed pregnancy, the birth fathers rarely were. Birth fathers like Adams never spoke to anyone about their children and harbored their secrets as closely as we birth mothers did. The birth father's parents often knew nothing about their grandchild, and neither did the rest of the extended paternal birth family.

Some men disappeared unknowingly, having no idea that they had become fathers long ago, because their partners did not want them involved. It was, and remains, the view of many birth mothers that the baby is "theirs." Other men knew their mate was pregnant but were forced aside by the woman's family. Roger Hanson was nineteen in 1972 when his fifteen-year-old girlfriend became pregnant. He says her mother was adamant that nobody should find out. She removed her from school immediately and did not let her daughter out of the house. Roger suggested that he and his family raise the child, but she would not hear of it because they were living in a small town and everyone would know. "She told me if I pursued it, she would charge me with rape," says Roger. "So I dropped it, and they went on with the adoption without my consent. Well, I agreed to it, but I didn't sign any paperwork. I didn't have much of a choice." Roger and his girlfriend continued to see each other secretly throughout the pregnancy, even when she was sent to a maternity home over a hundred miles away. Afterward, Roger says, "I moved away, because we knew that nothing was going to be able to materialize between us, because of her mother."

Agencies also often reinforce the notion that the birth mother is the true client, and fathers might show more interest if they did not lag behind birth mothers in receiving social services, legal counseling, and education about their options as a parent. Helping biological fathers find their place, especially in the growing climate of greater openness, is one of the greatest challenges facing adoption professionals today. Sharon Kaplan Roszia, who counsels birth fathers, says, "Because the birth father does not experience the pregnancy, it takes a long time for him to realize that there is a real person involved. We have to work very hard to bring them into the process because they don't know what their role is." If they are not named, we first need to locate them. Then we can work to change their *and* society's view of single fathering.

Jon Ryan, a birth father and president of the National Organization for Birthfathers and Adoption Reform (NOBAR), relinquished his daughter in 1969 and has been reunited with her since 1984. Since then, he has become an advocate for birth fathers' rights. "After my reunion," says Jon, "I began to find out how abusive that system can be, not only in terms of trying to coerce mothers to put their babies up for adoption, but also in trying to push fathers to the periphery of the situation." Jon married his daughter's birth mother, but she did not want to keep the child for fear that her family would find out she had gotten pregnant before the two wed. Jon, who says that he did not even know at the time that fathers could legally raise their children as single parents, signed the relinquishment papers along with his wife and never knew what happened to their child. "We stayed married for ten years," he says, "and after the day we signed the papers, we never once talked about our daughter. We never even discussed the possibility of having other children, which is not an unusual response for married couples who have given a child up for adoption."

Mary Martin Mason explains in her book *Out of the Shadows* that "a baby creates a permanent connection between two persons who may have had no intention of permanence. In cases of an unplanned pregnancy, 'fatherhood' looms before a man who may not have anticipated or desired such a role. Even if the relationship is one that suggests a future together, the strain of the unplanned pregnancy may cause a breakup." Tom tried to do the right thing when he flew back to the States to marry me, but our relationship did not have a strong enough foundation. From that point on, there was no question but that my family would decide the fate of our child. For Roger Hanson, however, it was his girlfriend's mother, rather than the strain of the pregnancy, that caused the breakup and rendered him powerless.

According to Jon Ryan, several studies and his own experience working with birth fathers show that, contrary to popular belief, men have a high degree of interest in their children, whether it involves parenting the child or being involved in the adoption. "I've found," he says, "that a lot of fathers who originally were against adoption because they thought it was the typical closed adoption where they would never know where the baby went, are more receptive to an open adoption, where they can still be a part of the child's life."

Birth Fathers Fight for Their Rights

> We are after all a nation of laws, and to believe that
> we do not have to obey laws is a strong statement
> that would not fly in any but adoption cases.
>
> Annette Baran

Several high-profile media cases that have swayed the public's perception of how adoptions are handled have involved fathers fighting to retain their parental rights after the birth mother has relinquished. The two most prominent of these are the Baby Jessica and Baby Richard cases, both of which were private adoptions. In the case of Baby Jessica, the birth mother falsified the identity of the father. Soon after signing relinquishment papers, she had a change of heart and mind and sought a way to get her daughter back. When the actual birth father learned that Baby Jessica was his daughter, he immediately sought a reversal of the adoption process. The case was complicated by a number of factors including differences in state law between Michigan, where the adoptive parents reside, and Iowa, where the baby was born, and the birth father's checkered history of failure to provide child support for two older children. The adoptive parents' legal advisors encouraged them to resist the birth parents' efforts, and that, coupled with the adoptive parents' concerns about the birth father's fitness to parent, caused them to expend every effort to maintain custody. By the time the fight was over, Baby Jessica was two and a half years old. In the case of Baby Richard, who was four years old when he was taken from his adoptive parents, the birth mother had told the birth father the baby had died. She had believed he had left her for another woman. As soon as he learned the baby was alive, he filed a petition to gain custody. The case was heard by various courts, and it dragged on for four years before it was determined that the birth father's parental right had not been legally terminated.

There are many opinions about how the courts and the attorneys handled these cases as there are about all emotional court rulings, but some professionals, like child welfare advocate and adoptee Kate Burke, believe "the trouble with both these cases is that all the parties knew within six weeks that there was big-time trouble, and both of these children should have been returned because the birth fathers exercised their rights." Burke notes that had an agency been involved, and had the birth parents and adoptive parents been properly counseled, neither of these protracted battles might ever have been fought.

It is obvious to any one of us seeing a child being forcibly removed from his parents that the child's best interests were not served. It is easy to side with the adoptive parents, who have loved and nurtured the child since infancy, especially in the case of Baby Richard, whose adoption had been finalized. I myself wrote an op-ed editorial asserting that justice had not been served and that in the best interests of the child, birth mothers have to accept the consequences of their decisions. Today, I have a more complex view, and I could just as easily say that it is not in the child's interest for adoptive parents to fight for years to retain custody and risk their child's well-being if they lose. There are usually some red flags early in the process signaling, at the very least, a need to proceed with caution toward finalizing an adoption. It is easy, too, to blame the courts; but in both cases, final decisions were rendered in strict accordance with the laws as they stand. It is hardly constructive, though, to assign blame to any one party so arbitrarily.

Professional preadoption/prerelinquishment counseling helps both sets of parents understand adoption before final decisions are made. And in the rare instance of a disrupted adoption, properly counseled adoptive parents usually choose to return the children to the birth parents without a legal struggle (although there will always be some cases where a suit does proceed). Psychologist and adoption reform advocate Annette Baran also identifies other measures that would safeguard the child's welfare:

> Basically, birth mothers need to be instructed as to the awful consequences for the child if they in any way equivocate about the true identity of the father before placement, and if there is any question DNA tests must be given. It is expensive, but is ultimately cheaper than the damage to the lives involved if there is a false identification. If a suit is filed, the case should be adjudicated quickly, and any appeals should be accelerated to protect the child. During a suit, the adoption should be open with birth parents available to make attachments to help ease the transition if a move becomes necessary.

These cases, though rare in adoption practice, are heart wrenching, creating turmoil and pain for everyone. It is especially tragic for adoptive parents who are helplessly in love with their child. As a birth parent, I can well understand the depth of their pain at the loss of their child. Unfortunately, the media surrounding these high-profile cases helps foster demeaning stereotypes of birth mothers and causes prospective adoptive parents and their families to be more fearful of adopting domestically. At the same time, cases like these serve to narrow our focus on where we need to turn our collective attention to begin reforming the adoption system. State legislatures are looking at ways of identifying the criteria for determining legitimate rights and responsibilities of biological fathers.

Roger Hanson, who is a longtime member of CUB (Concerned United Birthparents), says that there are birth fathers who want to take responsibility for their children but are marginalized and are not acknowledged as having any rights. They are generally seen as an obstacle to an adoption and have to prove through a lengthy bureaucratic process that they are worthy to parent their child. He says, "I feel, if the birth mother wants to relinquish that child, and the birth father is a suitable parent, there is no reason he can't have that child. But it's not that way in the real world. You have to prove that you're the parent; you have to prove that you're fit. Other people have kids, and they don't have to prove that they're financially stable."

Ironically, adoptive parents argue similarly that they are subjected to scrutiny that biological parents are not.

Some states now require that birth fathers take responsibility for knowing about the pregnancy and for offering support during the pregnancy in order to qualify for consideration of their parental rights. In light of such policies, Tom came forward and was prepared to parent—at least in legal terms. He would have more rights today, and knowing, as I do now, his parents' distress on learning of the adoption, I am quite certain I would have a dilemma if I were faced anew with the decision of what to do. I can only hypothesize in a vacuum that it would be very difficult to convince him to waive his parental rights, and I would honestly find it difficult psychologically to have my baby living with the paternal birth family. That would certainly be a factor in whether or not I ultimately placed. The issue is complex for young people trying to make adoption plans, and it presents an added burden for women who may feel it would not be healthy for their child to be with the birth father. At the same time, rationally, I sympathize with the birth father who genuinely cares about his child and would like to parent. There are no easy solutions.

The Family Extends Beyond Mother and Father

> People who are parents and grandparents have the easiest time of perceiving meaning and continuity to their lives. It is all there: they had children, their children had children, the continuation of their genetic legacy is assured.
>
> David M. Brodzinsky, Marshall D. Schechter, and Robin Marantz Henig, *Being Adopted*

Birth grandparents, siblings, aunts, uncles, cousins, and other relatives are also deeply affected when a woman makes an adoptive placement. At the time I relinquished Andrew, maternal grandparents were usually the guiding force in steering their daughters toward adoption. Sadly, many concealed their own feelings not only from their daughters but also from themselves. It was only after Andrew contacted me that I learned that my mother had harbored tremendous guilt through all those years, feeling that she had pushed me into the adoption. "In 1966 you cared what people thought," she says. "It was such nonsense, and today I wouldn't give a hoot. Had it all happened now, I probably would have said 'to heck with it, we're keeping this child, and I'm going to bring him up.' But in those days it was different; it was a very different thing and it was just heartbreaking." In her book *Synchronicity & Reunion,* LaVonne Stiffler also reports that in some cases, a grandmother may have wanted to help her daughter keep the baby, but instead deferred to her husband's authority, and like her daughter, was left to deal with years of lingering anger, guilt, and grief.

Siblings, while they may have played a relatively minor role throughout the pregnancy and adoption arrangements, were often equally scarred by the events surrounding them. One woman I know, whose older sister relinquished a child, decided to have an abortion when she became pregnant in order to avoid the turmoil and pain another unwanted pregnancy would cause her family. Brothers and sisters often express confusion and shock if they learn of the pregnancy later in their lives, and they wonder what other secrets have been kept from them. My sister knew of my pregnancy but remembers feeling very separate from what was going on and being upset about what was happening to me.

Cynthia Beals's parents were too emotionally stressed by events in their own lives to understand what their daughter was experiencing. It was her grandmother who sensed the hurt and shock that she felt. "My grandmother knew somehow that I was raped," she says, "and tried to tell my parents. I don't know how they reacted, but I don't think they believed her." We can see that it is not only the pregnant women who are affected by the dilemma of an ill-timed pregnancy, but also entire families, across generations.

While they have enormous influence, grandparents do not have the ultimate say, legally, in what happens to the child. In America you cannot vote until you are eighteen and you cannot drink until you are twenty-one, but you can sign the papers to relinquish a child at any age. It is one of the only contracts a minor can sign, and it is important for parents of a young mother to help their daughter reach her own decision. "When the parents take charge and negotiate everything," says Judy Greene, director of Birth Parent Services at Spence-Chapin, "the girl doesn't get a chance to process or understand what she's going through; she can't experience it, and lots of times she will get pregnant again."

Nevertheless, relatives strongly affect the adoptive decision, and a woman or young teen desperately needs her family's unconditional love and support when she is faced with the overwhelming situation of trying to decide what to do. Joanne Remy, deputy executive director of Spence-

Chapin, recalls a situation where one family struggled together to figure out what was best for their daughter:

> They were ready at one point to disown her and kick her out of the house if she placed, but they weren't necessarily going to parent the child, so they had put her in a no-win situation. Then they went back and renegotiated and realized they had a choice to make as a family. The daughter was not ready to parent this baby, so it was either the family who could parent, or she was going to look into placement. It touched a lot of issues for them and they really had to work very hard.

The complicated issues surrounding adoption loss often manifest in patterns that run through an extended family. Jan Waldron, author of *Giving Away Simone,* was the fourth woman in her family to relinquish her daughter. In her memoir, she ponders the underlying dynamic causing the women in her family to repeat the cycle of loss: "Why did we keep losing our mothers? My blood-related great-great-grandmother, great-grandmother, grandmother, and mother had all turned away from their children. Fifth in line, I fought an undertow of conditioned exiting, an affliction of easy farewells." But the farewells are never "easy," and they last a lifetime.

Hide Us No More from Ourselves

> By openly acknowledging their relinquishments and
> coming out with their secrets, some have begun to
> confront their fears of rejection and judgment and to
> deem themselves worthy of respect.
>
> Merry Bloch Jones, *Birthmothers*

Jim Gritter, who has worked with triad members for over twenty years, remembers how people generally perceived and portrayed birth parents when he first began in the field. "I was tremendously annoyed when I began in 1974, that the day and age really pegged birth parents as wild, reckless people from the wrong side of the tracks, when in fact I was dealing with truly delightful individuals. In some ways things haven't changed that much. Birth parents still live under a pretty stereotypic shadow, but it was more pronounced then. All I knew was that I wanted to roll up my sleeves and do what I could to make life better for them." Gritter became appalled at how society admonished young women for succumbing to human impulses. "It just struck me," he says, "that the adoption system was something pretty close to our society's method of punishing them. It was part of the price they had to pay for their wayward behavior."

Many support groups now exist for birth mothers as well as for other triad members. Telling our stories and supporting one another is one way to battle the isolation and to find our lost selves. While we have individual stories, birth mothers share a common profile, including the feelings of dissociation, isolation, loss, prolonged grief, shame, and poor self-esteem. Communicating with one another in a supportive group helps new birth mothers avoid the damage caused by maintaining silence and secrecy, and helps older birth mothers heal that pain.

Ronny Diamond of Spence-Chapin says that as society has changed, triad members no longer need to be protected from the truth. "Without the stigma connected with premarital sex," she says of birth mothers, "and a greater acceptance of single, unmarried parenthood, they no longer need to lead lives cloaked in silence and secrecy." It takes time, though, for this to sink in. Despite changes in our society, a single parent is viewed differently from a woman who has given up her child. Even young birth mothers struggle with issues of guilt and shame and may be reluctant to speak openly of having relinquished a child for adoption. Judy Greene says she does not want birth mothers "to be ashamed to be this unique person that nobody knows. It's very interesting that once somebody comes out of the closet or talks about it, they usually find somebody else. But it's not going to happen if they're in their own isolation and pain."

Melissa Kramer relinquished her son in 1993, and she feels her support group has been a vital lifeline for her. "It's the one and only place where I'm surrounded by people who have walked in my shoes and who understand. I feel I can cry in front of them and share intimate feelings without judgment, without criticism, and without remoteness. They've been there. They understand without me having to explain." I was also relieved to find a support group where there is a warm sense of community that I know I can count on. Perhaps trust and intimacy would not have become or have remained such large issues in my life if I had shared some of my hurt with others over the years.

How Do I Decide?

"Oh God! That one might read the book of fate."

Shakespeare, Henry IV, Part III

We have looked closely into some of the issues affecting birth parents who surrendered their children generations ago; we have seen how for many the decision was mandated by the social mores of the time. We have also seen that as our society is gradually becoming more open, birth parents are finding greater support. The fundamental issues surrounding relinquishment remain, however. Adoption practices also vary across the country, and not everyone is adequately counseled about the options that are available. In some cases, too, having more of a choice, in a way, makes the decision more difficult.

The stigma of being pregnant out-of-wedlock that haunted birth mothers of my generation has been largely replaced with a stigma associated with birth mothers "giving away their baby," and people today are quick to condemn a woman for making an adoptive placement. Judy Greene worries "that most people feel (especially if the woman is seventeen or older), that the birth mother is cold, uncaring, and selfish. They ask: 'How could she separate from her baby?' They think 'She must have no feelings; she must be a calculating woman.' They don't understand for the most part what a loving, caring decision this is and how emotional and how involved and how difficult a decision placement is for these women to make."

Before placing her son with a couple she chose and got to know, Melissa went to great lengths to explore all the possibilities and tried to imagine herself parenting in different situations:

> I had a job, I had benefits, I had the financial ability to be a parent, to mother and raise my son. It would have stretched me out, but it's not like I didn't have a college degree. I pictured myself marrying my son's father, who was my boyfriend and wanted me to keep the baby, but I didn't feel in my heart that he was the right one for me. So then I'm a single parent and what does that mean for me now? I know I can be a single mother, but I'd be jumping through hoops to be a good mother and a good father.

Melissa found that she had to face the hardest questions she could imagine about herself. "I had to ask," she says, "could I emotionally sustain, get through, giving away my child? Am I going to survive? Am I going to get beyond this? Is there life after placement? What does it mean about me that I'm giving up my child? How can I do it? Am I heartless? Am I human?" As she worked through the process, she understood that it was a decision requiring that her heart, emotions, head, and spirit all come together, because it would affect so many lives.

Naomi Brand was romantically involved with Bob, her son's birth father, for many years, but she was not ready to marry him when she learned she was pregnant. Initially, Bob wanted Naomi to have an abortion, because he felt it would be easier. "I told him I didn't need it to be that easy," she says. "I didn't think I could live with that kind of easy. I could, and would, struggle through the nine months of pregnancy. The only thing I knew for certain at a very early point, was that at the end of my pregnancy, barring any unforeseen disaster, our child would be alive." Although Naomi felt from the beginning that she was going to place her baby for adoption, it was a painful decision. She still questions that decision, but in her heart trusts that her son is where he is supposed to be:

> I honestly feel that Bob wanted to parent our child, and he was waiting for me to change my mind. I was kind of counting on him to come forward. If he had even said, "Maybe we should try," who knows what might have happened. It's the biggest regret I'll ever have. Neither of us came forward, and so we went through with the adoption. No one thought we would. Everyone thought we'd decide to keep and raise the baby. Maybe we should have, but one thing I've known and believed from the earliest stages of my life is that everything happens for a reason. My son was conceived and born and went to live with his family for a reason. It happened too recently to see and really know what that reason is, but I have no doubt there is one. If my son was meant to be with me and Bob, then we would be raising him. And that is an amazingly comforting thought. It's really the only thing that makes all the doubts, questions, and eternal "what ifs" bearable. That, and the thought that I will see him again someday.

Many women in such a crisis are impressionable and can be emotionally swayed, and certain groups have made it their practice to push women aggressively toward adoption in an attempt to "save" the babies that may be aborted. In her paper "Adoption's Impact on Birthmothers: Can a Mother Forget Her Child?," LaVonne H. Stiffler says, "In Christian circles, there has been a recent renewal in the maternity home concept of the 1950s and 1960s, and workers are encouraged to 'recruit' young women in high school settings. Hundreds of 'crisis pregnancy centers' have been set up in an effort to curb the number of abortions being performed. Volunteer counselors are presenting 'the adoption option' as a desirable choice." While for some it will certainly be a good choice, these "counselors" often fail to tell these teens how deeply they will feel the loss, and how relinquishment irrevocably alters the future of both mother and child. Adoption *is* an option, and it can be a positive choice, but it should not be presented as the only option.

Not too long ago, author and publisher Jeanne Warren Lindsay visited a well-established adoption agency in Texas. She says, "I was in the Fort Worth area and had missed the official tour of the agency, so I went there late in the day. The director took me around and showed me everything. And I said, 'What happens if a girl here changes her mind and decides she'll keep?' 'Oh, she goes right home,' the director told me. 'This is for those who are placing.' I was appalled because you haven't truly made up your mind until after you deliver." The not-so-tacit message that such practices convey to women who are pregnant and unsure not only about what to do but also about what their choices are, is that there is no help unless you hand over the baby.

Twenty-year-old Maria Baez received conflicting pressure from her family, her friends, and her church as she struggled with the decision:

> The first thing my father did when he found out I was pregnant was call abortion clinics, but I was already six months along. I hid my pregnancy from my parents for six months, and when they found out, my stomach just popped out. The clinic suggested adoption as an "option," one we had never thought about. My mother said if I kept the baby, she wouldn't help me out, and I was so young and wanted to finish school. The adoption agency told me about being able to choose the parents, but once my grandmother and my church found out I was pregnant, they were pressuring and saying in God's eyes adoption is wrong and I should do what I have to do to keep the baby. After the baby was born, it was real hard on me. I put the baby in foster care while I decided. My father and I would go see her all the time, and I would talk to the adoptive mom for hours on the phone. I felt like I knew her for a long time and that eased me, but then again I was still feeling like I don't want to give my baby up.

It took Maria six weeks to decide to place her daughter with the adoptive parents she picked, and she could not have done it without time and support. Since then, Maria has tried to share her experiences with pregnant teen groups, but she found the criticism she received from her peers too difficult to bear. "I was telling them about a different option," she says. "I wasn't telling them to do it. But they were doing a lot of stereotyping, and it made me feel very uncomfortable. I went home crying." Jeanne Warren Lindsay, who began a program in Los Angeles County for teen mothers in 1972, feels strongly that in the programs for pregnant teens adoption is an issue that needs to be discussed, not only because they might decide to make an adoptive placement, but also because adoptees have a tendency to think they were throwaway babies.

> They don't have any idea what goes into placing a child for adoption. And that's very important. I think it's very important that everybody, not just pregnant teens, know the way adoption has drastically changed in the last ten years, and the wild differences between open adoption versus closed. If there is someone in the class that is considering adoption, she needs the support of her friends. If you don't know anything about adoption, you can be real quick to think either a girl should place, she's too young to parent—or how could she give away her flesh and blood? It's an awful lot to ask a teenager to look at all that's going on when she's considering what to do, but that's the only way it's going to work.

If women are receiving good counseling, they are encouraged to wait to make a decision until after the birth of the baby. No matter how sure a woman is that she wants to place her child, things can change radically when the baby is in its mother's arms. As Margaret Moorman says in *Waiting to Forget,* "A baby is more lovable than a pregnancy, especially an accidental pregnancy." Somehow the kicking creature inside a womb is abstract until you can examine the features of its face and count its toes. In order to say "good-bye" we first have to say "hello." Melissa Kramer considered placing her child from early on in her pregnancy, but she knew that while she "was walking in the direction of placement," she would not make the final decision until she had a chance to be with her baby. Even if people fear a change of heart, it is essential that women be informed of all their choices and supported in making a decision that is right for them.

A new mother is particularly vulnerable while she is in the hospital. The time before, during, and just after birth is traumatic, even if you are looking forward to having a baby. Birth parent caseworker Judy Link says she constantly tells birth mothers, "You don't make a final decision about the baby until after it is born, and even then you don't make it in the hospital. All you have to decide in the hospital is whether you want to take the baby home or whether you want us to take the baby into temporary care." Unfortunately, hospital staff may have their own point of view that it is wrong to place a baby for adoption, or they may simply be unsophisticated about adoption. Judy Greene says she is astounded at the emotional ignorance of some hospital social workers:

> We'll get a call from the hospital social worker who'll say, "Oh, did you know Debbie isn't placing because she's breast-feeding the baby." And, quite honestly, that is not indicative of her final decision. Or they say a mother isn't placing because she sobbed all night and morning. We'll say that's great because we'd much rather have someone sobbing than being stoic about relinquishment. It's amazing that the social workers don't understand the need for these women to express their feelings.

Kate Burke, who helps reunite adoptees and birth parents, says, "If the birth mother is unsure, then I say let her have at that kid, let her be with the child, and let her be real sure what she wants to do. And let's wait to place that kid until we know it can be permanent." The information kit given to expectant mothers who come to Spence-Chapin includes a "Birth Parent's Bill of Rights," which encourages them to explore all their options and advises them that they have the right to change their mind. Judy Greene says, in fact, that a lot of the women who change their minds had, until twenty minutes prior, planned an adoption:

> Now they've had the baby, and suddenly tomorrow morning with ten hours' notice, they're taking the baby home and they're unprepared. A lot of times the family, the grandparents, the aunts, the uncles, the siblings, who maybe didn't want her to keep the baby, suddenly see the child and fall in love. They rally around and sometimes come through for the mother and sometimes they don't. So we try to prepare them. We try and let them know what some of the issues and problems are so that maybe taking care of the baby won't be such a shock.

Spence-Chapin reported that during 1995 and 1996, they received 944 calls from would-be parents inquiring about adoption for their as yet unborn children. Of these, 565 met with a counselor at the agency and ultimately 185 placed.

More Information Is Better

> Birth parents do not move on with their lives more
> easily in the absence of information about the child.
>
> Ronny Diamond

Women making an adoptive placement today ideally choose the parents for their children, and they have some measure of contact with the family. There was, however, an ambiguous period into which many birth mothers fall between the closed system when I relinquished and the current climate of openness. Melissa says that at the agency where she placed, "Ten years ago, you could ask for a letter. You could ask for a photo, but you couldn't choose the parents. Then you could choose the parents, but couldn't ask for contact. The evolution toward greater contact was just beginning. Birth mothers from that time don't have the relationships with their children that we have today. I think it must be hardest for that group."

Elaine Davis placed her daughter in 1977 when birth parents were given little if any information about their children. "My daughter's adoption was totally closed," she says. "There were no options. About the only thing I was offered were a few pictures at the very beginning. Shortly thereafter, Catholic Social Services, where I placed, began semiopen, and now they do open adoptions." Elaine says that "coming from my perspective of a closed adoption, it's very difficult to live with because all you have is your imagination. It's probably what a parent who has lost a child to death goes through." Birth mothers who are too young to search, but too old to have had an open adoption, are caught, at least for now, in a limbo not unlike that of the birth mothers of my generation, with the added frustration of knowing that others who came through the process more recently have fared much better.

Choosing the parents who will raise her child is empowering for the birth mother and allows her to determine to some extent her baby's future. Melissa chose a couple she felt a connection with after examining their letter and photo in the adoption agency's book of family profiles. She met them after she delivered her son:

> It was very emotional, we hugged, there were a lot of tears, but it was good. My requests for them were letters and photos on his birthday. I told the adoptive mother that "I think with my genes and your upbringing, he's going to be a nice, really charming young man, and I want to know him. So, I can't promise you twenty years from now that I won't

try to find him." She accepted this, but I don't think she was entirely comfortable with it, but it was my honest answer. I know I'm never going to be his "Mom," and that's a truth I have to accept.

When birth mothers of my era relinquished our children, the agencies told us as little as they could about the adoptive families. We had no point of reference, no idea if the people we had entrusted our babies to would deliver them to safe and loving homes. Birth mothers like Melissa, Maria, and Naomi now have the advantage of placing their children in what they hope is the ideal setting. How do they decide which couple it will be? Naomi says, "The couple I picked reminded me of the good things about my parents, things that I remember fondly and things that I cherish. They're really active on the school board and they're involved in the church. They do the same things that my parents did, the things I recall and thought were important from my childhood." Maria remembers that the adoptive mom she ultimately picked told her about her favorite activities. She says, "She was telling me things that she likes to do, like camping and biking, and those are things that my father, my mother, and I like to do together. For some reason it made me feel at ease." I, on the other hand, had no information in advance about the family chosen by the agency. I was told when Andrew was adopted that the parents were in their late twenties, that the father was a corporate businessman, and the mother was a teacher. Now that I have met them and am developing a relationship, I know Andrew was lucky. Although I was not given the option of choosing them myself, I doubt that I could have made a more appropriate choice. It has been important for me to acknowledge this and not hold on unnecessarily to bitterness about my fate and the ills of the system.

To Keep You Close in My Arms

She went her unremembering way,
　　She went and left in me
The pang of all the partings gone,
　　And partings yet to be.

Francis Thompson

For decades the premise in adoption philosophy has been that it is better for a child to be raised by strangers than by a mother who is ill prepared to parent. However, Grace Hsu reports in her paper "Why Do So Few Unmarried Pregnant Women Make Adoption Plans," that "46 percent of all the non-marital pregnancies in 1991 ended in induced abortion, 10 percent ended in miscarriage, and 44 percent were carried to term, of which only 2 percent were placed for adoption."

Today, many adoption professionals, intent on reforming a system that has too long served primarily the needs of those *in search* of children, strongly encourage birth parents to consider ways to keep their child. Sharon Kaplan Roszia, who counsels birth parents and adoptive families, and consults on adoption policy around the world, says, "Family preservation is the place at which you start because children need to stay with their families. Adoption should always be the last resort." To favor family preservation as a first choice does not equate with being antiadoption. There are of course instances where it is clearly in the best interest of the child to be placed in an adoptive home, and there will always be biological parents who are unable to parent and *whose children are in need of a family* who wants them and will love them as their own. Nevertheless, the premise of family preservation is that people should consider fully the possibility of keeping a child in its family of origin as a first choice, just as adoptive parents' first choice is generally to parent biological children.

In order to help families stay together, we need a different mind-set that would open us to creating structures and paradigms, both governmental and familial, that on the most basic level celebrate a new life rather than punish a sexual act. Our society has not been sufficiently protective of its children, and money is a large factor in whether women choose to raise their children or not. Recent legislation has cut funding and diminished vital services to single mothers, and we are paying the price in more disrupted families. In particular, there is a surge in the number of relinquishments from married couples raising other children. In England, mothers are given more support and are encouraged to stay with their children before making a decision, and this has resulted in far fewer adoptions. The same is true in other countries with broad social welfare programs, like Sweden, where mothers have at least a year of paid maternity leave and more governmental funding of day care. Thus there is little need for babies to be relinquished because of financial hardship.

Jeanne Warren Lindsay offers some key questions that a pregnant woman needs to ask her adoption facilitators before she makes any plans: "What will you do if I decide to keep? Will you be there to tell me what is available in social services? To tell me where I can get medical help? If groups only want birth mothers who are placing, then they are at risk of being swayed towards adoption." It is vital that you know from the start how the professional assisting you feels. Annette Baran counsels groups of prospective birth and adoptive parents, and she says, "I give them my bias before I start, that I think it's better for mothers to keep their babies, and we take it from there."

Bonnie Bis says, "I think if birth mothers really looked at the long-term consequences, they could figure out some way to do it. But a lot of times, that way is through family support and many people are too proud to ask for help. Wouldn't it be ideal if we had maternity homes where women could band together and help each other out for the first few years because that's really the most critical time." There are some programs for teen mothers, but the idea of helping women keep their children has not taken root in America, where much more emphasis is placed on providing tax credits and other incentives for prospective adoptive parents. In the meantime, says Kate Burke, "The clock is ticking on the child," and some decision has to be made.

We are not all equipped with enlightened emotional intelligence, and it is not realistic to think that everything will work out fine if we just all get together to make a decision, especially if we do not have good professional help. Eleanor Oakley, an adoptive parent who has been a social worker for over twenty-five years and in the adoption field for more than five, has seen birth mothers who have chosen to parent and feels that the woman can figure out the practical aspects, but the emotional needs are sometimes overlooked. "I have to admit," she says, "there are times when a birth mother has chosen to parent and it has really upset me because I just felt she had no emotional resources. There is just so much personal need, the need to be parented herself, and the attention she got while pregnant that she thought was going to continue after the baby was born. You just get frightened about what's going to happen when it goes away and there are no supports."

According to the article "Adoption Law" by Joan Heifetz Hollinger, included in *The Future of Children* (vol. 3, no. 1, Spring 1993), there are now as many as five million adoptees living in America. Each year states grant anywhere between 100,000 and 160,000 new adoptions, including infants and older children. A remarkable feature of these adoptions is "the variety of contexts in which they occur. . . . Half or more of all adoptions are by stepparents or other relatives." Hollinger says further, "In contrast to the increase in intrafamily adoptions is the sharp decrease, both proportionately and in absolute numbers, in adoptions of infants by unrelated adults." (This is due in part to fewer voluntary relinquishments overall, as well as to a reluctance by prospective adoptive parents to adopting a special needs infant, especially one who may have been exposed prenatally to drugs or alcohol, or who may be HIV positive.) Our government supports and encourages finding adoptive homes for children in need, especially for those languishing in the foster care system. Many professionals, however, continue to advocate in favor of working to keep families together whenever possible and finding other kin if the children have to be removed out of harm's way.

Kinship adoption can in fact be the best solution for a family as it maintains intact the adopted person's genealogical heritage and identity. There are compelling reasons for considering this option whenever a woman is faced with a decision about who will parent her child. At the same time, kinship adoption comes with its own set of complexities. What sounds ideal is not always what is possible or in practical terms even preferable. In Maria Baez's Hispanic culture, adoption by nonrelatives is not a widely accepted practice. She and her family thought seriously about keeping her baby in the family, but it was not the right choice for her:

> First of all, if my mother's brother was here, maybe I would have considered it if he lived around here, but he lives all the way in New England. And he even said he would have taken care of the baby, but I didn't want to be so far a distance. So that's why that was out of the question. And my father's sister, she has five kids already, and then for her to have mine, I don't like the way her kids live, and I wouldn't want my daughter to live there either. Before that, I would keep her at my house.

Counselors and social workers can encourage families to come forward in support of the mother. Ultimately, however, in the case of voluntary relinquishment, the final decision is the mother's, and care needs to be taken so that support does not cross the line and become excessive pressure in one direction or another.

Constantly Re-creating Ourselves

To exist is to change; to change is to mature;
to mature is to create oneself endlessly.

Henri Bergson

I and many other birth parents have to live with the reality that we have children we were not able to parent. Assigning blame is not useful to our children, or to their adoptive parents. Adoption is with us to stay, and it remains one of the valid ways in which families are created and in which loving homes are found for children in need. At the same time, it is misguided to deny the fundamental mother/child relationship by suggesting that adoption should automatically be a first choice for teenagers and women desperately looking for a solution to an untimely pregnancy. As we consider the best interest of the child, it behooves us as a society to look at the services that a mother under stress may need in order to raise her child responsibly.

There are many professionals dedicated to ensuring quality care for all members of the adoption triad and to creating an environment where birth parents, as well as all other triad members, can come together in an open dialogue. We can help by working to increase the awareness in the general public of the complex issues facing women who have to decide whether or not to parent their children. When we accept ourselves for who we are, we *can* move forward—with strength and hope in place of guilt and shame.

In the next chapter, I will examine the issues surrounding the impact on the infant of separation from his biological mother. There is a growing body of research into how an infant adapts to his world, and I will look at how a baby's first experiences can influence his future relationships. Children who have moved through the foster care system also experience difficulties forming attachments, and I will review some of the problems caused by the disruption in their young lives, and how, as we develop new adoption policies, we might learn from their experience. I will also explore how the ongoing debate on nature versus nurture relates to children who are adopted.

TWO

AND MILES TO GO BEFORE
I SLEEP

Adoptees Find a Way Home

Born to Whom?

> O, wonder:
> How many goodly creatures are there here:
> How beauteous mankind is: O brave new world
> That has such people in't.
>
> William Shakespeare

THERE IS NOTHING more miraculous and vulnerable than a newborn child. Unlike most newly born animals, they are truly helpless, unable to feed or protect themselves. In fact, experts agree that when human infants are born, they are basically still developing fetuses. Evolution dictated a compromise to accommodate the infant's head. Otherwise, female pelvises would have to be so large that women could not walk. Our babies are therefore delivered to us completely dependent, and requiring constant care and attention for their very sustenance and survival. Ideally, the biological mother is the source of that maternal love and nurturing. For the mother-child bond, says Linda Gray Sexton in her memoir *Searching for Mercy Street,* "is the most important of all our relationships, the one upon which all others are based."

Although I hope that the time I spent loving him in the hospital made a difference in both our lives, Andrew entered the world after nine months in the womb of an immature and ambivalent mother, unsure of her infant's place in society—or her own. After my mother and I brought Andrew to Spence-Chapin, my mother and I walked out of the halls of the "establishment" and were gone from Andrew's life for nearly three decades. The agency then placed him in foster care until they worked out the final arrangements with his adoptive parents, Katherine and Bill. What happened to Andrew the first month of his life, how he slept, ate, interacted, and behaved with his foster parents, is lost to all of us, hidden deep inside Andrew's unconscious, probably never to be uncovered. He was most likely treated "well" in his temporary home, but how did he feel when held by a stranger, cuddled by a mother unknown to him, but to whom he may have started to attach when the agency came to place him with Katherine and Bill?

The newborn child's preverbal state makes it difficult to assess accurately the emotional response to separation from the biological mother and the effect of relinquishment on his life. Later, the adopted child has no conscious memory of the separation. Marcy Wineman Axness, an adoptee and doctoral student in perinatology, points out that this does not mean that the child has not experienced the loss, or that he does not retain what is called "behavioral memory" of a primal trauma that is mentally unrememberable, while somatically and behaviorally unforgettable. From Freud's perspective, the patient does not remember anything of what he has forgotten and repressed but acts it out, repeating it not as a memory, but as an action. Hopefully, with greater insight into and sensitivity to the surprising perceptive and sensory abilities of newborns, people will become more aware of the needs of an infant separated at birth from his biological mother, whether that be through adoption or some other traumatic event.

Aware from the Start of the World Around Me

Such a knot of little purposeful nature!

Richard Eberhart

Until eminent child specialists D. W. Winnicott and Dr. Daniel Stern developed their groundbreaking theories about infant development, people generally believed that newborn babies had little ability to perceive the world around them. This has been disproved by countless research studies and clinical tests indicating that although the baby's brain is still developing after it has left the womb, the baby is far more aware than was once believed. In a special edition of *Newsweek* (Spring/Summer 1997) devoted to early child development, Susan Greenberg reports that "even in utero, they begin to recognize the muffled voices of those who will care for them," and many parents enjoy telling stories of how their babies responded in the womb to them. I learned recently that Andrew sang one song repeatedly to his daughter before she was born, and he and his wife, Chloe, are certain she recognized it after her birth.

In her novel *Behind the Scenes at the Museum*, Kate Atkinson goes so far as to create a meaningful miniature universe for an embryo by beginning the book at the very conception of the main character's life. Ruby expounds, hypothesizes, and wonders as she swims around in her amniotic soup, wishing her mother would cheer up and celebrate the pregnancy. Ruby has already become quite attached to her highly ambivalent and self-centered mother by the time she pops into the world, fighting from that moment on to fit into the many generations of her family described in the story. In *The Secret Life of the Unborn Child*, Thomas Verny discusses how unborn children feel, remember, think, and are aware of what goes on around them from conception to birth. By the sixth or seventh month of pregnancy, the fetus is able to discern subtle changes in his mother's mood and attitude.

Adoptee Joan Cummings believes that she "absorbed a lot of what her mother was feeling during the pregnancy." She says, "I think I was really connected to her while I was developing and that it actually helped me out later in life." Joan's mother, Diane, with whom she is now reunited, told her that during the pregnancy, even though she was under tremendous stress, she visualized them bonding and felt like she already knew her daughter when she was born. In his book *The First Relationship: Infant and Mother*, Daniel Stern writes about how we begin as newborns to navigate our way through the complicated topography of human interaction:

> The infant's first exposure to the human world consists simply of whatever his mother actually does with her face, voice, body and hands. The ongoing flow of her acts provides for the infant his emerging experience with the stuff of human communication and relatedness. This choreography of maternal behavior is the raw material from the outside world

with which the infant begins to construct his knowledge and experience of all things human: the human presence; the human face and voice, their forms and changes that make up expressions; the units and meaning of human behaviors; the relationship between his own behavior and someone else's.

It is essential to us and to our very survival to develop a sense of trust with those caring for us in the first months of infancy. Erik Erikson tells us that the psychosocial task of infancy is to develop this trust in order to move on to each challenging new phase that life presents. When the mother, whose voice we have come to recognize in the womb, suddenly disappears soon after birth, a rupture occurs that many adoptees feel is never completely healed. The trauma of separation from mother at birth also affects babies incubated for long periods, or babies whose mothers die in childbirth.

Though a child intrinsically forms a bond to her mother before and immediately after birth, research and experience show us, nevertheless, that this does not preclude her ability to attach to others. As Winnicott writes, "We can now say why we think the baby's mother is the most suitable person for the care of that baby; it is she who can reach this special state of primary maternal preoccupation without being ill. But an adoptive mother, or any woman who can be ill in the sense of 'primary maternal preoccupation,' may be in a position to adapt well enough, on account of having some capacity for identification with the baby." In more contemporary language we can say that babies attach readily to whoever becomes their primary caretaker. That is reassuring for adoptive parents. However, acknowledging the principal bond that exists between a child and the woman who gives birth to him is necessary, and while painful at times, need not be feared. On the contrary, some research shows that attachment with the adoptive parent happens more easily when birth mother and adoptee have time together before being separated. Allowing them to resolve to some degree the "primary maternal preoccupation" allows for a smoother transition to the adoptive parents. Recognizing that this is important helps adoptive parents attend to the special needs of their children.

How to Make Sense of This Primal Wound

What the child has missed is the security and serenity of oneness with the person who gave birth to him, a

continuum of bonding from prenatal to postnatal life.
This is a profound connection for which the adoptee
forever yearns.

Nancy Verrier, *The Primal Wound*

The journey back to when adoptee and birth mother separated, under whatever circumstances, is painful and difficult but of great importance in our attempts to learn how the two groups cope with their losses. In her book, *Synchronicity & Reunion,* LaVonne H. Stiffler says, "The loss of self and the identification phenomena, as commonly felt after the death of a loved one, are complicated and confounded in adoption loss, because of the physical and emotional bond created during pregnancy." Many professionals make a distinction between bonding and attachment. Bonding is a biological process that begins during pregnancy, whereas attachment happens with primary caretakers after birth who wholeheartedly love and care for the infant and develop their own "spiritual bond" with their children.

Winnicott's theory of *primary maternal preoccupation* asserts that the "condition" does not resolve itself for about a month after the child's birth, and as indicated above, babies who spend time with their birth mothers may actually attach more securely to their adoptive parents. We might well question then what harm can be caused by separating mother and child abruptly and prematurely. Annette Baran says, "The first month after the birth of the child is a time when the mother and the child are still connected as one. It's at both ends; the mother has to finish her business, and the child is not ready to separate yet. If you take the child away from the mother that quickly, what you have done is to cause an amputation for both the mother and the child." It is not hard to imagine how a baby might be more agitated and anxious if separated too soon from his biological mother, and how that underlying anxiety might affect the baby's initial experience with his adoptive parents.

Right after I relinquished Andrew, I remember walking around feeling that there was a hole, literally, inside me. Some sense of loss is not that uncommon for most women who give birth, and the empty womb and changing hormones do sometimes lead to postpartum blues. However, mothers who are parenting their babies have that baby there to hold close to their hearts, whereas women who relinquish their babies are stuck with the feelings of emptiness. What I initially felt acutely, both physically and emotionally, gradually slipped into my unconscious, and the hollowness I had felt silently became part of the fabric of my existence. When I first learned of the concept of the "primal wound," it resonated deeply for me as a birth mother. Baran also says, "You see a lot of birth mothers who really go through life feeling the pain of a nonexistent limb." Carol Schaefer too believes that "there's a primal wound for women who have given up their children. It doesn't mean they can't heal or that they haven't learned something tremendous from the experience, but it's at a great cost." It is significant to me that almost immediately after Andrew reappeared in my life, I once again became aware of that hole as it began to fill at last.

Many adoptees, without always being able to articulate the feeling, have ventured through their childhood, adolescence, and adult life never developing a sense of trust in their personal relationships. "Children are known to be resilient," writes Betty Jean Lifton in *Journey of the Adopted Self*, "to suffer all kinds of early abandonments and other traumas and to recover. But when the adopted child learns that he both *is* and *is not* the child of his parents, the shock connects to that earlier preverbal trauma that the baby had at separation from the mother and has retained as an inner experience." Adoptive mother and author of the book *The Primal Wound,* Nancy Verrier began her research after struggling with her adoptive daughter and striving to find a way to comprehend her hidden demons and fears. It was only after years of therapy that the family became aware of what she has termed "the primal wound, a wound which is physical, emotional, psychological, and spiritual, a wound which causes pain so profound as to have been described as cellular by those adoptees who allowed themselves to go that deeply into their pain."

The societal lack of understanding of her daughter's problems and the overrepresentation of adoptees in residential treatment centers, juvenile halls, and special schools induced Verrier to present her ideas in a book. Her intent was not to offer excuses or to place blame, but to elucidate and heal. Although for years parents were told that all their children needed was love and affection, it is now generally accepted that if we do not confront the pain of separation and adoption, it will lie dormant, only to emerge at various times in an adoptee's life expressed as numbness, a fear of intimacy, or a detachment from others. In her essay "In Defense of 'The Primal Wound,'" Marcy Wineman Axness recalls her first reading of the principles of Verrier's work: "I felt a sense of relief down to my bones, a tearful epiphany of oh God, someone finally knows me, sees me, understands this impossible ache/not-ache, this me/not me that I've been living with all these years, in solitary, the loneliness of not being understood, and moreover, the exasperation of the narrow halls of life when one is not conversant with one's full spectrum of being. Confined, and puzzled as to why." Axness felt that in the primal wound she found a crucial "key" to herself, but not all adoptees may feel this way. The sheer will and force it takes to delve into the hurt is not a task for which everyone is prepared, and many simply have no interest in such an exercise.

I remember feeling shaken as people I interviewed talked to me about the primal wound and its effect on the adopted person. I had always taken for granted that although complicated, adoption was fundamentally good for the child, and this new wrinkle in the complexity of the adoption experience gave me serious pause. Were our children irreparably damaged? What about Andrew? Then I read Nancy Verrier's book myself, and while some anxiety lingered, the raw fear subsided, and I could acknowledge that it makes sense that relinquishment and separation are traumatic for the pre-verbal infant, and that the imprint of that experience would be profound. It impressed me as a birth mother that an adoptive parent's love for her child would take her that distance in her quest to understand and help her daughter. I can fully appreciate the desire of adoptive parents (any parents really) to believe that their love alone can provide everything their child needs, that there is no history to reconcile. At the same time, it can be a relief for the parent to know she is not responsible for her daughter's pain, that she can simply acknowledge it is there and parent her child armed with a deeper understanding of her needs.

None of us comes through life unscathed. Illness, death, divorce, abuse, and alcoholism are among the many challenges faced by any of us. To admit that separation from the mother at birth has a profound effect on the infant simply moves us into previously unexplored territory that once understood and confronted need not be deemed devastating. Lois Melina, the author of *Raising Adopted Children* and publisher of the newsletter "Adopted Child," has said that the problem may lie not with the description of what occurs, but with the label given to it. She says that calling it a "primal wound" seems to make it sound unhealable—"a wound, but a *primal* one —one that we can never recover from, because it goes to the very core of who we are." She says that labeling it as such in effect legitimizes the theory, and that if it has a name, it must be real. At the same time she agrees that what Verrier describes *does* resonate with adoptees and birth parents—and even adoptive parents. If we can transcend the issue of the label given to it, perhaps we can break through our personal barriers and accept that the phenomenon exists and can be reckoned with much as we deal with any other challenge life brings us.

Many in the adoption community agree with Verrier's theories and actively address issues related to the so-called primal wound. Annette Baran says that if you take a child away from its mother, you're adding to an already traumatic situation:

> Birth is quite an ordeal, and kids are born with terrible headaches. They're pounding on the door to get out, you open it and out they come, and are they tired! If you then take the child away from what they know and is soft and the same, we're talking about the smell, the sound, the heartbeat, and you give them to a stranger, I think that's a great blow to the child. And it's a blow to the birth mother. Her breasts are swelling, hormones raging, and there's nowhere to go with it.

Health professionals too are beginning to place emphasis on the importance of the entire natal experience. "Many doctors and psychologists," writes Verrier, "now understand that bonding doesn't begin at birth, but is a continuum of physiological, psychological, and spiritual events which begin in utero and continue throughout the postnatal bonding period."

How an Infant Responds

Where do you connect with the human condition
when you are chosen and everyone else is born?

Betty Jean Lifton, *Lost and Found*

Carol Schaefer feels she did bond with her son while she was pregnant. "If I hadn't been in a home for unwed mothers," she says, "isolated from everyone else, I wouldn't have tuned into the spirit of my child, but I did." Schaefer, who has been reunited with her son for many years, feels that the love and connection with him she carried during her pregnancy is at least partly responsible for his well-adjusted outlook on life.

Other women, from the very moment they learned of their pregnancy, panicked, became suicidal, prayed for a miscarriage, considered ways to abort the fetus, made adoption plans, and hid themselves in shame until their secret made itself known. How could all these stressful preoccupations not adversely affect the incipient life growing inside? The special baby issue of *Newsweek* cites the research of Dr. Bruce Perry of Baylor College of Medicine, who says that "experience literally provides the organizing framework" for the brain of the developing child. Stress and trauma increase levels of cortisol, which, according to Perry, are particularly hazardous for children from birth to age three and affect areas in the brain associated with vigilance and arousal. After an original trauma, the brain is rigged to be hyperalert for any new stressful experience that would trigger another surge of cortisol. An early experience of trauma often causes hyperactivity and impulsive disorders. Although Dr. Perry's work refers to postnatal experiences, babies whose mothers were very stressed during pregnancy and babies separated at birth from their biological mother experience the same kind of trauma he describes. Once the baby is born, adoptee Joe Soll says, the "most basic connection in the world is broken. That bond that there can only be with the woman who brings you into this world is broken. It's irreplaceable."

When a newborn is taken away from its mother it naturally grieves, just as anyone would when separated from the person to whom they are closest. Many babies refuse to mold to their caretakers, crying and arching away, as though searching for someone else. Others' survival instinct may cause them to adapt by being outwardly submissive and docile. Adoptive parent and codirector of the Center for Family Connections, Michael Colberg, says that he thought his daughter was the ideal infant, because she slept almost all the time. "As a professional looking back," says Michael, "I now know she was shut down. It was a very significant change to be taken out of her environment, to go from being inside and outside the same person with the consistencies in sound and sensory information. Being moved from the biological mother to someone else is a big deal."

Adoptive parents as the new primary caretakers need to hold and massage their baby to help them become more emotionally secure, and to reassure on the deepest level that they are not going away too. *Newsweek* reports that Dr. Tiffany Field of the University of Miami Touch Research Institute has shown that touch decreases stress, and that infants who are massaged regularly have lower levels of stress hormones. Touch therapy is rapidly gaining respect in the medical community, and parent-infant massage classes have become very popular. These are excellent resources for adoptive parents seeking to build trust with their children. In his book *The*

Seven Spiritual Laws for Parents, Dr. Deepak Chopra refers to an infant as "pure spiritual gold." He says, "Spiritual bonding with your infant comes through touching, holding, providing security from harm, playing, and giving attention." All people need this response from their environment to flourish. As adoptive parents undertake their own spiritual journey with their baby, they can massage her and hold her. They can tell her that they understand she is hurting and misses her birth mother. They can say "I know you lost something very important to you and that you mourn that connection." On some nonverbal, energetic level, she will perceive the message and feel secure in her parents' arms.

While adoptive parents cannot change the essential reality of the birth mother's abandonment, with greater awareness, they can be sensitive to the pain that is at the core of this rejection. Adoptive mothers often worry that their role as parents is always in question, and they fear that they are not adequate because they did not give birth. It is understandable that the "primal wound" concept would at first increase their fear. In my view, however, their role as parents is enhanced, not diminished, when they are able to set aside their fear and accept the usefulness of this kind of information. Armed with knowledge of findings that can contribute to the well-being of their children, they have a greater opportunity to help their children grow into productive, healthy adults.

When I Choose to Mother

> Trust builds very slowly after a profound separation
> such as that which all adoptees experience. This is not
> a rejection of the person who is trying to give love; it
> is a way in which the child protects against further
> loss.
>
> Nancy Verrier, *The Primal Wound*

It is no surprise that when an adoptee becomes a parent, the trauma of her own birth can inhibit the growing relationship with her new child. If the adoptee has never acknowledged or mourned the loss of her birth mother, then her own experience as a mother is likely to be affected. In her insightful essay, "Many Hands: An Adoptee's Healing Journey," adoptee Marcy Wineman Axness tells of her experience at the death of her adoptive mother, and she connects the beginning of her healing journey to the birth of her first child:

> My real healing, I've often thought, began on the breezy morning when I watched my adoptive mother's ashes sink into the endless blue of Maui's friendly waves. Even as I sobbed the deepest of soul-shaking tears—had I ever cried so hard before?—I was puzzled, for these waves of grief were out of proportion to my rather detached, superficial relationship with my dead mother. . . . Even as I wept convulsively, the part of me that always watched from afar wondered why. I wasn't to find out for many years to come, for my body/mind/soul wasn't about to let go of their driving secrets without a struggle, without a threat.
>
> That threat came in the form an 8 lb., 14½ oz. bundle of unbridled needs and wants, born to my husband, John, and me when I was thirty, whom we named Ian. The experience of mothering relentlessly chipped away at the artificial self I had presented to the world—and myself— for 30 years. Mothering broke me open.

It took many years for Marcy to realize what actually happened to her, and until she consciously recognized her "primal wound," it affected her ability to relate intimately with her baby son: "It was *this* deep sorrow, unearthed for just a moment, that flowed in those tears so long ago when I buried my mother, sorrow for the original mother, and also the stark realization, unspoken until all these years later, that 'I never had a mother and I never will.'" The primal wound theory resonates profoundly for those who have been wandering through a landscape of twilight, unsure why they have difficulty connecting to the people around them. Once recognized, Marcy was able to address her loss therapeutically so that she could enjoy the full experience of motherhood.

Several voices question the degree of impact of the primal wound, and some like Lois Melina are troubled by the name given to the condition. There is also more anecdotal evidence rather than empirical research to document its effect. Others are concerned that it may be a catchall concept used to explain all the "ills" of adoption. In her essay "In Defense of 'The Primal Wound,'" Marcy Axness says that "to worry that the hapless adoptee will remain in the grip of this archetype-based idea of the primal wound, so that everything for that person will forevermore be explained by that theory, is to reveal a cynicism about the emotional and spiritual resources of the adopted person to continue the process of integration, the process of pursuing wholeness along whatever paths lead the way." She also says that paradoxically, it is only now, after being able to look back and grieve over what she lost, grieve over what her adoptive mother was *not* able to give her, that she can truly appreciate who her adoptive mother was, and what she *did* get from her. I am reminded here of people's arguments against psychotherapy, because it can cause the patient to dwell on the pain and to "hate" their parents, when in fact good therapy helps the person acknowledge the pain, move through it, and ultimately establish healthier relationships.

Some adoptive parents resist the idea that their children have such a permanent connection to someone they fear and would prefer to forget exists. Birth parents, on the other hand, sense a mounting wall of blame directed toward them for creating a wound that can never fully mend. When we can cut through these fears and issues of blame, we can begin to heal ourselves and our children. "What adoptees need to know," writes Verrier, "is that their experience was real." What we need to do is recognize that reality and start from there. Verrier also counsels us that love is a form of "communication" that must be received as well as given. Ultimately, acknowledging the pain is part of finding our place in the universe. Coming to some psychic and spiritual peace about what has happened in the past helps us determine how to go forward in the future.

What Happened After Birth?

> I felt nauseous, suddenly.
> "We did not get Jack until he was eight months old."
> I swallowed hard. Salty tears instantly burned my eyes.
> Oh, my little baby. What happened to you?
>
> Carol Schaefer, *The Other Mother*

After I said good-bye to Andrew, I had no idea that he was going to spend his first month in foster care. The numbness that had characterized my pregnancy and delivery kept a firm hold on my body and spirit, not allowing me to wonder where and with whom my new baby was destined to spend his life. When I got a call from the agency a month later announcing that he had been placed with a family, I was surprised and upset that he had been in a temporary home all that time. Some instinctive maternal concern sensed a red flag and sounded an alarm that penetrated my shield. I voiced my concern that he had been without parents for so long. They told me this was normal, but in my heart I knew otherwise.

Other birth mothers, like Carol Schaefer, said good-bye to their infants, only to learn decades later how the child spent his first weeks and months before agency workers and adoptive parents finalized arrangements. She writes in *The Other Mother* of hearing her son's fate from his adoptive mother: "Rosemary said Jack had been placed with another couple first. And he had spent six weeks in a foster home before that couple got him. I asked if she was sure. That was one thing I had demanded of Sister Dominic, that he go to his adoptive family right away. . . . He had been only twenty-five miles away when I was in college. He should have been in my arms."

In my generation, it was common practice for babies to be put in foster care for a month even if the biological mother had signed papers of relinquishment. Now, the baby is often in foster care until the mother determines whether she is going to parent or relinquish the child. Opting to place a baby in temporary care while deliberating over the decision is more empowering to the birth parents of today, but it does not necessarily make the choice any easier, and some feel it does not help the baby.

Melissa says it took her five weeks to decide whether or not to give her son to his adoptive parents: "My caseworker came to the hospital and took him down to New York City to put him in foster care while I made my decision. I had the option to have him at home with me anytime I wanted, but I wasn't so sure that if I brought him home, I'd have the strength to give him away. I knew I had to do it this way, so I didn't see him."

Melissa spent some time with her brother's family during those five weeks, and it confirmed her feelings that she wanted her child to have two parents. "I want all my children to have a mother and a father," she says, "who are financially and emotionally prepared to raise a child." As with birth mothers who did not see their babies at all in the hospital for fear of not being able to go through with the decision to relinquish, Melissa tells us she might not have had the strength to relinquish if she had kept the baby with her or had gone to see him. While she was with her family, her son was being cared for by people he was not connected to and from whom he would also be separated in another few weeks. This is accepted practice in most traditional agency adoptions. In view of what we now know, however, about the lifelong effect of separation on the child, we might begin to ask ourselves some questions about the system we have and see if there might be a better way.

Why Age Matters: Domestic versus International

And God stands winding His lonely
horn,
And time and the world are ever in
flight.

William Butler Yeats

Most domestic adoptions, depending on whether they are facilitated by a licensed agency or an independent operator and whether open or closed, tend to follow a standard protocol. In independent adoptions, babies generally go straight home with their adoptive parents, whereas agencies usually place infants in foster care for anywhere from a few weeks to several months. Children adopted from other countries are generally older, and many have been in crowded orphanages. In "Adoption and Stages of Development," Elaine Frank says, "When older babies or children are adopted, their capacity to form relationships may have been disturbed." A number of the parents who eagerly adopted Romanian orphans who had been languishing in the horribly maintained state-run facilities have discovered only a few years later that their children often harbor and exhibit severe attachment disorders. Some of these parents find it impossible to care for these children and adopt them away to others, thus rupturing the children's lives once again. It is apparent that the sooner children find a permanent home and begin attaching to their new parents, the better they are likely to adapt. In other words, the length of time before placement can affect their outcome, and a child's age at adoption plays an important role.

In later chapters, we will look further into some of the issues of international adoption as they relate to the adoptees and the parents who adopt them. For now, however, it is important to note that these children have suffered an even greater and more obvious trauma than children adopted domestically as infants. In some extreme situations, the children are unable to thrive or to attach at all to their parents, who find themselves helpless and unable to cope. Generally though, adoptive parents help their foreign-born adopted children adjust to their new surroundings by understanding themselves that the child is grieving and is disoriented, and by educating themselves about what they might expect in the way of attachment difficulties. Adoptive mother Dawn Gelder comments in the article "Becoming an Adoptive Family," "My daughter Lanae was four months old when we brought her home from Korea. She cried inconsolably. Our second child had been colicky and often cried in pain, but Lanae's cry was different. It wasn't angry; it seemed sad. Once I understood that she was grieving—that she needed to express these feelings—it was easier for me to relate to what she was going through." The pain and loss are more apparent in older children and therefore easier to admit. Although it is less visible in infants, they need the same understanding and empathy.

So Many Children in Need: The Foster Care System

> While his childhood slips away, John's social workers debate his best interests and the programs they hope will address them. But this skinny kid who loves baseball knows better: "I'm all wrapped up in programs," he says. "What I need is a mom."
>
> Conna Craig, *What I Need Is a Mom*

In the previous pages, we have examined how babies are affected by separation from their birth mothers and from extended delays in placement. We also know that when older children are adopted, they are more likely to have attachment problems. We can easily understand then that children coming out of foster care have demonstrable problems, which become more serious the longer they live without a permanent home. Large numbers of children in our foster care system are caught, nevertheless, in what has become a bureaucratic tragedy. At the end of fiscal year 1995, there were 483,000 children in foster care. This number represents a 72 percent increase over the number of children in 1986. According to the report *The Future of Children,* as many as 85,000 of the children in foster care in 1993 were "waiting" for a permanent placement.

Ironically, there are thousands of infants, including those with special needs, languishing in state-run homes and facilities. Years can go by before they are available for adoption, and by then their chances of finding a permanent home are diminished. This fact is confirmed by a University of

Chicago study that found that children who enter foster care as infants remain in the system 22 percent longer than other young children. Another study, conducted by the Center for the Study of Youth Policy in Michigan, indicated that one in three children enter the foster care system as infants, and that they generally have only a 50 percent chance of finding a permanent home, either through adoption or by returning to their original home, by the time they reach their fourth birthday. The data show that the younger a child is, the more likely the child is to be adopted. According to statistics provided by Voluntary Cooperative Information System in 1993, almost 55 percent of finalized adoptions in 1990 were of children between birth and five years of age.

The reasons why so few children in temporary care will find stable, permanent homes are as vast and complex as the foster care system itself. Most often, they do not actually enter the system available to be adopted because parental rights have not been terminated. In addition, many of the children are considered to have "special needs" if they are older, are of diverse racial or ethnic backgrounds, are part of a sibling group, or have specific emotional, physical, or mental disabilities. Many prospective adoptive parents do not feel that they are able to or want to adopt children who have such "special needs." Others who do seek to adopt are often turned down by agency workers because of, among other things, racial considerations. A good number are discouraged by protracted waiting periods and complicated state rules and regulations. Meanwhile, the longer a child remains in temporary care, the harder it will be not only for him to be adopted but also for him to adapt successfully to an adoptive family. Unfortunately, as Dr. Eileen Bazelon writes in "A Psychiatrist Comments," "Politics, rather than an understanding of children's needs, often dictates decisions about child placement."

The foster care process, until very recently, has moved in a linear fashion, with reunification with biological parents and kin as the primary goal of caseworkers. It is now clear, as those who have worked in the child welfare system can attest, that the old method of reunification first, preparation for adoption planning second, and adoption planning third, is just not working. There is a near complete "lack of coordination," according to Judith K. McKenzie in her paper "Adoption of Children with Special Needs," "between family preservation, foster care, adoption, and legal services, which contributes to duplication of efforts and prolongs a child's stay in foster care."

Since the Adoption and Safe Families Act of 1997 has been signed into law, new federal and state initiatives are being instituted to speed up the process of terminating parental rights. The law actively promotes adoption of children in foster care by providing fiscal incentives to states to achieve adoptive placements. The new law also extends through 2001 the provision and funding for "Family Preservation and Support Services" to be allocated on a time-limited basis during "the fifteen-month period that begins on the date that the child . . . is considered to have entered foster care." Under this umbrella is a stipulation for "adoption promotion and support," but it remains to be worked out state by state how funds are to be allocated for pre- and postadoption services, including quality counseling.

An approach known as concurrent planning, whereby the biological parent whose child is removed from the home is counseled about requirements for family reunification and is also offered the possibility of making an adoption plan, is being used in places across the country. The theory is that parents will be more likely to consider voluntary relinquishment, but if not, after a specified time if they are not making progress, the parental rights will be involuntarily terminated so that the child becomes available for adoption sooner than was was previously the custom, thereby affording him a better chance of being adopted. This approach has the advantage of being compatible with the provisions of the Adoption and Safe Families Act of 1997, which allows funding for "Family Preservation and Support Services" for no more than fifteen months. According to Kathy Legg, executive director of Spence-Chapin, who is recommending concurrent planning be undertaken by New York City's Child Welfare Agency, this would allow the mother or guardian to participate in the decision of what happens to her child. Legg says, "You're giving the mother the opportunity to do something good for her child and not lose complete contact. And that's not to say that we want to twist her arm, but you can't hold the child hostage for the parent getting ready, it's just not fair."

While this move to speed up adoptions is needed, it is not a panacea for our family welfare ills. The issues behind why birth parents are unable to care for their children should not disappear in the new wave of adoption frenzy. Martha Allen, who has worked in foster care and adoption for over twenty-five years, presented a paper at the 1996 AAC conference citing some of the reasons why many parents cannot responsibly take care of their children. In her presentation, she flags such critical factors as unemployment, inadequate schooling, poor parenting models, and growing up in dysfunctional homes as crucial to one's own inability to parent. Many parents turn to drugs, sex, and crime to deal with their own pain, reenacting patterns of abuse that they themselves may have experienced. Agency workers may not be able to save a family, but it is important for the child to understand why his parents could not care for him. When talking about these issues with children, care needs to be taken not to cast their biological parents in a wholly negative light, because the birth mother and father remain very much a part of the child.

Older children, especially, usually know their birth parents, and they and their adoptive families need good counseling to help them understand and integrate their history so that they can establish a healthy individual identity. When these older foster care children are adopted, they are usually cut off from their birth family and/or from their foster family, to whom they have become attached, and that can adversely affect their adjustment to their adoptive families. Instead of completely depriving a child of having any contact, why not—when it is feasible and safety permits—try to create a placement where there can be some communication with supervision.

While the various provisions that are being considered or implemented should help remedy the system, there is no doubt the current situation is desperate. As Rachel L. Swarns reported recently in the *New York Times,* "Hundreds of New York City's most troubled children are stranded in city offices, psychiatric hospitals and private homes because the child welfare system is virtually filled to capacity." And we all hear of the tragic deaths of children who slip through the cracks of the child welfare system. Clearly, steps have to be taken quickly to help these children.

Nature versus Nurture

> Adoptees are not clones of either their adoptive or
> biologic parents. They are unique individuals created
> and nurtured by two sets of parents.
>
> Lois Melina, *Adopted Child* newsletter

In recognizing that relinquishment has a fundamental impact on a child whether it be at birth or some years later, we are in fact acknowledging the importance of the biological component in an individual's life. This in turn raises the long-standing question of whether nature dictates the course of a person's development, or whether nurture makes a more significant differ-ence. According to Marlou Russell's book, *Adoption Wisdom:* "This debate has special significance in adoption. People want to know how much of a child's personality and behavior is due to genetics and how much is due to the way a child is being raised." Behavioral geneticists and environmental-ists have been searching for years for a definitive answer. Recently, there has been a shift away from the long-held assumption that environment plays a larger role in a person's life, and current research involving identical twins and adoptees points convincingly to a greater influence of genetics.

Lois Melina interviewed Linda Claxton, a social worker at Children's Home Society of Minnesota, for the September 1989 issue of *Adopted Child,* which was devoted to the subject of nature versus nurture. In Clax-ton's view this new appreciation of the importance of heredity helps adop-tive parents recognize that their children come to them with their own genealogy and have a need to feel connected to their genetic heritage. Melina suggests though that "it should not be necessary to show that genet-ics is more than 50 percent influential to explain this need, justify contact between birthparents and adoptees, or recognize that birthparents have made a significant contribution to their children." Melina also points out that the downside of emphasizing genetics is that adoptive parents can just as easily fall back on the "bad seed" theory. This way, they can take pride in what they like in their child and distance themselves from behavior they feel stems from the "bad blood." These are false assumptions that can adversely influence parents' expectations for their children. It is easy, for instance, to mistake a predisposition to a particular illness for a certainty that the child will develop that illness. Melina cites Joseph Horn, Ph.D., a researcher involved in the large study known as the Texas Adoption Project, who asserts that having information about genetics only indicates "probabilities not certainties." She offers as an example Huntington's disease, where a carrier has a fifty-fifty chance of passing the disease to offspring, and sug-gests that the risk of inheriting any number of other conditions is signifi-cantly less.

In *Talking with Young Children About Adoption,* authors Mary Watkins and Susan Fisher cite several studies of the late 1980s and early 1990s by a number of researchers, including Plomin, DeFries, Fulker, Reiss, Hethering-ton, and Daniels, in which they compared adopted and biological offspring as they related to their environment. Watkins and Fisher report, "The find-ings emerging from this large body of research support the hypothesis that whatever the genetics may be, the environment potentiates them—any child becomes more musical if he has musical lessons, but a musically gifted child raised in a musically indifferent family may never develop his musical talent." At the same time they say the research seems to indicate that "the genetic effect reveals itself increasingly with age." Other researchers, including Scarr and Weinberg, who studied a group of adopted adolescents from infancy, as well as Horn of the Texas Adoption Project, also conclude that as people grow older and have more control over their lives, they appear to be genetically predisposed toward certain choices.

Studies of identical twins are perhaps the most revealing. Lawrence Wright's August 7, 1995, article for *The New Yorker* examines the histories of a number of sets of identical twins who had been reared apart. The similarities in personalities and life experiences were startling, and the research findings from studies of twins as well as of adoptees have shaken the foundation of our previously held beliefs and have affected the debate on social policy. Leon Kamin, Ph.D., coauthor of *Not in Our Genes,* has been critical of the adoption-related research and asserts that the research was flawed because the groups studied were not comprised of families with both adopted and biological children, and also because some of the adoptive families were the product of agency "matching" practices, which placed children with parents with similar physical characteristics and genealogical backgrounds and therefore skewed the results. According to Melina's newsletter, he is particularly concerned that the findings can be used to justify racial bias and prejudice against minorities. Lawrence Wright's *New Yorker* article also reflects on how, in the current political climate, arguments favoring the influence of genes go to the core of the debate between conservatives and liberals and can adversely affect public funding for social welfare programs.

While there are cases where adopted children do not overcome a serious genetic history, overall the message for adoptive families need not be interpreted negatively, and parents need not use the "gene" theory as a reason to fear their children's birth heritage—and more importantly their birth families. There is no need at all to pit one group against the other. After citing all the various research findings, Watkins and Fisher conclude that the mystery of how a baby develops into adulthood exists for all families. Only adoptive families have to "look it in the eye from the very beginning." In advising parents on how to talk to their children about adoption, they say, "We need to allow the *child* to teach *us* about his unfolding sense of adoption. . . . We would do well to begin anew in understanding adoption alongside of him, leaving behind some of our fears, embarking on this adventure together." Lois Melina also concludes that what kind of person a child becomes "says more about them than it says about either their adoptive or biologic parents."

Andrew is his parents' son, and his adult life is reflective of the upbringing he has enjoyed. Looking at him, though, I delight in recognizing physical and personality traits that he has inherited from me. For me there is no conflict, only appreciation of the qualities of both nature *and* nurture.

Finding a Way Home

> And he who gives a child a home
> Builds palaces in Kingdom come.

John Masefield

From the time we are in our mother's womb, to the moment we take our first breath, we are aware. We are here. The months prior to and just after birth are absolutely crucial to how adoptees perceive and inhabit their world. As they grow, parents help them find their unique gifts and talents. We cannot take anything for granted with the life of a child. Understanding how and why adoptive parents receive other women's children in their lives is part of the circle of learning. In the next chapter, beginning with the story of Andrew's adoptive parents, I will examine the personal issues and the ways in which people come to parent children not biologically their own.

THREE

SOUL CLAP ITS HANDS

Adoptive Parents Welcome a Child

One Family Begins

Who would have thought my shrivel'd
  heart
Could have recover'd greenness?

George Herbert

THE DILEMMAS AND issues for each member of the triad are equally complex. While I can only provide an angle that, at its core, derives from a birth mother's experience, I have grown to appreciate the concerns of adoptees and their adoptive parents since I met Andrew and his parents, Katherine and Bill. As Andrew's parents and I get to know one another, we are finding that our love for him unites us. My conversations with them have also broadened my understanding of why adoptive parents welcome other people's children into their lives.

Katherine told me that she and Bill met while she was still in college, and they married before she graduated. They moved to New York after Bill got a job there, and she finished her degree in early childhood education before deciding to start a family:

I taught second grade at a public school and not soon after marrying, both of us felt that it was time to begin our family. Children were definitely a part of our vision of a complete and fulfilling life together, and we decided that moving to the country would be a better place to establish a home. We moved to Connecticut, where grass, trees, and flowers were a part of our daily lives.

I soon became pregnant and we began preparing for a child in our home. Unfortunately, there were many problems during the pregnancy, including endometriosis and toxemia. The baby was stillborn, delivered with the cord wrapped around its neck, and never took a breath. We were both devastated, and the excitement we had felt as my belly had expanded quickly gave way to a black and despairing depression after the death of our child. We moved back to New York City, where I completed my master's degree in early childhood education and taught nursery school again. After a little time, when we felt that we had regained our emotional strength, Bill and I decided to try again. The next pregnancy lasted for five months, when I had what is known as a missed abortion. I was supposed to have miscarried earlier in the pregnancy, the doctors told us, but did not for some reason.

After losing the second baby, we started to think about adoption. I never gave up hope that I would deliver a full-term baby, but I was anxious to start our family and could not handle the loss of yet another child at that time. The doctors were afraid for my health after the toxemia and agreed that a break from pregnancy was wise. Bill and I agreed that we would investigate adoption, and in September 1965 we submitted our application to Spence-Chapin.

When I talked with Bill, he explained to me that in the 1960s, where you sought to adopt in New York City was often based on religion. There was Catholic Charities, and if you were Jewish, Louise Wise. Spence-Chapin was the nonsectarian alternative and was even then one of the foremost adoption agencies in the country. When they came to the agency, Bill said they were welcomed graciously, and he and Katherine discussed with the social worker their desire to adopt two boys and a girl:

Neither Katherine nor I had a brother, and we thought it would be fun to have boys in our lives. We were able to complete two-thirds of that plan and adopted two boys with little problem. The agency had no difficulty with a supply of infants when we began adopting, but by the time we were ready for a third in the early 1970s, the agency had fewer children to place.

I was very impressed by the compassion and thoroughness of the interviews at Spence-Chapin. One woman who talked with us was very specific about making sure adoption was not a secondary choice for us, considering our disappointment with our own childbirth process. Of course, we had tried to have biological children, but she wanted to know, I suppose, if we had emotionally dealt with our pain over the losses. I now believe that it was entirely appropriate and legitimate for her to ensure that we were absolutely committed to adopting a child and taking care of it every bit as much as if that child were of our own genetic background. They checked our home very carefully, visiting a number of times to see that we were well equipped and prepared for a baby.

When they were approved to be adoptive parents, Katherine and Bill joined a list of other couples waiting anxiously to receive a baby. Although they felt assured the call would come, they did not know how long it would take. Katherine remembers what it was like when they got the news there was a baby for them:

I was teaching nursery school in the spring of 1966 when I received a call from Spence saying that they had a baby boy for us. He was born March 20 and spent the first month in foster care. Exactly nine months after sending in our application and three days after the phone call from the agency, we met Andrew. Bill and I could barely contain our joy as we got into a cab near our home on the East Side and headed up Madison Avenue toward Spence. We were both so nervous and excited that we just chattered away the entire trip to the agency. Upon arrival, we were shown into a room where we met a social worker who greeted us and then promptly told us she was going to get the baby and bring him in. And there he was, this beautiful one-month-old baby with big brown eyes, dark brown hair, and a small cleft in his chin. The social worker handed him to me, and I just sobbed as I held him. Andrew was crying too, but eventually fell into a deep and nourishing sleep.

I cannot help but contrast Katherine and Bill's happiness in the taxi as they went to pick up Andrew with the heavy sadness my mother and I carried, as we rode through the same city streets to deliver him to the agency.

Presumably they were greeted by a more welcoming social worker and were escorted through a door reserved for adoptive parents—one where there would be no risk of running into weeping birth parents. The dichotomy between my sorrow and their joy is an incontrovertible reality of all adoptions. Bill and I talked about our experiences, and he acknowledged the obvious differences in the mood inside each taxi: "The one I was in with Katherine was one of just enormous joy. You know giddiness is the only way I can put it. And to be sensitive now, in talking with you, to be aware that the mood in the other conveyance would be so different is really sobering, and I've reflected a lot on that since we've talked about it."

Recently, some agencies and professionals have become more aware of a need to create an environment where both parties recognize each other's contribution and responsibility. At Spence-Chapin, as well as at other agencies, birth parents and adoptive parents are invited to exchange vows acknowledging each other. Birth parents need adoptive parents to know the love they have for their baby, and the great trust they place in them by giving them their child. Adoptive parents want birth parents to know they accept the responsibility of parenting their new baby, and acknowledge the birth parents' love and pain. These rituals of mutual respect and recognition help set the stage for a positive adoption in the long term.

When Katherine and Bill adopted Andrew, they were given nonidentifying information about the birth family that is the standard fare of closed adoptions, and then quickly went about the business of becoming parents. Katherine said that she was so excited that most of the information she was given flew out of her mind. She did, however, retain some of the basic details:

> I remember we were told by the agency the birth parents were a young couple who had met outside of the United States, were going to be married, but had decided to give the child up for adoption. We did not have any specific criteria that we submitted to the agency, but we were happy to hear that the birth mother was in college, and that they were young and healthy. We were told that the birth mother had the baby over spring vacation and then returned to school. I felt good knowing that the birth father and birth grandparents knew about the baby, because the birth mother would not have been all alone, going through this by herself; she had some kind of support during the process.
>
> After finalizing details with the agency, we dressed Andrew in clothes we had brought and took him back to our apartment. Our family had been devastated at the loss of our first two pregnancies and was

absolutely thrilled when we brought the baby home. My mother stayed with us for the first week and helped with the adjustment of a new baby. The agency had given us formula to feed Andrew, and for some reason, it kept clogging the nipple, so he was not getting any food. I kept sterilizing a sewing needle and trying to make the hole bigger by poking it, and Andrew was screaming bloody murder because he was so hungry. A friend came by and helped me try to figure out what to do, and I just looked at her at one point and said, "I think I've made a terrible mistake." I was just so frustrated.

We got through that difficult moment, and the care became easier. Andrew was such an easy baby, and it was just thrilling to have him in our lives. It was fortunate that he was an easy baby, because we were really never thoroughly counseled by anyone as to how to care for a baby, what their needs were, and how an adopted baby might be different from a baby that I had given birth to. I often thought about Andrew's birth mother and would say to myself, "How could anybody have given up such a beautiful child?" And I always thought about her on his birthday. I thought, "Gee, this must have been really hard and I wonder how she is feeling right now." I was sure that the birth mother was thinking about him on his birthdays.

These words from Katherine were gratifying. Knowing that she thought of me and was aware that I must be missing Andrew was important to me. I am sure her willingness to acknowledge me in her heart helped Andrew grow up understanding that he wasn't simply abandoned. When I talked again with Bill, he shared some of his memories of the early years with Andrew:

From roughly April of 1966 to February of 1969, it was just Katherine, Andrew, and me, and we had a wonderful time together. Andrew's maternal grandparents (my parents were no longer alive) adored him, and we saw them for all the major holidays and on many weekends. My memories are not just of Katherine and me loving him, but of our whole family having embraced Andrew and bringing him into their lives. He had one great aunt, Auntie Abby, whom he truly cherished, as he did his grandparents. It was a very happy time, a honeymoon period.

When people adopt a child, that child joins the extended adoptive family and is embraced by grandparents and aunts and uncles. Kenneth L. Woodward, writing for *Newsweek,* cites Arthur Kornhaber, a child psychiatrist, who has shown that "attachment between grandparent and grandchild is second in emotional power and influence only to the relationship between parents and children." Clearly, Andrew attached from the first days to his grandparents and to his Auntie Abby. These many years later, he has talked to me of them with pride and obvious love. He has also shared precious archival records of prominent people in Katherine's family history, a heritage he has wholeheartedly embraced as his own.

In biological and adoptive families alike, the arrival of new siblings changes the family dynamic. When Katherine and Bill adopted Jason, Bill remembers things changed considerably:

> One area where the agency had counseled us well was when to start talking about adoption, and that was from the very beginning. We used the word with Andrew from the very start, so when we adopted Jason, even though he might not have understood, Andrew had an idea where the new baby came from. In fact he came with us to the agency to pick up Jason, but he was so young, he doesn't remember it. We also adopted Jason when he was about a month old, and I think Andrew really never got over the fact that we had gotten another baby. I do think he noticed that children in his cousins' and friends' families were born and not picked up from an agency and that this fact stood out for him. Andrew and Jason are very different people, and the first thing I think Andrew noticed was the physical difference.
>
> We loved them both intensely and were so grateful to have them in our lives, that perhaps we did not pay close enough attention to their differences from the very beginning. We had created a family through adoption where we could not biologically. The early years were rich in new experiences and discoveries for us that we will always cherish, even though Katherine and I eventually divorced.

The Need for Children in Our Lives: Infertility Leads to Adoption

> For many the discovery of infertility cuts to the very core of being, destroying their sense of self-worth, and indeed of self.
>
> Elizabeth Bartholet, *Family Bonds*

For most people, the instinct to bear children is as fundamental as earth, water, fire, and air. Women talk of heat surges, hormonal pulls, psychological and physiological yearnings, and a nearly magnetic attraction toward babies. Men, while generally not as physically drawn to pregnancy as women, do feel the instinct to have a family, to create a connection to the human legacy that will continue after they are gone, and to strive for immortality through their offspring. When an individual or couple learns that they are unable to conceive or carry a biological child, it is as if the very ground on which they stand has imploded and all that remains is a large void in their universe. The shock of infertility, however it manifests itself, often wreaks havoc on personal relationships, self-esteem, and a person's faith. The eternal "Why me?" that birth mothers and adoptees constantly ask themselves is also a pressing question for men and women unable to have biological children.

Couples are often told when trying to conceive that if they "just relax and enjoy themselves," then they will get pregnant without a problem. Unfortunately, a serious effort to relax generally produces that much more anxiety and stress. Most women begin worrying about their fertility if they do not conceive after one or two tries and start to measure out their lives in two-week cycles. They get their periods, they mourn for a few days, take a short break, and then begin plotting when they think they will next ovulate. The doctors say not to worry until at least a year has passed, but few women can stand to feel so out of control of their bodies for such a long stretch of time. According to some reports, one in seven couples trying to get pregnant are unsuccessful. Many in the field believe that this figure grossly underestimates the scope of the situation.

Women are basically schooled from childhood to believe that their identities are linked to their ability to have children, and not being able to conceive or give birth can cause them to feel insecure about their maternal role. Birth and adoptive mother Cynthia Beals tells of the desperation she felt after relinquishing her first child and then not being able to get pregnant with another:

> I just couldn't imagine giving up my only child and then not being able to have another. I guess I thought all along that my bad luck had ended and that this couldn't be happening to me. As time went on and I learned that it was happening, I was devastated, to say the least. I just didn't know what to do. There weren't a lot of options out there for us

then. Artificial insemination was fairly new and it wasn't highly recommended. The other choice was adoption, which was fine with me. I
wanted a family.

Beth Lake, who felt that she had always been able to get what she wanted
in life, had to reassess her self-image and life plan in order to live with being
infertile. She and her husband went through several years of infertility treatments before deciding to adopt:

> We tried every available procedure that was known at the time, but
> nothing worked. Things are a lot more sophisticated now, but we
> jumped through the hoops of what was available then. After a certain
> point, we decided that if none of this worked, we would adopt. We
> were always open to the idea, especially, since I come from what I con-
> sider a "blended" family, full of stepchildren and wayward folks. It
> was just easy for me to understand the concept of nonblood relatives in
> your family. It didn't matter where they came from. They were a part
> of your family.

People hoping to get pregnant have a much better chance today than they
did formerly. Still, not everyone gets pregnant, even with the use of more
advanced technologies, or succeeds in carrying a child to term. Ginny
Graves reports in her article "Goodbye to Bio-Baby" that "of the estimated
three million couples currently seeing a doctor for help with conception,
about half will bear a child after the simplest kind of intervention. . . .
Couples who are unsuccessful after twelve months of basic intervention,
however, face ever-diminishing odds of success." For those who keep trying,
modern medicine tends not to offer greater comfort, only more frustration.
"The promise of pregnancy taunted us every month for years," says Jana
Wolff in *Secret Thoughts of an Adoptive Mother.* "Basal temperature
charts, LH surges, laparoscopy, Clomid, hCG injections, sperm washing,
insemination, asexual sex, and many other steps along the continuum. . . .
We were victims of fertility humility." Today, the prospect of custom-made
embryos adds yet another debatable option to the host of possibilities made
possible by modern technology.

When couples conclude they have had enough of the fertility roller
coaster, it is a very personal and difficult decision. Adoptive father David
Adler says, "Fertility work is very stressful. You can get involved with it for
a certain amount of time and then you say, 'We can't take this anymore.'

And you stop the process. But often you start it again and several years can go by. For us, it was something like five or six years in different incarnations." David and his wife came to a point finally where they started thinking about adoption. They knew adoption might not be easy, but they could no longer live with the disappointment of their medical ordeal. In "Goodbye to Bio-Baby," Ginny Graves writes, "Accepting the idea of adoption is a turning point for many infertile couples, who come to the realization that, for them, surefire parenthood is a saner goal than the dream of pregnancy."

A Bittersweet Solution: The Need for Counseling

For the adoptive parents, good counseling means embarking on an inner journey to confront the most destructive force in adoption—their own insecurities, their own profound losses through infertility or death or miscarriage of a child, and especially their own fears.

Marcy Wineman Axness

For those unable to conceive (or carry a child to term), adoption becomes an option that many hope will be the answer to their problems. Andrew's parents turned to adoption when they could no longer stand the pain of another lost baby. When they adopted their boys, they were prepared to love them as they would any child who might have been born to them. Nevertheless, the decision to adopt is a second choice for most people, and it is important for them to mourn and heal the loss of their fertility before moving headlong into adoption.

Diane Nemes, who has type I diabetes, managed to give birth to a daughter, but it was at the risk of grave physical harm to herself and her child. After her daughter was born, Diane knew she wanted more children, but her doctors advised her that there was a strong chance another pregnancy would result in the death of the child. After many months of therapy, Diane decided to have her tubes tied. Though it happens extremely rarely, two years after her surgery, she became pregnant again:

It was absolutely agonizing to try to decide what to do. And I kept saying, "Well, maybe this is a message from God that I'm supposed to have a child. It'll be different this time." I like to think that everything in life has a meaning, like when my brother died of cancer, and I began to wonder what this pregnancy was supposed to mean. And I realized that I really hadn't dealt with the fact that I wasn't going to have any more children, which meant to me forced infertility. I finally decided to have an abortion and then I miscarried. I made the choice and then it was made for me. I had my tubes removed and had to have major surgery. Then I really mourned the loss of that potential person and my fertility. Before I could even think about adoption, I had to figure out why I wanted more children and did I really want to raise someone else's child?

When couples adopt a child, they have to some extent resolved the pain caused by not being able to give birth to biological children. But like the birth mother whose child is lost to her, and the adoptee who has lost his birth parents, adoptive parents also carry the loss of their fertility through-out their life. In *Journey of the Adopted Self,* adoptee Betty Jean Lifton says that it is important to deal with the loss associated with being unable to conceive or give birth so as to prevent projecting any unconscious anger or fantasies onto the child. Adoptive parents need to resolve the feelings not only for themselves but also for the sake of their children.

Sharon Rhodes withstood a decade of tests, infertility treatments, surgery, fibroids, and endometriosis until her doctors finally checked her hormone levels and discovered that she had experienced early menopause. After months of psychotherapy, Sharon says she eventually realized that in spite of not being able to conceive, she still really wanted a child:

> At that time, my closest friend had a child and I was at the birth. I had been to other births, but my joy at this birth turned into a black hole. I couldn't see my friend, I couldn't see the baby, and it was clear to me that I needed a child in my life. We began looking into adoption, and it was incredibly overwhelming. There were domestic adoptions, foreign adoptions, interracial issues, agency regulations. We didn't know where to turn until my gynecologist told us about a progressive agency in Vermont called Friends in Adoption. We went to an introductory weekend and met a birth mother, other adoptive parents, and other prospective adoptive parents. The agency really promotes open adoption and they advocate for birth mothers. I was very moved by their philosophy and their support system. I spent the whole weekend sobbing and felt like I had finally come home.

Sharon felt that the months prior to adopting her son were very important in coming to terms with her own pain and the feelings of others in the
triad. "Along the way," she remembers, "there was hope, fear, and resis-
tance, and the turmoil of feelings was just overwhelming. I think, because
my husband and I are both therapists and spiritual people, we were very in
touch with the fear. I know that I was keenly aware of my loss and having
to let go of the idea of having a biological child." When Sharon did get the
call from the hospital that a birth mother had just literally run out of
the building, and there was a child in need of a home, she felt ready to begin
the next leg of the journey.

Reports show that many people move rapidly from infertility treatments
to trying to adopt, sometimes without giving themselves enough time to
grieve. Gretchen Viederman of Spence-Chapin says each situation is different, and the degree of counseling needed ranges from useful to absolutely
essential, depending on the family:

> Some families come having done lots of homework, in having really
> thought and looked and struggled and been in therapy and had coun-
> seling and are quite informed and in a good spot. Others are just begin-
> ners. So I think our response depends on all of that. I find that even with
> the most informed families, they will still talk about how isolated they
> feel, how alone, how different they feel from their siblings and their col-
> leagues at work who are achieving pregnancy pretty easily. They like
> the sense here of being able to connect with other adoptive families who
> are in the same boat and share the same feelings.

Although it may seem like torture after the years of struggling to conceive,
the protracted process of adopting provides the space needed to work
through feelings, reflect on decisions, and review expectations.

Not Simply an Event

> Adoption is a lifelong process which has to be inte-
> grated in different ways at different points in the lives
> of birthparents and adoptive parents.
>
> Jeanne Warren Lindsay, *Open Adoption: A Caring Option*

The task of dealing with infertility is followed by the task of learning about
adoption and learning that raising adopted children is different from raising

biological children. Prospective adoptive parents are naturally impatient to have a child, and they are not happy having to deal with the new difficulties and uncertainties that are part of the adoption process.

At this juncture, they are also confronted with the fundamental fact that the child they hope to adopt has biological parents. That alone presents the greatest emotional challenge, as they are asked to acknowledge in their hearts a lifelong link to birth parents, whether or not they ever meet them. At the time when Andrew was born, prospective adoptive parents did not have to think much about birth parents. Adoption professionals assured them there was no difference between a birth and adoptive family. Agency workers "matched" children to their new parents so that no one would ever question the child's origins. "Adoption workers believed that adoptive parents were better off without information on their child's medical and social background," says Ronny Diamond. "The adoptive placement was a new beginning, a blank slate. Adoptive parents were counseled to tell their child about adoption, and answer all his/her questions. And that once this was established, all the child's needs would be met. A good adoptive home and love were all the child needed." She explains to clients that experience and research have shown that in fact children need to know much more, and that it is important for adoptive parents to understand that "adoption brings losses, and that the best adoptive family and all the love in the world won't make up for those losses." She stresses the need for ongoing communication with the children to help them understand what it means to be adopted and to allow them, too, to grieve for their losses. If parents can show that they understand why their children wonder about their birth family, children will be more comfortable asking questions and sharing their feelings. By shying away from acknowledging the blood bond, adoptive parents may well communicate to their children that their birth family is not only inferior to the adoptive family—or perhaps simply irrelevant—but also, as far as they are concerned, does not exist.

In order to be eligibile to adopt, prospective adoptive parents have to be evaluated to determine their suitability to parent. This evaluation process is part of what is commonly known as the home study, a prerequisite for adoption across the country. It entails providing intimate details about their life and home, and many people are afraid of being judged unacceptable. It also feels like an imposition and an intrusion on their privacy, and many complain they are victims of a double standard, because biological parents are not required to submit themselves to the same scrutiny when they want to have children. In a sense this is true, but our society deems it necessary to place the needs of the child first when a child becomes available for adoption, and those entrusted with the child's care are obligated to ensure that every precaution has been taken when making a permanent placement. In addition, birth parents who voluntarily terminate their parental rights are not just abandoning their child. They want to know that they are handing him over to parents who they feel are best suited to provide the kind of home they want for him.

Although prospective adoptive parents approach preadoption counseling and home studies with mixed emotions, it is actually a vital way for them to educate and prepare themselves for the challenges of adoption, and to be sure they understand the toll infertility may have had on their life and how it can affect their children. Katherine and Bill's home study was very rigorous, and Bill feels that although it was difficult for them, he believes they were helped by the thoroughness of the study. They understood better how their child-bearing problems had influenced their decision to adopt, and they were prepared to handle the commitment. They were ready to be parents. Today, the process usually includes meetings with other members of the triad so that they can become more aware of the issues facing them as they become parents of adopted children.

When adoptive parents begin including birth parents in the scope of their child's family, they confront their worst fear, that the birth family will change their mind or will want their child back. Many cannot imagine giving up a child in the first place and can well understand why the mother might have a change of heart. David Adler experienced what he felt was an adoptive parent's worst nightmare about open adoption and contact with birth mothers. He and his wife received little or no counseling regarding the possibility that the birth mother they were in contact with, and had come to love, would keep her baby. He says people need to realize in advance that this can happen:

> All I'm saying is that it's common, and when it happens the adoptive
> family perceives it as a cataclysmic tragedy. The adoption service we
> were working with gave us no emotional preparation that this might
> happen. The birth mother basically stopped answering the telephone.
> We became very frightened that she was thinking about keeping. And
> she was. It was one of the worst things that happened to us since we
> were married. It was like the death of a loved one. Looking back now,
> I'm glad we didn't adopt the child because I think the birth mother was

looking at us to also be her parents, but at the time it just felt like our world had collapsed.

Even before a child is physically in the custody of his adoptive parents, many couples feel that the child is theirs. If a birth mother then decides to keep her baby, they feel almost as though someone has died.

Preadoption counseling is essential for prospective adoptive parents in order to prepare them for this possibility, even if they have developed a close relationship with the birth mother. Sharon Kaplan Roszia says this is so important because people need to realize that adoption is not just about getting a child. They really need to look at what it means for the child:

> What's the long-term picture here? Is it just about getting a kid and keeping it, or is it about having a story for that child so that as he grows up he can feel good about how he got here and who he is connected to and how the choices were made. It's about raising a person, not securing a baby. Tragically few people are counseled about bonding and attachment so that when something goes wrong, they have no point of reference, they feel hopeless and don't know where to turn.

Annette Baran adds that "I think one of the biggest problems is families' desperation for kids. If you think about it, they'll take any baby. And that's sad for them and the child. And if it's a bad mix, then nobody wins."

Although it is risky emotionally for adoptive parents to meet birth parents, with good counseling they are helped to understand the value of getting to know the birth mother as a real person, not as a shadowy disruptive figure. Eleanor Oakley counsels adoptive parents that life for the adoptive child starts before adoption and that meeting the birth mother offers them an opportunity to engage in a relationship. "It could be for only an hour," she says, "but if they personally see the birth mother and exchange ideas that revolve around the child, then the adoptive parent can be the one who shares that information and helps pull together the birth mother and the child so in some measure they create a partnership." In time some adoptive parents come to feel a sense of kinship with the birth parents of their child. Society offers no name for this connection, but the more I know Andrew's adoptive parents, the more certain I am that they are part of my family, as I am in some way a part of theirs.

Like most people, adoptive parents are fearful of the unknown, but once adoptive parents are able to acknowledge the importance of the birth family for their children they are better able to appreciate the benefits of more contact. In *The Spirit of Open Adoption,* Jim Gritter says that despite the risks inherent in open adoption, he has found that adoptive parents enjoy it. "They liked the candor. They liked the greater control over the experience that open adoption gave them. They liked the improved information they received. They liked the chance to be involved with the baby in the hospital. They liked being able to express gratitude to the people who deserved it. They just plain liked it."

Finally the day approaches when the long wait is over, and people seeking to adopt at last become parents. All their attention has been focused on getting their child, and there may have been little time to become familiar with the basics of baby care. Agencies may provide some rudimentary information, but usually the baby arrives suddenly, and families have to scramble to pull everything together. First-time parents are always somewhat nervous and worried. New adoptive parents just have a little more to deal with when they are abruptly thrust into caretaking after waiting for so long. Katherine's first panicky days of caring for Andrew are typical for most new moms. Her family rallied round her and Bill as they all embraced Andrew. This early period is crucial for adoptive parents and their child as they begin to establish their life as a family.

In *The Story of David* author Dion Howells says: "When David was done with his bottle and had burped enough to please Carey, she just sat with him in her arms. We hadn't yet gotten all the assorted baby accessories we would need. There was no downstairs bassinet or cradle to put him in. None of that bothered Carey. She probably would have chosen to hold him in her arms even if we had every baby item ever made. Carey had already fallen in love with David, and as along as he was in her arms, they were both completely satisfied with life."

The attachment of a baby to her new parents is the first step in what will be a lifelong process. It is a precious time, and adoptive parents are rightfully very protective of it. It is hard enough for parents of newborns to cope with grandparents or siblings who tell them what they should do. Every parent is insecure about whether they will be a good parent. Adoptive parents, even more so, struggle with questions of inadequacy. In these vulnerable early days, as they begin to establish their identity as parents, adoptive parents need to have a chance to experience the joy of new parenthood. Most have looked forward to this time for years and have endured tremendous loss in the process. They may be reluctant to admit at this time that their child is grieving the loss of its birth mother. Nancy Verrier reminds us in *The Primal Wound* that "it is very difficult for the adoptive mother of a newborn baby to take in the concept of the primal wound. It is abhorrent; it is heartbreaking; it is something she would rather not think about. And many adoptive mothers don't think about it."

While it is true that most new adoptive parents are not thinking about the "primal wound" per se, there are many who do think about how that baby came to them and do appreciate that there are birth parents who also love him. They will have many opportunities during the months and years to help their child deal with these feelings of loss. I have addressed groups of adoptive parents and prospective parents who understand that in gaining a new home, their children have been separated from their birth family. They express a real concern from the start of how best to convey to the children how much their birth parents love them. I remember how moved I was the first time an adoptive mother told me about her baby album, which opens with pictures of the birth family. Time and again, I am struck by the love adoptive parents express for their children in all the small ways they attend to their needs.

Gay and Lesbian Adoptions

> My major wish is that my kids can grow up with the same chances, opportunities, and support systems all children have, and that they not be discriminated against.
>
> Michael Elsasser, a gay adoptive parent in "For Daddy and Pappy, a 'Fantastic' Decision," *Newsweek*, 1995

In the 1960s when I was pregnant with Andrew, agencies placed the babies with two-parent, generally white families that best matched the prevailing idea of what was a "normal" parental situation. Changes in American culture, including gay rights, more special needs children, and unmarried women opting to raise rather than relinquish their children, have resulted in increasing numbers of "nontraditional" families. Coupled with the rise of these families has been an ever-growing movement giving voice to their unique situations. Some of these include advocacy for adoption of children by both members of a gay couple and for government-subsidized child care programs for single parents.

Jack Steadman, a single, gay adoptive parent, explains how he came to adopt his son in the early 1970s:

> I was close to thirty years old. I was a gay man who had just gone through the whole beginnings of the gay liberation movement and I had been trying to make a life on the model that straight people presented because it was the only model around. And that model was that you fall in love, you get married, you have kids. I had a strong support system around me of friends and family and I thought that for me the best thing I could do was raise a kid. I had raised other people's kids in institutions; I was a child care worker for many years, so I was used to kids from the age of about eight up through the teenage years. I thought I would like to try to raise a child of my own from infancy on, so I just did.

Jack was able to create what he calls "an invisible village" of support that he maintained throughout the years he was raising his son, but there are not many systems in place in or out of the gay community that assist or support gay adoptive parents.

Some reports state that there are from two million to eight million gay parents in the United States, but it is very difficult to pinpoint an accurate number. The assumption remains that there are from four million to fourteen million children being cared for by gay parents in what is known as the Gayby Boom. The biases that gay and lesbian parents fight against include the ideas that gays are mentally ill, that lesbians are not maternal, and that homosexuals are hypersexual beings and are therefore unfit parents.

States have begun to pass some progressive legislation, but some judges will still rule in favor of biological parents who are convicted felons rather than a gay couple who want to adopt a child. One example, however, of a case where the courts ruled in favor of a gay adoption was when the New Jersey appellate court allowed a lesbian partner of a mother of twins to be granted all the legal rights of a parent. And in a breakthrough decision in December 1997, New Jersey has become the first state to specifically allow adoption by gay and unmarried couples jointly, no longer requiring them to go through a two-step adoption process individually. In another case, the Washington, D.C., court of appeals allowed two homosexual men in what they deemed a committed relationship to adopt a four-year-old girl. Two states, Florida and New Hampshire, ban gay adoptions altogether, but twenty-three have granted second-parent adoptions (for the other member in a gay couple).

One of the arguments against gay and lesbian adoptions is that the parents' sexuality will influence the child's. In a study entitled "Do Parents Influence the Sexual Orientation of Their Children? Findings from a Longitudinal Study of Lesbian Families," Susan Golombok and Fiona Tasker reported that their findings show there is no basis for the commonly held assumption that children raised by lesbian mothers will also become lesbian or gay. "The majority of children who grew up in lesbian families identified as heterosexual in adulthood, and there was no statistically significant difference between young adults from lesbian and heterosexual family backgrounds with respect to sexual orientation." The children of gay and lesbian parents, not surprisingly, were found to be more open to alternative types of lifestyles and parenting options.

Many gay adoptions are arranged through independent, nonagency facilitators, generally lawyers, although a number of adoption agencies have begun their own programs. Many of the children that gay men adopt have special needs because there are few birth parents who want a gay adoption for their child. Though rare, occasionally a birth mother will request a gay couple over a heterosexual one for her child. Clinical psychologist and author of *Getting Simon*, Kenneth Morgan, and his partner received their child from a woman who did not want another woman taking her place as mother.

When Michael Colberg and his partner, Gene, decided to adopt, they asked people they knew how they became adoptive parents. They were led to an agency in Brooklyn where they attended a number of orientation meetings. When they were called for their seventh orientation, Michael says, "I told them the only way I would go would be if I could give it, since I could probably do it better than they could." Nobody had told them that their status created a problem and that people in the agency who were trying to help them were possibly risking their jobs, because they were bucking unwritten policy. In their ongoing quest to adopt, they also met with a number of attorneys in New York and Los Angeles:

> One of them said through intermediaries that he had no problem working with us, but it was not in our best interest, because no one would ever choose us. Another was happy to take our retainer, and then wouldn't return phone calls. My favorite, an attorney in Los Angeles, took our money, placed ads, and said she would be in touch. After a

period of time, the ads were running out, and she wanted additional money. She said that she had almost called us about a child born with a tumor, because the couple in place had backed away. Then, she said they found out it was operable so she didn't need us. I realized then that the people who were putting themselves in charge of my future and any child I would let into our lives, I wouldn't let open a can of soup for me.

Eventually, Michael and Gene were assisted by Dawn Smith Pliner at Friends of Adoption agency in Vermont, who taught them the mechanics of how to go about things, and within three months they were offered five firm situations. Michael was determined to meet each of the women, and when he met Diane, he decided he would wait for her to give birth even if it meant risking the possibility she might not go through with an adoptive placement. Michael says he will always remember being present for the delivery. "There were a lot of people chattering and pointing as I and my partner took care of our daughter," says Michael. "I suddenly understood that we were going to be the subject of a lot of whispering, but I knew my job was to care for this baby. By the time we left thirty-five hours later, a lot of these people were rushing at us with supplies, and they stuffed their phone numbers into our pockets. I realized at that moment that we were really ambassadors. How we would be received would be dependent on the tone that we set, and we're still in touch with some of these people through the birth mother's family."

Although it is a struggle, lesbian and gay singles and parents are managing to overcome the many obstacles that they encounter on their journey to adoption. Nevertheless, there is no denying that adopted children growing up in lesbian and gay families have unique challenges, including handling being different from their peers in yet one more way. Michael Colberg says that because his daughter, Julie, has two fathers, it is always present that she is different. I have also heard of cases where children love their parents but are reluctant to bring friends home. One way parents can help their children is by including a diverse group of friends and role models in their support network. Gay adoptive parents know better than most how hurtful people can be, and some children are better able than others to cope with the pressures they will face. At the same time, much of parenting revolves around normal everyday activities, and as one adoptive parent has remarked, "I don't make gay breakfasts, I just make breakfast." A stable and loving home is critical for children no matter how many parents are called "daddy" or "mommy."

Single-Parent Adoptions

Mommy wanted a child very much, but it takes a
mommy and a daddy to make a baby and I didn't have
a husband.

Lois Ruskai Melina, from *Making Sense of Adoption*

Formerly, single-parent adoptions were relatively rare, and agencies were not likely to choose singles over couples. It was not considered socially appropriate to encourage single-parent households, and singles were most likely discouraged from applying. Research conducted during the 1970s found that only .5 percent to 4 percent of single persons seeking to adopt completed those adoptions. Studies in the 1980s, however, showed a steep increase, with 8 percent to 34 percent of single parents completing adoptions. Along with increased acceptance of single parenting in general came more acceptance of single-parent adoptions.

Most single adoptive parents are women who, despite not being married, still want to have a child. White singles who wish to adopt domestically still have a relatively difficult time adopting a healthy white infant, since most white single birth parents prefer not to relinquish their baby to another single parent. Many private agencies do not offer white single women much hope for a domestic, healthy white baby, and as a result they tend to adopt older children.

The experience is often different, however, for African-American women seeking to adopt, independently or through an agency, because many African-American households are headed by women, and African-American birth parents may have been raised by their mothers or grandmothers. They trust that the adoptive mother will be there for their child and worry less about the presence of an adoptive father.

Adopting a child is costly, and this can be a discouraging factor for single women wishing to adopt. Not only do they have to have resources to afford the adoption fees, but they will also need enough income to support the child on their own. Ironically, while they might have a better chance of finding a child through an independent attorney or facilitator, the expense is usually greater than through a not-for-profit agency. The financial picture may, however, be more flexibile for African-American singles working with agencies that are actively looking for parents for African-American children in need of a permanent home.

Many single people who want to adopt do so through the foster care system, where the need for parents far outweighs the desirability of two-parent homes. Navigating the public child welfare system is not easy, and a completed adoption can take enormous time and energy. Single parents can make a difference in special needs adoptions, an area that is finally getting more attention as the availability of healthy infants has declined. In 1995, only fourteen thousand special needs adoptions were finalized out of the roughly hundred thousand adoptions nationwide. Of course, raising any child as a single parent is difficult, and a child with special needs will place greater demands on the parent, both emotional and financial.

The international arena is another avenue that people who do not have a partner explore when seeking to adopt. China and some Latin American countries have relaxed rules on single-parent adoptions, and we will explore further in this and other chapters the particular concerns pertaining to international adoption.

Once they have a child, single adoptive parents, like any single parent, will have to face their child's inevitable questions. They will ask their parents not only why they were adopted but also why they do not have a father or a mother. Single adoptive parents face the same challenges as other adoptive parents, except of course they have to handle it on their own.

Agency versus Independent Adoption

We have a big business in California that has usurped the world of adoption and taken it away from the professionals.

Sharon Kaplan Roszia

Adoption is a field that draws professionals with the best of intentions and the desire to aid children in need, but it is also an arena that attracts those seeking to profit from the desperate circumstances of many triad members. In the current climate, there are a plethora of attorneys, adoption "facilitators," and even doctors who convince gullible women and their partners to relinquish their children to couples who, not coincidentally, have very deep pockets. Ironically, these facilitators found their niche when birth parents began demanding open adoptions, a move that would ideally benefit the adoptee, birth parents, and adoptive parents. Because so many agencies did not offer progressive programs that included open adoptions, some birth parents believed they had found their answer with attorneys. Unfortunately, there is no established authority to regulate private, independent adoptions, and too few attorneys and independent facilitators make efforts to secure good counseling for both prospective adoptive parents and birth parents. Many offer little or no counseling to adoptive parents, and in some places may even conduct the home study over the phone. They may also neglect to inform birth parents of all their options, and too often problems ensue. Adoptee Kate Burke has advocated extensively in California to protect the rights of birth parents in independent adoption. She says, "I would much prefer to have an agency work with a young woman or young man, birth mother or father, and make sure this is what they want to do. And if they're not sure, then let's not disrupt their lives. I think we need to look at the whole model of what's happening in adoption."

In agency adoptions, in addition to providing generally better counseling services for birth parents, babies are usually in the legal care of the agency until relinquishment papers are signed (even if they are being physically cared for by the adoptive parents, who may have chosen to risk possible disruption), and this buys birth parents more time to consider if they want to go through with the placement. When they do decide to place, they are more sure of their decision, and this is a relief for worried adoptive parents. Agencies are also more inclined to work with special needs children, so birth parents do not have to worry as much if they have a child who requires greater attention. In independent adoption, the agreement and placement are directly negotiated, and many poorly counseled birth and adoptive parents perceive the "hands-off" approach of an independent facilitator to be advantageous. However, they may not get the quality of service they need to make sound decisions, and this can come back to haunt them.

Many professionals and triad members believe that no one should profit financially from adoption. Nancy Verrier writes in *The Primal Wound* that "state-controlled, non-profit agencies, which would be required to provide adequate pre- and post-adoption counseling for the birth and adoptive parents, would assure an impartial setting for adoptions." Currently states are so overwhelmed with the child welfare crisis that overseeing all adoptions is not a realistic goal for the near future. Nevertheless, the more oversight there is, the better the chances that children are placed in homes that have been extensively evaluated and that are prepared to receive a child. In my view, agencies do this best. In addition, properly licensed nonprofit agency adoptions help assure that no one has a financial edge when adopting a child.

The business of finding children for wealthy couples is a nationwide system, but in California, where some of the streets *are* paved with gold, the market has exploded. Now, despite the fact that full disclosure of identifying information is now required by California state law, and agencies have rallied to embrace it, the independent facilitators have more or less captured the market. Annette Baran confirms that agencies are not placing many newborn babies. They have gone on to placing the special needs children, the hard-to-place-children:

> It's these entrepreneurs, these middlemen, these billable-hour attorneys, who have really taken over the world of newborns. What the attorneys, and middlemen figured out was the ploy that you could promise young, immature, unready women their cake and the ability to eat it too. They sold them an open adoption at relinquishment, but there is nothing in the law that says it has to stay open.

Jim Gritter worries about what he calls "the commercialization of adoption." He says, "I think the field has shifted from a professionally delivered system to a business. It's a consumer-beware, buyer-beware sort of situation and it's a huge step backward. Where we've gained on diminishing secrecy, we've lost on creating dignity. Children are now too often a commodity. Nobody would use that word, but that's the fact of how they're treated."

Adoptive parents need to consider thoroughly all of their options before choosing an agency or a third-party independent. When looking into agencies, I encourage finding out whether they are public or private, profit or nonprofit, and what kinds of pre- and post-adoption counseling they offer for both birth parents and adoptive families. If independent adoption is legal in your state, before engaging an attorney or working with a facilitator, it will be important to gather as much background information as possible, and to take the time to seek out good adoption counseling. In the short term, it may seem like extra work and a waste of time, but in the long term, this will be in the best interest of the child, and of the family.

Adoptive Parents and International Adoption

I feel as though we have so much Guatemala in our
life that there's never going to be a question of
whether he's going to speak Spanish. We'll go to

Guatemala again and introduce him to his heritage
because our life is rich and full of people and things of
Guatemala.

Diane Nemes, adoptive mother

Currently some 10,000 American singles and couples each year are adopting children from abroad. After World War II, most of the children adopted into the United States were of European descent. Between 1948 and 1953, Americans adopted close to 6,000 children from Europe. These adoptees were almost always white children adopted by white parents, so their integration into the American mainstream was made with minimal attention drawn to their adopted status. During the same time, some 2,500 Asian children, mostly of Japanese origin, were also adopted. These adoptees had a more difficult time assimilating into the racially divided culture of the United States. This was especially true because America had just fought a war against the Japanese.

The Korean War left another ravaged culture with orphans in need of homes. Coinciding with this event was the drop in availability for adoption in the United States of healthy, white infants. The adoption of Korean children in the 1950s (and in greater numbers in the 1970s and 1980s) and then Vietnamese in the 1960s (and now in the 1990s, as our political relations with Vietnam have improved) firmly established the pattern of white Americans adopting from racially different cultures. Currently, it is estimated that the total number of children adopted from Korea exceeds 85,000, and in 1991, immigration statistics indicated about 2,500 adoptions from Central and South America. Political and social unrest in Central and Eastern Europe during the late 1980s and early 1990s made white infants available for the first time since the end of World War II. Between 1989 and 1991, some 1,500 Romanian children were adopted by Americans. However, following an exposé of certain black market operations, Romania closed down all foreign adoptions in July of 1991 and has only recently begun to allow them to resume.

International adoptions are likely to continue in significant numbers. Though there is the usual red tape and the uncertainty of fluctuating politics, adopting an infant from a foreign country may be easier and faster than adopting domestically. Many of those who are adopting internationally also do so because they do not want to deal with birth parents. They simply do not want to be judged by the birth parents or feel they need to prove that they are fit to care for the child. We know, however, that no matter how distant these birth parents may be, they continue to exist in the hearts and minds of the children. Parents adopting from abroad may avoid their scrutiny, but they cannot eradicate their influence in their children's lives. Those wishing to hide in the imaginary safety net of international adoptions create what Jim Gritter calls "an amazing irony." He says, "I find it unbelievable that in the name of safety people would turn to the international arena, where there are so many unknowns, so many more variables. Things can take so many wild turns, that it's just mind-boggling to me." However, some adoptive parents have experienced a mother's change of heart and cannot face another possible loss. The decision to adopt internationally assures them that there will be a child for them in a predictable amount of time.

Once the infant or child is brought to the United States, it is important to take into account their ethnic and cultural background. Even as young infants they have to adapt and adjust to an entirely different set of cultural codes, a new language, and in many cases a lack of awareness and information about their heritage. While it may be true that adoption offers these children their only chance for a permanent family life, rescuing them from their impoverished circumstances is not necessarily a guarantee for a stable future.

David Adler and his wife decided not to try to adopt a child domestically after the woman they had been working with opted to keep her child. Though they adopted their daughter from Paraguay, they did meet her birth mother. That was important to them, and he and his wife are committed to honoring their daughter's heritage. David says, "It's a complex issue of how we're going to deal with her cultural roots. A lot of people ask us if we're going to speak Spanish to her, and I have to tell them that Spanish isn't actually the language of her birth mother. Gharani is the language. So it just isn't that simple." Other people have asked if they are going to celebrate Cinco de Mayo, and David has to explain that Cinco de Mayo is a Mexican holiday and his child is not from Mexico. Since I met with David, he and his wife have adopted another little girl, from China. The diversity of cultures their children bring with them will surely enrich their family life.

Eleanor Oakley admits that when she adopted her child from abroad there was initially a certain element of rescue involved. Later, after visiting several other adoption-friendly countries, her perspective changed:

> Having gone to the countries, I really came to understand how painful it is for the people to have children leave for adoption, how much they

love their children, how important the culture is for them in terms of having the children have a Russian, Chinese, or Guatemalan identity, and that really touched me. I think it also increased in me the commitment that when I work with couples who want to adopt from abroad, that it just be essential that they know that the children are always going to be of the country they came from, and how important it is for the family to embrace the culture. This means not just sending the child off to a language lesson or celebrating an annual holiday, but that it be an ongoing part of their life so that the child will value it when they see their parents value it. It's almost like religion. You don't just get sent off to Sunday school, it has to be something you live.

Diane Nemes puts it simply about her toddler son Sam from Guatemala. "I hope to encourage him to do whatever he needs to do to feel good about himself."

International adoptions are often a wonderfully fulfilling and successful way for foreign-born children and adoptive parents to create nurturing families. However, attachment and health problems can sometimes pose very real difficulties, and the situation varies, depending on how long and in what conditions children have been kept in their home country. Currently, nearly a third of all children adopted from abroad come from China, most of them girls. The children are still fairly young when they arrive in the United States, and the fact that they spend less time in rudimentary orphanage conditions helps them attach more easily to their American adoptive parents. Korean children, who comprise 14 percent of foreign adoptions, also fair well for the most part, thanks to a well-run foster care network. Children from Latin America, largely adopted during infancy, often have curable infectious diseases like hepatitis and tuberculosis. While there is no guarantee that these children will not develop other emotional and physical health problems, the research shows that they tend to adjust and adapt quite well to life in the United States.

Children from orphanages in Eastern Europe and the former Soviet republics often have more immediately apparent difficulties in the short term, because of the conditions in the orphanages and because they are usually older when they are adopted. The lack of physical contact and affection in the orphanages also significantly influences a child's ability to develop a sense of trust in the people around them and contributes to attachment problems. There have also been reports of abuse by adoptive parents who are not equipped or properly counseled to deal with a population of children suffering from severe emotional disturbances, developmental delays, and attachment disorders. Obviously, not all international adoptions are troubled, but there have been too many reported to ignore the issue. On June 16, 1997, *Newsweek* reported that "some horror stories are not exaggerated, and the fears that these tales inspire are based on some sad truths."

One of the ways that agencies that handle international adoptions can assure good standards in adoption practice is to establish connections with reputable organizations in each country, and to send personnel regularly to assess the quality of care of the children. Kathy Legg, executive director of Spence-Chapin, has worked to develop the agency's international department under the direction of Flicka van Praagh, who travels extensively to meet with adoption officials and to visit orphanages. International adoptions are handled differently in every country. "In some countries," says Kathy Legg, "you're working with an agency, in another you're working directly with the government, and in yet others you're dealing with attorneys. It varies across the map." In each area they try to determine how the children are being taken care of, what information is available about the birth families, and how the children are being relinquished.

Responsible agencies also consider the needs of the majority of children who remain in orphanages and provide some support in the form of medical or other much needed supplies. Unfortunately, there are many for-profit groups that set up shop with little regard for anything but getting children out of the country for people ready to pay any price. Kate Burke, who advocates in favor of family preservation, feels that adoption out of one's culture of origin should be a last resort:

> A child's culture is very important to the child, to his or her evolution
> and growing process. One agency that I know of does international
> adoptions in a proper fashion. They go to the country of origin, try to
> find the birth family, and see if they can reunite the child with his family.
> They try to help the family keep the child. If the family is unable,
> then the agency tries to have the child adopted within the birth country.
> They only bring a child to the United States when they've failed at both
> of the other things. I think that's the appropriate way to go.

A number of foreign governments are concerned about the flow of children being taken out of their culture. Despite the fact that there may not yet be an infrastructure in place to keep children in families in their country of origin, there are strong national sentiments that affect how many children may be adopted out of a country. International politics also play a role, and doors for international adoption open and close regularly. It makes sense, however, that as countries develop better child welfare programs, adoptions out of the country will become fewer. In India, children are first offered to Indian families, and then to nonresident Indians, before they can be adopted by a foreigner. In countries like Korea, foreign adoptions have dropped primarily because of improvements in the economy along with government policies encouraging birth control and legalizing abortions. Negative press about "exporting" children also put political pressure on politicians. At the same time, although Koreans do not adopt at anywhere near the rate that Americans do, there have been increased efforts to foster in-country adoptions. In other countries there are criteria that the children must have special needs before they can be adopted out of the country. Sometimes, however, that is a technicality that is easily circumvented.

When seeking to adopt overseas, it is important to go through a licensed and experienced agency that has performed many adoptions and has legitimate and legal contacts in the country of origin. Finding out as much about a child's birth family as is possible will also be invaluable to parents when children begin asking questions.

Using the Internet

> Adoption advocates across the country, working to find permanent homes for thousands of hard-to-place U.S. and foreign children, are trying a new marketing tool. They're going on the Internet.
>
> Mark Potok, *USA Today*

The Internet has revolutionized the way we disseminate information and has created endless possibilities for making connections with people we might never otherwise know. Triad members and adoption professionals have begun realizing the Internet's potential, using it for everything from searching for birth parents and adoptees to placing special needs children. Spence-Chapin has begun a program they call ASAP for children who are more challenging to place. The Internet is used for outreach and answering inquiries from people who are interested in adopting a hard-to-place child.

It enables the agency to touch base with network organizations and other agencies across the country.

In late 1994, a Waco, Texas, homemaker was the first person to establish a site on the World Wide Web of computerized photographs of children in need of homes. Agencies soon followed, as did several states, with Texas and New York leading the way. The Internet does have great potential to educate and demystify the adoption process, not only for prospective parents but also for birth parents and adoptees as well. However, there are those concerned that access to information about children to such a large number of people could lead to abuses, since users are able to download images from their computers and alter them. Privacy issues are also a worry, but when browsers search the Web sites for information about children, generally only a first name or identification number is offered.

Prospective parents who find a child they are interested in learning more about or possibly adopting still have to go through the home study and intense scrutiny that responsible agencies require. If a couple or individual eventually does adopt a child after finding him on the Internet, they will one day have to explain to him how the process began. Many adult adoptees retain the sense of being "chosen" or "bought" from a store. The Internet has the potential to aggravate this sense some have of being a possession, and adoptive parents can clarify how the Internet was a fundamental tool in helping them create their family, and how the birth parents still had to decide that they were the right parents for their child.

A Family of Our Own

> We are a family that came together through a different means than biological conception. That is the message I want to communicate to my son. I want him to know that there are different means by which families come together.
>
> Sharon Rhodes, adoptive mother

Not everyone who wishes to create a family can do so biologically. While this may be unfair and life shattering to the couple or individual experiencing it, denial tends to increase the duration of pain and longing. When a person finally arrives at the decision to establish a family through adoption, in addition to thinking about what a child will add to their life, they, like all good parents, need to think: "How can I do what is best for the child I will be welcoming into my life?" In the case of an adopted child, this means being available to the child to help her grow in understanding about adoption.

Realizing that the joys and heartbreaks of adoption coexist within each adoptive situation provides a positive frame for viewing the extended process. The moment when an adoptee legally becomes the child of parents to which he was not born is an event, but the life of the adoption continues eternally. Michael Colberg aptly says that adoption begins the day you come home after placement.

In Part Two I will look at how the lives of triad members progress in the years following the finalization of an adoption, and I will begin by exploring how birth parents can live with the past and yet move forward in their lives. During the years Katherine and Bill were raising Andrew and his brother, I grew up and created a life for myself. Andrew was always in my psyche, and was an integral part of my being. The loss I experienced when I said good-bye to him as an infant was with me not only in moments of crisis and soul-searching but also in my daily existence.

PART TWO

LET US LIVE IN AS SMALL A CIRCLE AS WE WILL

GOETHE

FOUR

SURELY SOME REVELATION
IS AT HAND

Birth Parents Wonder

Finding My Place in the World

> Yes it hurts when buds burst,
> There is pain when something grows.

Karin Boye

WE ALL HAVE choices to make about how to handle what happens to us, and how to go on living afterward. In the process, we may deepen our understanding of who we are and learn more about what our lives mean. After placing Andrew in what ended up being very good hands, I finished college, became engaged and "disengaged" to another young man, and moved to San Francisco, where for a short time I lived on the fringes of the hippie counterculture. The late 1960s were heady and confusing times, and after graduation I wanted to escape to a new life and perhaps leave behind my memories of what had happened to me. In the summer of 1968, after the deaths of Martin Luther King Jr. and Bobby Kennedy, a friend and I headed west in a 1964 Volvo my parents had given me to commute to work. We traveled through Chicago during the riots, swam in the Great Salt Lake wearing our

MCCARTHY FOR PRESIDENT and MAKE PEACE NOT WAR hats, and landed in the streets of Haight-Ashbury ready to take on the world. I embraced the city's colorful lifestyle by rejecting my first job offer in a bank, because they wouldn't let me wear fishnet stockings. I subsequently found work I enjoyed in a foreign-language bookstore, and by the time I left six months later, in April of 1969, I had acquired a taste for my independence and had a growing sense that I could be self-sufficient.

I went back to Washington, D.C., after an adventurous trip to Morocco and found work at Sidney Kramer Books, where in those days the store closed for important political demonstrations. That summer, on my way to Woodstock, I stopped in New York for a job interview, and as they say, the rest is history. I moved to the city in September 1969, just three and a half years after giving birth to Andrew, and although I travel frequently, I have made New York my home. For the first few years, I lived on the Upper East Side and had no idea Andrew was growing up just blocks away from me.

Literature and language have always been a part of my life. In New York, I worked first as a bilingual secretary for a French publisher and then moved on within the company into marketing and promotion. When I left six years later, I was ready for a new phase of my life to begin. My latent entrepreneurial nature took over, and I gradually established a literary agency helping foreign publishers acquire the rights to translate and publish American books abroad. Whether I was conscious of it or not, I began to draw strength from my new family of publishing colleagues. I brought my foreign clients together for "family dinners" and enjoyed it when they thought of me as "Mama Lynn." Few could empathize with my innermost feelings, as I shared the knowledge of my son's existence with only a small circle of intimates during this time. I suppose I hoped to minimize the effects of the relinquishment upon my life. The imprint of my experience would become more apparent in the following decade, but for now I focused intensively on nurturing my career.

On some level, however, I was struggling with the internal trauma of having been separated from my son, and I only semiconsciously connected that turmoil with a pull toward Eastern philosophy and meditation and a desire to figure out how we are all related in this cosmos. I was looking for some deeper awareness, and perhaps more importantly, acceptance of self. I had given up my child and had to find a way to live with that and not believe I was a terrible person. My spiritual journey has its roots in my early adult years in San Francisco and has continued and evolved over the years. I have drawn courage from my Jewish heritage, a sense of interrelatedness and universal acceptance from the silence of my meditative practice, and a feeling of self-acceptance and self-love when I dare to accept in my heart the Christian promise of forgiveness and unconditional love.

Though I still question endlessly, I have an inner core that tells me there is a big picture, and I have my place within it. I have taken that proverbial leap of faith. I will never know if I was not "meant" to parent Andrew, or whether, as one friend suggested, someone else was "supposed" to be the mother of my child. I do not know what kind of mother I would have been to Andrew, especially if I had found myself in an unhappy marriage to Tom, his birth father. The fact is it did not work out that way, and I do my best to trust that life is somehow unfolding as it should.

Over the years, I would sometimes catch myself thinking about Andrew, occasionally fantasizing about running into him on the street, imagining what he would look like, wondering if he was happy, and if he ever thought about me. His birthday never passed without recollections of his actual birth and our short time together as parent and child. I questioned whether Mother's Day ever found him curious about his birth mother, and if he had asked his adoptive parents about me. Whether I consciously thought about my child or simply let his memory rest deep inside my soul, his absence from my life was always significant.

Illness Forces Me to Return to the Past

And in my heart there stirs a quiet pain.

Edna St. Vincent Millay

There is nothing like even the slightest hint of death to induce us to come to terms with our personal demons. In 1985, my silent wall of pain and loss began to crumble from within when I received a positive Pap smear indicating I had advanced cervical dysplasia. I had physical evidence of the possibility that somewhere inside me, potentially, a cancer was lurking. I had held myself together for years without therapy, supported by my fulfilling career, a growing faith, and a nurturing community of international friends and clients, but the mere idea of a serious illness prompted me to seek help.

I did not intend to work with a psychotherapist; I fell into it when I sought the advice of a nutritionist, hoping to initiate some sort of preemptive, noninvasive treatment. The nutritionist recommended I see someone who uses visualization techniques as an adjunct to traditional medical treatment. I made an appointment with Claire Young, and when I was face-to-face with her for the first time was shocked to discover she was a Gestalt therapist. Trying not to overintellectualize the situation or run in the other direction, I decided I had been guided there and would give it a try. No one in our family had ever sought therapeutic counseling, and my parents were initially uncomfortable when I told them what I was doing. Once I began working with Claire, I realized how closed in on myself I had been, and the emotional release was explosive. When I began writing this book, I went back to Claire to check what she had thought about me when I came to her. She remembers that I did not tell her right away about Andrew, and when I did, I had difficulty bringing up my feelings. "You could barely talk about the pain of the loss," she says. "But your concerns about your health reignited those issues of loss surrounding your child. You began to express long hidden anger toward your parents, and with some coaxing were able to experience the grief you felt at the time of the relinquishment."

Sharon Kaplan Roszia and her colleague Deborah Silverstein have developed a list of what they call "the seven core issues of adoption," which offers those working their way through the maze of adoption-related issues a context that relates to everyone in the triad. They pose the question: "How can we celebrate our similarities, rather than highlight our differences?" Roszia and Silverstein advise that each of us in the triad needs to recognize our sense of *loss, rejection,* and *guilt* before we can achieve any *mastery* or *control* over our lives. We have to allow ourselves to *grieve* and mourn before we can come to terms with what we have lost. By working through this process, we forge an *identity* that is truly our own, and the strength we derive from being more sure of ourselves will help us overcome our fear of other members of the triad. Roszia points out that it is important to remember that everyone's pain is real; no one's pain hurts more than anyone else's. We are all seeking *intimacy* with the people we love. This is the seventh core issue, and without first dealing with the other six, it is bound to remain a problem. A birth mother who has relinquished her child may have felt abandoned by those closest to her, and she may not trust herself to hold on to a loving relationship. Often an adopted person will not know where to place his trust, because he is fearful of being abandoned again. Adoptive parents, still plagued by their infertility, may feel at their core a sense of inadequacy that inhibits their communication with their children.

Through my therapy I began to uncover how these key issues applied directly to my life. As I dealt with my immediate physical problems, I drew the parallels with the loss I had experienced some twenty years before. In the end, I had to grieve the reality that my womb would never hold another child within its walls. After my positive Pap smear, I had the first of two surgical conizations, and within two years I was faced with having a hysterectomy. I was forty years old, and the decision was taken out of my hands; I would not have any more biological children. A major and persistent question had finally been answered, and while I was terrified at the thought of cancer, there was a part of me that was relieved to put the uncertainty about childbearing to rest. On some level, too, I felt like I deserved to be punished, and that I did not deserve someone's continuous love. Deep down I was prepared to believe I was not good enough to have another child. It was obvious I needed Claire's help in untangling a web of complicated and negative emotions, and we worked together for four fruitful years.

The holistic view of health promotes the idea that repressed emotions are held in the body and are a causal factor in diseases that can develop years later. My own medical problems have been centered around the uterus and breast. It is not a stretch for me to believe that the feelings I held so tightly after I relinquished Andrew ultimately affected my health, despite the fact that I was not fully conscious of them. While it may not be as simplistic as an eye for an eye, or a uterus for a child given for adoption, I do feel that my unresolved feelings caused a lack of harmony in my body in areas directly related to the issues I was dealing with, in particular those centered around my poor self-image as a woman.

Mind/body therapist John Beaulieu has another view on the healing I did surrounding the loss of both my fertility and my child. Sometime after the surgery, he advised me: "I think through your psychotherapeutic work dealing with the pain and hurt in your life, that there is no doubt you have arrived at a stage where you can declare for yourself that you are your son's birth mother no matter what. You have let go and given up enough to send energy to the universe acknowledging on the deepest level that you accept who you are, regardless of whether you and Andrew ever meet. Whether he is with you or not, you are his birth mother, and you honor your responsibility to him to respect the sacredness of that connection." That simple energetic affirmation of my relationship to Andrew opened a channel for me to begin imagining that I might actually see him again one day.

Two other women I have previously mentioned, Cynthia Beals and Diane

Nemes, also had to mourn their fertility after having had only one child. Both women knew they still wanted to be a mother, and both eventually became adoptive parents. For me, my work continued to be an outlet for my creative and maternal energies. Soon after I had recovered from the surgery, I decided to shift the focus of my activities from working primarily with foreign publishers to representing authors directly and helping them with their books from their inception through to publication. It remains a special thrill for me each time we receive the finished printed copy of an author's work. Like a baby, a book comes through a long and arduous birthing experience.

Somehow in facing the reality of my mortality, and the end of any dream of having more biological children, I came to embrace the blessings in my life instead of dwelling on a multitude of shortcomings. I also realized that while there may be time in life for everything, there is no point in wasting it. It was time to think big, to be bold, and to take risks. This was a turning point in my life, and I gave myself permission to contemplate the possibility of a reunion with Andrew. A few years would pass before that would happen, but I know I started getting ready then. I have since met many other birth mothers, and I have come to realize how we travel some of the same roads in our journey toward wholeness.

Out of Sight, but Not of Mind

> Today, as every day
> I send you blessings
>
> Becky Cagle, from "Wondering"

It is hard to fathom how anyone could have counseled a birth parent to forget about their child. Like myself, all of the birth parents I have since spoken with spent years (and many still do) wondering where and what their children were doing, what they looked like, how they felt about school, their family, and if they knew they were adopted. For the birth parents who have recently relinquished in semiopen or open adoptions, the questions are fewer because they do have some information about their children. However, they also find themselves pausing in the midst of their regular activities to imagine what their child is doing at that very moment.

Elaine Davis has no contact with the daughter she placed in the late

1970s. She feels that when birth parents relinquish a child, a small piece of them goes with that child. She always thinks of her daughter on her birthday (which happens to coincide with her parents' wedding anniversary) and often wonders what she is like. "I wonder if she's in college. I wonder if she's interested in a guy right now. I was thinking about her the other day and wondering, 'Geez, you know, she's the age I was when I was pregnant.' I was hoping that she's not had to deal with some of the things that I was having to contend with at that point in my life."

Holidays, birthdays, and anniversaries are particularly difficult because they serve to remind birth parents of the family member who is absent from the celebrations, and many of us look for special ways to remember our children. Naomi Brand celebrates her son's birthday by baking a cake and sharing it with the women in her support group. Mother's Day is always painful for birth mothers, and recently the idea has caught on of establishing a "Birth Mother's Day" to be observed on the Saturday before Mother's Day. It is a way of creating a ritual of celebration to help us honor our ongoing connection to our children. In a lecture at the 1997 Open Adoption Conference in Traverse City, Michigan, Brenda Romanchik said that birth mothers have to respect themselves. Otherwise, they cannot feel truly important to their children and cannot expect others to accept them. She says that after placement, birth mothers have the task of adapting to a new life without forgetting the old. They have to let go of their role as a parent and get on with being a birth parent. She said she now feels proud when her son Matthew introduces her as his birth mother.

Even when birth parents establish an open or semiopen adoption, they still have to deal with the pain of being separated from their child. "No matter what the circumstance," says Brenda Romanchik, "the birth mother is transformed by the grief of relinquishment." Longing and depression are to be expected in the first year or two after placement. Gradually though, birth parents like Melissa Kramer can allow themselves to remember their children, and at the same time begin to move on with their lives:

> In the first year after placement, I was depressed. I don't know how from one day to the next I kept going. I was in tears a lot, but I also knew that I had to get it out, that I didn't want to suppress it. I felt like a part of my heart had been cut out, like a part of me was missing. It's an unnatural separation and it's odd because your child is alive, but he's not with you. And you're a mother. You have a mother's heart and you

want to shed this love on someone and you don't have the object of this love to shed it upon. As the pain subsided by the second year, I wasn't crying all the time. It was starting to ease and it became easier. Every once in a while I got back to the whys: "Why did I place?" But then I'd recall I was very much aware of what I was doing, that I made a decision when I was twenty-six. It wasn't like I was sixteen. It would have been difficult, but I could have taken care of him somehow. So when I place myself back at the decision, I wonder, "What if?" I don't regret my decision. I wish I didn't have to make it, but I'm proud of the choice I made.

Melissa sometimes projects and fantasizes about the future and the hope she has of seeing her son again. The image she has of him is as a young man in his twenties, and he is a handsome, intelligent person. "That's the boy I want to meet," she says. "I don't hold so many images at this point of him growing up through his teenage years."

Maria Baez, who relinquished her daughter even after members of both her family and church pressured her against it, feels generally relieved about her decision, and is for the most part happy. "There are times," she says, "when I get depressed and I have mood swings, but there is always somebody there to help me now, like my mom, dad, or boyfriend. In some ways, the adoption has made me and my father closer. Before I wouldn't talk to my dad about feelings, but now I notice that we have a tight bond." Maria's father takes her dancing each year on her daughter's birthday to celebrate the child's life. And when Maria wants to know how her daughter is doing, when the wondering and her curiosity overtake her, she is able to call her child's adoptive mother directly: "She still keeps in contact with me. I call her. She calls me."

Jane Leeds, on the other hand, placed her son in the late 1960s and did not have the advantage of being able to call her son's adoptive parents. Nevertheless, she kept him alive in her heart: "Every night of my life, I prayed that he would be safe and that whoever had him would love him, and that someday I would see him."

Some birth parents do not think about their children for many years after they relinquish, because they have repressed or sublimated the painful memories. The births of subsequent children often break down barriers and lay fresh ground for memories of the firstborn to surface. Bonnie Bis, president of CUB, did not start to have thoughts about the two children she relinquished until her third child, a son, was six years old. "I had a lot of memory loss," she says. "I even forgot their birthdays, because I did such a good job of pushing all the pain down." Bonnie had such a wonderful experience with the son she had after she married that she began to think, I wonder how my other kids are, and where they are. When Bonnie broached the idea to her husband of looking for her earlier children, he could not handle it. It took eight more years of ruminating and wondering until she decided to take action and search for them.

After Jane Leeds had more children, she thought of finding her son and trying to reclaim him:

> I always dreamed that I would be able to get him back. And I thought if I could do it while he was young, it wouldn't make such a big difference. Then I realized after watching my own children that trying to get him back would be horribly unfair, to drag him out of the only family situation he had ever known. However, that didn't mean I gave up thinking about him, but I gave up the idea that I could ever take him out of there because I realized that it would be awful for him.

Carol Schaefer felt the loss of her first son most poignantly when she conceived and carried her second. Normal fears that a pregnant woman faces were exaggerated for her to the extent that she was not sure if she would be a responsible and capable mother. In *The Other Mother*, she wrote about worries and wondered, "Would my 'sin' hurt my second child somehow? Was I the only ex-unwed mother to react so inappropriately? Had all the others blithely erased the fact? Was I the only one who could not?" Carol thought of her first son many times as she watched the other boys grow. It was not until many years after their births and a near brush with cancer, that she seriously thought again about locating her firstborn child.

Birth fathers, too, think of their children if they know about them. Roger Hanson says that after his daughter was relinquished he spent the first year trying to "drink and drug" himself into unconsciousness about it. "I was very sad, and the alcohol and drugs did not help at all. I thought about my daughter daily, and I cried almost every day. About a year later, I ruptured a blood vessel in my stomach and almost bled to death. I stopped abusing then and vowed I would someday find my daughter." I have wondered sometimes whether Tom has gone on to have other children and whether he thinks about Andrew. How does the fact of having a first son affect the fathering of his subsequent offspring? Does he ever think about the "what ifs?" in his life?

Faith and Healing

> There is always a moment in any kind of struggle
> when one feels in full bloom. Vivid. Alive. One might
> be blown to bits in such a moment, and still be at
> peace. . . . To be such a person or to witness anyone
> at this moment of transcendent presence is to know
> that what is human is linked, by a daring compassion,
> to what is divine.
>
> Alice Walker, *Anything We Love Can Be Saved*

The wounds that an adoption can create for birth parents often force them to question their belief in God or a higher power as well as the integrity of their spiritual and religious advisors. The reality of relinquishing a child creates a crisis of faith like none other. Religious institutions traditionally provide sanctuary for those in need, but sometimes they fail to uphold the trust placed in them. Instead of being supported and loved by those from whom they sought guidance, many of the birth mothers of my day who asked for help from their churches or other religious institutions were made to feel ashamed for their "sin." At their worst, these institutions can foster a judgmental and critical environment that does more harm than good. According to Maria, many in her congregation insisted that "in God's eyes, it is wrong to place the baby and I should do whatever I could to keep it." Maria's strong inner faith allowed her, at a young age, to withstand the pressure of church elders and come to a decision that she felt was right for her and her daughter.

When birth parents are confident in their decisions, and when they have achieved a sense of inner resolve about their choices, they usually find that their faith remains unshaken. Melissa Kramer firmly believes that good things can come out of difficult situations and that her decisions will ultimately lead to a stronger, healthier relationship between her and her son. "I know I can stand right before the Lord," she states, "not having had an abortion, knowing that my son is alive, and I'm sure there are more blessings to come in my life because I made the right decision." Melissa prays each day for her son and his adoptive parents, and hopes he will want to meet her one day. "I believe, I have faith, that I'm going to know him as a young man."

Melissa delved deep, seeking the best answer for herself and her child, never questioning her faith, because she was able to take an active role in his placement. Conversely, many birth mothers who were pressured to relinquish have to overcome a sense of betrayal before they regain their spiritual trust and begin healing. They see the relinquishment of their child as a great schism between them and God. For many of these women, forgiveness comes only once they uncover information about their children, or have a reunion. LaVonne H. Stiffler comments in her essay "Adoption's Impact on Birthmothers: 'Can a Mother Forget Her Child?'" that "forgiveness is seen as a major milestone in spiritual growth, resulting from the search and reunion process." Birth mothers must forgive not only a God who takes their children away, but also themselves for letting it happen.

The Reverend Thomas F. Brosnan, an adoptee, has said that "the world of adoption is always ripe for conversions of the heart." I take these words to mean that if our hearts are open, we can literally be transformed and can convert our pain into compassion for others in the triad who have also suffered. My faith has grown stronger from the physical and emotional challenges that brought me to a place where I could face the ghosts of my past. There is no doubt that as a result I have been better prepared to meet the new challenges of my postreunion relationship with Andrew and his family. From the stillness of my meditation experience also comes a sense of interconnectedness with others, and a spirit of openheartedness with no strings attached that seeps through to my everyday life. And in the struggle to understand and to handle emotional upheavals, I have found that prayer is a magical tool that allows me to let go and ask for divine guidance. I have no doubt that these practices have influenced the way I have sought to relate to Andrew and his family and to develop a relationship that is comfortable for them.

In this next section, we will see how the movement toward open adoption also allows for faith and forgiveness to flourish as relationships among triad members grow.

A Brief History of Adoption Leading to Greater Openness

It is hard to remember that until the last half-century, adoption was an open transaction in this country, often an informal arrangement between an unmarried pregnant woman and a childless couple who befriended her.

Betty Jean Lifton, *Journey of the Adopted Self*

We know that adoption has existed at least as long as there have been written records. References in the Bible and the writings from ancient Babylonia, China, Egypt, Israel, and India point to a practice that was created primarily to provide childless couples with male heirs. Families needed children for reasons of inheritance, certain religious rites, and in some societies like ancient Rome, political aspirations.

Adoption laws in the United States are largely based on ancient Roman codes with one significant difference—in centuries past, the interests of those adopting far outweighed those of the adoptees. Laws in America have always been enacted with the stated intention of protecting the welfare of the child. While adoption has persisted for several millennia, the debate surrounding open adoption practices and access to information about birth families is relatively new.

Although our adoption laws derive from Roman decree, our legal system is nearly analogous to that of British common law, which did not recognize adoption legally until 1926. Linda Bothun elaborates on the subject in her book *When Friends Ask about Adoption:*

> Blood ties were stressed by English nobility more so than by any other group in history. Property and titles passed from father to son, or to other male relatives if necessary. In the absence of male relatives, titles and property fell out of use. Informal adoptions were common, but informally adopted persons were left in legal limbo, and Heathcliffs abound in English literature.

Adoption nearly disappeared in Europe during the Middle Ages because it was replaced by indentured servitude, but it was then reintroduced in the mid-nineteenth century.

In some cultures like Hawaii, where there is a long tradition of adoption, known as *hanai,* families nevertheless trace their genealogical heritage back to mythical ancestors, and bloodlines are fundamental in securing an individual's identity. Children given in *hanai* would retain knowledge of their lineage, and the tradition was seen as a way of strengthening kinship in the community. Few of the early settlers on our shores, however, could boast about their pedigree genealogies, and they were more concerned with their immediate survival than they were with blood heritage.

The United States did not pass any laws regarding adoption until 1850, when Vermont and Texas made public the records of private adoption agreements. In 1851, Massachusetts enacted the first law that provided for a judge to preside over an adoption proceeding. The state wished to set a precedent that insured the ability of parents to care financially for their child. This statute was very significant, not only because of judicial intervention, but also because the child's interests were emphasized as a priority. Nevertheless, until the latter part of the nineteenth century, adoption arrangements remained generally informal in the United States.

Multitudes of orphans joined the great waves of immigration to America. The "orphan train" movement was conceived to relocate immigrant and indigent children between the ages of two to fourteen. Workers from the Children's Aid Society announced the arrival of forthcoming shipments to eager citizens who would choose the children they wanted from each trainload. The majority of these trains traveled from 1854 to 1904, but some ran as late as 1929. They carried as many as 100,000 children throughout the territories to farm communities that needed free labor to survive. The quality of their lives depended solely on who decided to "adopt" them. Because many of the children were never formally adopted by the families who chose them, they had no legal rights to any familial or inherited property. The Reverend Charles Brace, founder of the Children's Aid Society and initiator of the first orphan train movement, is considered a pioneer in the child welfare movement because he recognized early on that permanent placement was more beneficial to children than institutionalization. However, some of his practices did generate criticism from other child advocates. Many asserted that the children he relocated had biological parents who were never informed about placements, that the Children's Aid Society did not sufficiently screen families, and that the children's progress was never tracked after settling with their new parents.

Foundling homes in large urban areas were another response to the explosion of homeless children around the turn of the century. These homes quickly showed evidence of all the horrors of institutional life, and child advocates soon sought other solutions for parentless children. Abraham Jacobi, perhaps the most famous American pediatrician of his time, recommended that the institutions in New York City be closed and that infants live at the homes of wet nurses. Because it was impossible to secure enough milk for all the needy infants, many of the foundling institutions began experimenting with the development of a formula that infants could drink instead of human breast milk. When a recipe was finally created, it not only increased the survival rate of many orphaned babies but also established the foundation for adoptive infant placement in the early part of the twentieth century.

Adoption in Twentieth-Century America

> We could structure our laws to recognize adoption's
> positive potential as a family form and to make it
> work to expand life's potential for birth parents, their
> children, and the people who want to parent.
>
> Elizabeth Bartholet, *Family Bonds*

By the beginning of the twentieth century, agencies were placing fewer abandoned infants and children in institutions and more in adoptive homes. Concern grew that inadequate screening before adoptions and poor follow-up afterward did not ensure that children were living in suitable environments. Child welfare reformers pushed elected officials to pass legislation that would provide court supervision for adoption cases. By 1929, each of the United States had created some form of statute that regulated adoptions, but enforcing these laws was another matter. Adoptions had for centuries been practiced without much thought to how the child's lineage could affect the adoptive family's status in the immediate community or the greater society. In the early part of the twentieth century, that began to change. The stigma attached to being an unwed parent, a parentless child, and a childless parent became so great that people decided that hiding the facts was beneficial to all triad members.

The Minnesota Act of 1917 is recognized as the first legal step toward making adoption a secret and sealed process. It is generally believed that the inaccessibility to birth family information was created to insure the privacy of both birth and adoptive parents, but in reality legislators wanted to hide adoptions from the public eye. Initially all parties involved in an adoption were allowed to see the information, but from 1920 into the 1940s, states began denying everyone access unless a judge saw good reason to open the files. This trend toward secrecy is said to have been led by child welfare workers who wanted to prevent children from having the stigma of illegitimacy. Social workers also believed that if birth and adoptive parents were kept apart, and all information was changed to make it appear as though the child were born to the adoptive parents, then the child would integrate into the new family with less trauma. Physically and culturally matching babies to their adoptive parents had become a common practice by agency workers.

As the twentieth century progressed, more emphasis was placed on the needs and desires of adoptive couples. For years child welfare workers and childless couples did not believe that abandoned children could overcome their "bad blood," and very few people were willing to adopt a child from foster care. However, the development of formula, an influenza epidemic following World War I, and a drop in the birth rate created a surge of interest in infants during the 1920s. In this climate, baby brokers and black market operators became a common conduit for want-to-be parents to secure an infant. People were now more inclined to believe that environment, not genes, dictated whether a child would thrive or whither. According to Ronny Diamond at Spence-Chapin, the large-scale sealing of adoption records truly began in the 1930s and 1940s in response to the belief that social and psychological influences were primary in shaping who a person is and who they become:

> People were suspicious of the notion of genetics and connected genetic theories with the eugenics practiced by the Nazis. The role of the mother was considered the essential ingredient for healthy development. This meant that most childhood problems were directly related to a problem in the mother-child relationship. Conditions such as autism and schizophrenia were blamed on mothers, as was infertility, which was believed to reflect the infertile woman's unconscious hostility toward her mother.

In their efforts to ensure that the nurturing of the adoptive family far outweighed the genetic history of the birth family, agencies encouraged both parties to have nothing to do with each other.

During World War II, many women who worked in the war effort became pregnant, and with abortions not a legal option, adoption rates began to rise. Women in maternity homes during this time nursed their babies for five or six weeks after birth and were allowed to interact with their infants until adoptive parents took the child home. Because of the baby boom, the number of babies placed in the late 1940s and early 1950s almost equaled the number of people who wanted them. However, agency workers were still concerned that couples would not want a child from a questionable background, and they began sequestering infants in foster homes called "study homes." The babies were kept in the homes for six months to a year before being placed so that doctors and social workers could assess their developmental and physical progress.

By the mid-1950s, there were far more applicants than there were healthy and desirable infants. Agencies developed criteria that they hoped would best match adoptive parents and infants along religious, socioeconomic, intellectual, and physical lines. The outside world was never to know that an adoption had taken place.

By the time of *Roe v. Wade,* major societal shifts were already in full swing. The civil rights movement had paved the way for the women's rights movement. Women, too, were tired of being second-class citizens and yearned to make their contribution in the workplace, not just the home. One of the most hotly debated issues relating to women of the late 1960s and early 1970s was reproductive rights. Women wanted to say when they could have sex and when they could have babies, which meant they wanted safe, affordable birth control—and the right to choose an abortion. Gradually attitudes relating to unwed pregnancies began to shift, and women started parenting their babies. Women had more choices about what to do when faced with an untimely pregnancy. The increased accessibility to birth control and abortion, and the option to parent as a single woman, decreased the pool of healthy, white adoptable infants.

Annette Baran has worked in adoption since the late 1940s and is a pioneer of adoption reform. She says that suddenly it seemed the adoption world had changed:

> Pregnant women who used to come to the agencies were suddenly saying, "I'm not just going to give up my baby. If I'm going through with the pregnancy, I'm going to keep the baby. Otherwise, I'll terminate this pregnancy." Once this became inbred in the 1970s, women began to say to us, "If I give up a baby, I want to know who I'm giving it to." And they changed the complexion of the entire agency system. And there, with that, we didn't have any more babies to place.

Further changes were in the offing. On January 1, 1976, California legislators passed the Uniform Parentage Act, which asserts that every child is considered legitimate. Several other states have since passed the same legislation, sending a signal that every adoptee has a right to know that he holds within him two heritages and that both should be a part of his life. As these societal changes began to take hold, many agencies scrambled to devise ways of staying in business, even if that meant conceding to a potential birth parent's wishes, a practice that would have been laughed at a decade earlier.

As early as 1975 Annette Baran and Reuben Pannor, two of the authors of *The Adoption Triangle,* offered the then radical recommendation that adoptions should be practiced with a greater emphasis toward openness. They came to this conclusion after studying and documenting the psychological and emotional effects of secrecy and anonymity on triad members during the 1960s and 1970s. Initially, they suggested that open adoptions be practiced only in certain cases, but by 1984 they advocated for openness in all future proceedings. Different parts of the country have progressed toward opening adoption faster than others, but the movement has gained significant force since the early 1980s.

A View into Open Adoption

When open adoption is carried out with integrity, then it can really shine.

Jim Gritter

When an idea catches fire and spreads through a group of people there is no matching its energy or stopping its force. Open adoption is such an idea, and it has breathed new life into a field where for decades people were kept apart who needed to be in touch and communicating with one another. In these pages, my focus will be on the birth parents' experience of more openness. In succeeding chapters, adoptees and adoptive parents will have a chance to express how their experience with open adoption has enhanced and/or affected the relationships in their lives.

Agency workers who used to choose and match adoptees with adoptive parents soon discovered that birth parents made equally good choices for their children. Maxine Chalker, an adoptee and founder of Adoption from the Heart, an agency specializing in open adoptions, discovered that when she began doing semiopen adoptions in the early 1980s, "it turned out that birth parents were really as good a judge as any social worker in matching who their children belonged with." At the same time, choosing parents for a child is an awesome responsibility, and birth parents want guidance. Jane Leeds, who relinquished in the 1960s, says, "I can't imagine being a birth mother right now and having to choose parents for my child. How can you ever know what people are truly like and how life goes. That would be too overwhelming a decision for me." Birth parents are concerned about the choices they have to make, are worried that they will never find the right people, and that if their child is born with a problem, that no one will want him. Some are concerned that the adoptive parents will divorce and that a single parent will raise their child. Birth parents need to discuss all of these anxieties and uncertainties before and after placement, so that when and if a problem occurs, they are properly equipped to deal with their feelings. Kathleen Silber says that when adoptive parents split up, it's really hard for the birth parents. "The birth mother will call us up or come in and talk with a counselor about it. They often say, 'You know, I wanted my baby to have a two-parent family.' So they've got their feelings about it when it happens, but they can deal with it, and they can go on. They can also help their child in the situation."

In an open adoption, contact with birth parents is an ever-changing landscape, dictated by the course of events in a family's life. Adoptive parents have their own problems just like everyone else. I know that Katherine and Bill love Andrew and his brother as much as any parent loves a child, and yet their personal difficulties caused them to divorce. Finding out about that when Andrew was already an adult was something of a shock, so I know it would have been hard to be close to what was happening when he was a child going through his parents' divorce. I'm sure I would have had to deal with more conflict and guilt and would have needed help.

Maxine Chalker's agency practiced semiopen adoptions for five years before moving to fully disclosed adoptions where the adoptive parents and birth parents exchange identifying information and could determine themselves how much contact they wanted. This could include anything from a few letters to regular meetings while the child was growing up. The terms of an open adoption are set by the involved parties, and it is up to both sets of parents to honor their agreements.

Spence-Chapin is another agency that began doing semiopen adoptions in the early 1980s. Now birth and adoptive parents meet in over 95 percent of the cases, and some form of contact is encouraged by the agency, whether it be letters, photographs, telephone calls, or visits. When Melissa Kramer met her child's adoptive parents, she was able to give them some gifts for him:

> I had a few things prepared to give them, I had made a piece of crewel work that was my gift to my son and had framed it. I included a letter explaining why I was placing him, the decision I went through. His parents were to read it to him at a time when they felt he was old enough

to receive it. I had some photos taken from the hospital, from his first day of his life. When we first met we hugged, and it was tearful, but good. I told them I wanted photos on or near his birthday each year and that they use the name I had given him somewhere in his full name, which they did. I like his parents quite a lot and feel under different circumstances we'd probably be friends.

As I listened to Melissa tell her story, specifically the part about having photographs from the day her son was born, I remembered how often I had wished I had that picture of Andrew and me taken in the hospital. I could see that my experience might have been so much more positive if I had known how my son would be growing up. I did not have these same opportunities, but seeing that things can change is what has inspired my interest in being active in the adoption field.

In open adoptions, birth parents have a whole new set of ways to process and cope with their grief. They no longer have to say good-bye forever to their children. They feel they have some control, and the adoption turns into something positive because they are making responsible parental decisions for their child. They have less anxiety for their child and improved self-esteem because they feel good about their decision. Jim Gritter, a pioneer in open adoption, says that most of what he learned about birth parents before the days of open adoptions came from listening very closely to them, and that inspired him to look for a better approach:

> It occurred to me that they were trusting the professionals to such an extent that they felt they had cast their babies' fate to the wind. They felt very uncomfortable with it, to the point where it seemed they had simply abandoned their children. I sat for a while and was able to translate the issue into one of trust. So I decided to invite them to roll up their sleeves and to trust their own judgment instead of ours. And that was the turning point. That little bit of logic moved us from the secret system of adoption to the open system.

Gritter found that when birth parents confronted the fact that what they really were doing was "arranging" the adoption of their child, they could face the difficulties with a sense of purpose. They also recovered from the trauma faster, more effectively, and were better able to move forward with their lives.

Randolph Severson reminds us in his pamphlet *A Letter to Adoptive Par-*

ents on Open Adoption that in an open adoption "the grief is real. But the birthparents live through their grief. The grief is real but the sight of smiling eyes and a chance to touch sometimes quiet it. The grief is real, it is a loss, nobody can change that. But open adoption provides a way to work through that grief and go on living, so that it doesn't consume your heart."

In 1985, 131 teen mothers from a teenage mother program in Cerritos, California, responded to a survey regarding adoption. None of the girls had surrendered their children, but 10 percent said they would have been more likely to relinquish if they had been assured of some future contact. Sixty-three percent of the mothers felt that if more teenagers were given the choice of an open adoption, they would consider the option quite seriously. Maria Baez receives regular letters and photos and has talked with her daughter's adoptive parents about meeting one day. Although Maria says she's "just not up for it right now," knowing that meeting her daughter in the future is a very real possibility helped Maria decide in favor of adoption.

Naomi Brand was never sure that she wanted to be a parent until she had her son and made a plan for his future. She says, "having lived through a pregnancy, childbirth, and the placement of my son, and seeing my sister with her niece, and getting pictures of my son and letters from his adoptive mother, I think that I do want to parent my own child one day." Having contact with her son's parents and information about his life with them has enabled Naomi to see that she is capable of mothering more children when the time is right. She can also avoid some of the pitfalls of women of my generation whose negative memories later affected their marriages and their relationships with their other children.

As open adoption began to grow in the 1970s and 1980s, some old concepts about privacy had to be redefined. Editor and publisher of "Open Adoption Birthparent," Brenda Romanchik, writes "I now realize there is a big difference between privacy and secrecy. Secrecy is deliberately hiding information you are ashamed of, and usually you have to lie to keep the secret from being discovered. You can keep things private and still be an honest person." In open adoption, the shroud of secrecy is lifted. Birth parents in closed adoptions usually tell very few people about what happened to them, whereas birth parents in more open adoptions who feel they made a positive choice may not be ashamed of letting people know they relinquished a child. However, as Brenda suggests, it may not always be appropriate or comfortable to tell people the whole story, and it is an individual's choice whether or not to keep the information private.

Birth Fathers and Openness

Within the emerging trend of open adoption, more
and more adopted persons are hearing the legacy of
their first family and birth stories told by their birthmothers. Few, though, in either open or traditional
adoptions will hear that story told from the viewpoint
of their birthfathers. A half-told history is a haunting
half-truth of heritage, genetics and beginnings.

Mary Martin Mason, *Out of the Shadows*

Jon Ryan says that it is very important to educate birth fathers about the
possibility of open adoption. He says, "Many of them know they're not
ready to parent, but they're not ready to have their child leave their life forever. So when they hear about open adoption, they become more aware and
involved." Birth mothers like Melissa Kramer and Naomi Brand were in
close relationships with the men who fathered their children and, as Ryan
recommends, tried to keep them involved in the adoption process. Melissa
relates a meeting she arranged with her son's adoptive parents together with
herself and the birth father, Mafal:

We met for two hours and it was less emotionally charged than the first
time. We talked about our mutual love for our son and shared stories.
At that point he was fast on his legs and was running faster than kids
who were older than him. Mafal shared that he had run on the track
team and had won a number of awards in high school and college. I
know Mafal has had a harder time than I have with the adoption. He's
a much quieter person and told no one about our son. He really held it
inside and had no support. The year after placement, I was trying to
hold myself together and he was looking to me for help, but I just
couldn't give any. When I asked Mafal to meet with our son's parents, I
thought it would be very healing for him and it was. They're not
abstract to him now. He knows them and has met them. He has a sense
that they're good people, they're kind people, and that they love our
son like he is their own, which he is.

Bob was involved in making a semiopen adoption plan for his son with
birth mother Naomi Brand. He found himself dealing with emotions and

thoughts that he never imagined would be so painful. Naomi says that she had never seen him cry until the day they surrendered their child and he told her:

> For as much as I've always said I don't want kids, I really, really do want to have children, but I want to be able to be there for them one hundred percent, like my parents were for me. And right now I can't. I detest the thought of my child being out there somewhere and me not knowing where. I hate thinking about the fact that one day I'm going to wake up when he's ten and wonder how he's going to do in Little League that day? Or how's he going to do in school?

Bob was distraught when he expressed these feelings, and he has difficulty talking about how he feels since his son was adopted, but one day he may be thankful he can express his love and concern for his child. Birth fathers of the 1990s who help place their children in a more open adoption are made to confront the reality that they had an integral part in the relinquishment of their child. While this can be painful, it is beneficial for the child to know that his or her father cared enough to assume his share of the responsibility for the decision.

Unfortunately, birth fathers today are still not always involved in the adoption decision. Some like Paul Adams opt out early. Paul always knew that he had a child somewhere in the world whom he was not raising, but he only thought about it occasionally. "Quite frankly, before she called me," he says, "I didn't even know she was a she, so I wondered was my first child a son or a daughter. All I knew was that somewhere out there was some of my genetic material. I knew very little else because I never spoke to her mother again until my daughter was sitting in my kitchen."

Roger Hanson tried to stay involved with his daughther, but in 1972 he was not given the chance. Other men discover many years after the fact that they have fathered a child. I met a birth father at the 1997 American Adoption Congress conference who had only recently learned he had a grown daughter. He spoke of his shock and his attempts to integrate her into his life. He attended all the lectures, contributed during workshops, and struggled to reconcile all the years lost that he felt could never be regained.

We can see that the birth mother/father relationship strongly influences to what extent a birth father can remain involved in the placement decision, and in the case of an open adoption, in the child's life. When a man who wants to remain connected to his child is deprived of that possibility, the child is consequently also deprived of a close relationship with the birth father. Birth fathers also have to deal with the reluctance of some adoptive parents to welcome them into the extended family, especially when an angry birth mother insists that they promise not to have anything to do with the birth father. While it may at times be appropriate to approach birth fathers with reasonable caution, on the whole birth mothers need to examine their motives for wanting to exclude the birth father and look beyond their own resentment to the welfare of their child, much in the same way divorced couples need to control their personal feelings for each other for the sake of their children.

Open Adoption Takes Work

> I think open adoptions can be like a very good friendship or a good marriage. I think it can be fabulous with a lot of reward for each side. But it can also be as difficult as a marriage where the needs on each side aren't being met and aren't clearly spelled out.
>
> Sandra Ripberger, communications and public relations director at Spence-Chapin

Although there is no single definition of open adoption, the one essential ingredient for a fully open adoption is disclosure of identifying information between birth parents and adoptive parents. That does not always mean, however, that there will be frequent visits, especially if the birth parents and adoptive parents are living at a distance from each other. Each family's arrangement is different, varying from a picture or two once a year to visitation on a regular basis, but regardless of how friendly the families become, open adoption is *not* coparenting.

Birth parents have terminated their parental rights, and adoptive parents can establish healthy boundaries to ensure a stable home life for their child. Adoptive parent David Adler, who experienced a disrupted open adoption when the prospective birth mother decided to keep her child, shares the concerns of adoptive parents who are afraid of having difficulty with birth parents not respecting their boundaries. He says, "There are many birth parents who have serious problems in their lives and they are going to be a part of the adoptive family and child's life in an open adoption. I'm not saying they're good or bad people, I'm just saying there are going to be lots of complications." If a child's birth parents have problems, the adoptive parents and their advisors must decide how much if any contact should occur. Just as in any family where there are relatives or in-laws with serious problems like mental illness or substance abuse, it may be necessary to set limits without necessarily cutting off all contact or hiding the truth. When care has been taken with each party prior to the adoption, usually lines are not crossed. In fact, birth parents might be too careful not to overstep their welcome. They are for the most part responsible individuals who care about the substance of their children's lives.

There are few courts that recognize open adoption agreements. If the adoptive parents decide to change the terms after an adoption is finalized, birth parents have very little legal recourse, and it is important they do their best to create workable agreements. In his pamphlet *Looking Back, Looking Forward: An Adoptive Father's Sociological Testament,* H. David Kirk says that as currently practiced open adoption "covers widely different arrangements, some workable, others utopian and possibly harmful. The range of 'open' in open adoption has never been defined or delimited. This ambiguity camouflages the fact that the interests of birthparents, adoptees, and adoptive parents are by no means identical."

Maxine Chalker reports that even though prospective adoptive parents come to her agency with the knowledge that they must agree to some degree of openness, they do not always respect their commitment. "We've had some adoptive parents promise things," she says, "and then not follow through, which was really awful." With good counseling adoptive parents can be helped to understand the need to respect the spirit of the agreement with the birth parents and to honor their biological and emotional link to their child. Licensed nonprofit agencies are more likely to do the best job of interviewing and counseling all the involved parties, working with them to determine what kind of relationship is realistic for them. Maxine Chalker says this is important because "in some ways, open adoption is harder because you have to work on relationships."

Most professionals who specialize in open adoption believe that it leads to less psychological confusion among triad members. There are times, however, when birth parents involved in an open situation find it difficult to achieve closure and to reconcile feelings of guilt and shame surrounding the relinquishment of their child. In some cases, instead of easing her anxiety, ongoing contact between birth parent and adoptee can create an ambivalent and confusing situation for the birth mother. At such times, it might help her to maintain a little more distance while she sorts through her confusion and allows herself time to grieve.

Birth mothers commonly find it difficult to see their children in the first year or so after placement. Some even have difficulty receiving pictures. The pain is more intense in those first years, and adoptive parents can be helped to understand that their child's birth mother needs some time for healing, and may not be able to respond to letters or to be in direct contact until they have had time to process their loss and to establish themselves in their new life. Caseworkers and counselors who fully understand that many of the positives in open adoption are balanced by complex sets of expectations unique to every case can help all parties achieve some balance in their relations with one another.

Teenagers especially can be confused about their dual roles as parents and children, and they may not recognize the importance of maintaining contact with the adoptive family. Counseling to help these young mothers look toward the future and imagine how they will feel in five, ten, or twenty years is crucial. Sharon Kaplan Roszia says she has dealt with young birth mothers who are unable to see that although they feel they are in a hurry now to move on in their lives, they will one day want to know how their child is faring:

> I've had birth mothers who say, "I want to get on with my life. I don't want to be reminded about this time in my life. I don't want any connection to this rape. I don't think I can do it emotionally, it will be too painful." So the way we negotiate that is I try to have them imagine they're buying an insurance policy. I say to them, "That's how you're feeling now, but I don't know if that's how you're going to feel in a year or five years. So let's pick a family that will give you much more in the way of openness than you think you want. And in that way, if after you deliver, or after you've done your healing, or when life has treated you differently over time, when you feel the need to open those doors, the family is going to welcome you back." So we try and buy them a little bit of insurance. Ironically, I have a much harder time keeping birth families involved than I've ever had with adoptive families.

Some critics of open adoption fear that it increases a woman's willingness to relinquish her child even if she is not truly prepared to do so. Adoptee and president of the Council for Equal Rights in Adoption (CERA), Joe Soll, believes that agencies and independents are "using open adoption as a way of enticing a woman from her baby," without telling her how much she is going to hurt for the rest of her life. Studies do show, especially among teenage mothers, that women are more likely to relinquish if an open adoption is offered. As we have also seen, there are numerous instances of enticement of economically disadvantaged teens and other young women who are particularly vulnerable to offers of a quick solution and financial support or gain. It is important though to emphasize that when open adoption is offered with integrity, it can be a positive choice for numbers of women and their partners who would otherwise feel trapped in a situation they cannot handle. Open adoption is not easy for birth parents, but neither is parenting, and for some adoption is the right way to go. With more openness they are better able to live with the choices they make.

Brenda Romanchik has said that birth parents in open adoption not only have the privilege of knowing how their children are doing but also have the responsibility to assume a constructive role in their lives. No one can predict at the signing of papers what the ensuing years will bring, but with some form of steady, positive communication, I believe open adoption offers more benefits than adoptions that are loaded with secrecy and fear. In our culture, where each year the blended family becomes more a part of mainstream society, open adoption is another acceptable way of bringing families together. Melissa Kramer, who continues to correspond and visit with her son's adoptive parents, sums up this sentiment when she says, "I want to be a part of a new basis of understanding where there is communication between adoptive parents, birth parents, children, and society."

Birth Parents and the Choices They Live With

> Finally we shall place the Sun himself at the center of the Universe. All this is suggested by the systematic procession of events and the harmony of the whole Universe, if only we face the facts, as they say, "with both eyes open."
>
> Nicolaus Copernicus

We have established that birth parents do not forget about their children after relinquishment. Even if they are not in touch, they continue to wonder about them as years pass. With open adoption there are new opportunities for ongoing connections. Ideally, the more birth parents and adoptees communicate, the greater will be their understanding and compassion for the roles they play in each other's lives. Birth parents love their children no less because they allow others to raise them. Open adoption offers them the opportunity to express that love directly.

In the following chapter I will explore how adoptees feel about their birth parents as they grow up, how they fantasize about them, and how they adjust to openness in their lives.

FIVE

THEN FELT I LIKE SOME WATCHER OF THE SKIES

How It Feels to Grow Up Adopted

Discovering My Place

We Shall not cease from exploration
And in the end of all our exploring
Will be to arrive where we started
And know the place for the first time.

T. S. Eliot

I KNOW I cannot return to March 1966 and experience my son's infancy and youth. Fortunately, Andrew can tell me about significant moments and memories from his childhood. His words and stories have helped to shape our relationship and my understanding of how an adopted person feels within a family not biologically his own. He has grown into a man strong in his convictions and confident in his love for his wife and children. Katherine and Bill obviously have a great deal to do with his belief in hard work, honesty, and his ability to take care of others. I also see in him characteristics that flow through the generations of my family, and I know that he is a product of both his biological heritage and adoptive upbringing.

Andrew remembers his mother telling him that his first three years were very happy, and he speaks warmly of the influence of some of his close relatives:

> I had a wonderful extended family that included aunts and grandparents, and my father's surrogate parents whom I call Aunt Mary and Uncle Frank. I spent summers outdoors in New England, swimming in lakes, walking through the woods, and enjoying nature. I think those summers have a lot to do with my comfort in the country and my desire to raise a family away from big cities.
>
> I was told about adoption from the very beginning, probably before I could understand it. My mother always told me things in a very straightforward manner, so when she explained adoption to me, she didn't try to hide anything. She told me what adoption was and that that was how she and Dad had created our family. I had some idea that my family was not like other people's, because I have a younger brother, Jason, whom my parents adopted when I was three. I don't remember how I felt about my brother when he arrived. I just remember that my parents brought him home one day. There wasn't a lot of information, and without information it's hard to get answers to questions. My brother and I had our problems growing up, and I don't know whether it relates to both of us being adopted, but we are very different people.

Some children struggle more than others from an early age, but Andrew was comfortable with the information he had as a young child. Katherine and Bill were encouraged by the agency to make *adoption* a household word from the start, and it seemed to have helped Andrew accept being adopted as normal:

> Adoption did come up when I was a young kid, but I wasn't all that interested in learning about it until many years later. I remember when I was in second or third grade, the class was discussing a tribe of Indians and how babies were born and fed. I just stood up and said, "Well, my mom didn't breast-feed me because I'm adopted." There were a lot of kids in the class who didn't know what it meant, so I explained it as best I could. My teacher called my mother and told her she was very impressed with how much I knew and could convey. The teacher said that I seemed proud of who I was.
>
> I'm sure I let other people know that I was adopted, and I remember

that I knew another adopted kid, but I don't remember ever being teased. I think growing up in New York City, there are so many different types of people, that once someone knew you were adopted, it was no big deal. Some kids were curious more than anything, but most didn't make a big deal, which made me realize pretty quickly that being adopted was okay. I met some friends of my parents who were adopted, so that I knew others, even older folks, were too.

When Andrew's parents' marriage came apart, he struggled with the fact that they were getting a divorce, and he started to have problems dealing with his anger:

> My parents separated when I was nine and Jason was six. Mom, Jason, and I all stayed in the same apartment, and Dad moved to another place, but we were all in New York City. We lived in a neighborhood that was full of kids, and it helped to be able to stay with my friends. Jason and I had dinner with Dad on Wednesdays and spent every weekend with him. Things were settled for a while until Dad remarried. I had hoped, as all kids do, that my parents would get back together, but Dad's new marriage made my parents' divorce absolutely final. My parents seemed like such good friends, I couldn't understand why they weren't still married. Jason and I were fighting more than ever, and in some ways I suppose because he was younger, he was an easy target, and I took a lot of my resentment out on him. I had a hot temper and tended to blow up over small things. Mom got me to see a therapist for a little while, but I decided pretty quickly that I'd had enough. By the time I was in my teens, I was aware of how angry I was, but I think I needed to release it in my own way. That way didn't include therapy, at least not for me.
>
>   When I turned fourteen and was thinking about high school, I decided I wanted to go to a boarding school. My city school only went to eighth grade, and a lot of my friends were leaving home too. I also wanted to get away from shuttling back and forth between my parents. That's when I started to be more curious about my birth family. I just wanted to know more about the story . . . who these people were. I wasn't even sure that I wanted to meet my birth parents. I just wanted a more complete picture of who they were . . . and where I came from.

Katherine had told Andrew from an early age that when he wanted more information about his birth family she would help him, and that the caseworker at Spence-Chapin had said they could talk to him and provide nonidentifying information. Sometime in the years following the separation, he asked to go. It is funny how memory plays tricks on all of us. Katherine has clear memories of going with Andrew to Spence when he was still very young, shortly after the separation. Andrew, however, remembers it as being a number of years later, and that may be, because agencies did not generally release information to young children:

> I don't remember exactly which year it was, because I was feeling mixed up and angry about the divorce. When I went, I took paper and a pen and took notes feverishly from the social worker—three legal pages. I still have those notes. I also remember being irritated with her. The kid gloves were a little overwhelming. They were very condescending. I know she was probably uncomfortable, but I didn't like being talked to like I was going to turn into a basket case, like I was five or something. I felt like I was in a psychiatrist's office. I was enthusiastic. I was interested. And I just didn't feel that they did a good job relating to me personally and fulfilling my needs.

A week or so after Andrew and I spoke about his meeting at the agency, he called to tell me he had found his notes, and he faxed them to me. It gave me chills to look down on those few pages and see how carefully he had tried to record everything he was told. I was also pleased to see that although there were some inaccuracies in details about Tom's and my father's education, the information was mostly accurate—with only one very important exception:

> Mother: 19 yrs. old, pleasant-looking, intelligent, 5′ 4½″ tall, slender, brown hair, brown eyes, fair complexion, American nationality, born in middle-west city, half-English?, College student (2 years complete), her hope to enter international relations work, good physical health, warm and sensitive, shy w/friends.

> Her background:
>   medical background = o.k. (no problems)
>   g-mother: born in England; in early forties then a housewife, high school education, good health, 5′ 3″ tall, brown hair and eyes, fair complexion.
>   g-father: born in southern part of this country, in early fifties, colonel in U.S. Army. College graduate with 1 year of law school, 5′ 11″ tall with brown hair, blue eyes, and fair complexion, good physical health. 1 sister (14 years old), high school student

Father: 21 years old, German, white, born in Germany; Protestant family. When he was 18 moved to U.S. and lived here, 5′ 11″ and medium build, blond hair, blue eyes, fair complexion. High school education and went to trade school for 3 years and later entered U.S. Army, in army training program, stationed in Europe.

g-mother: early forties, good health, high school education, German, housewife, lived in Germany, 5′ 5″, brown hair, brown eyes, fair complexion.

g-father: born in Germany and lived there, major in German Air Force, mid forties, good health, completed college (?), brother, 3-year-old brother

sister: 18 yrs. old, high school graduate, lived in Germany and did clerical work

Relationship

Serious relationship = 1½ years

When mother became pregnant, they discussed marriage, they decided they weren't ready for responsibilities, mother wanted to finish college, I was given a name, both families knew about pregnancy and they supported adoption, she saw and cared for me. *She* brought me to agency when he was in England. She wanted me to go to a good family in late twenties or early thirties and could provide me with love and a college education, she wanted to know about my adopted [crossed out] new parents then but not now.

I was shaken when I saw the last line, suggesting that I had no ongoing interest in his parents—or by extension, him. Of course, nothing could be further from the truth. I have heard horror stories about adoption agencies purposely doctoring the nonidentifying information they provided to hide disturbing facts or to "help" adoptive families feel secure that birth mothers would not bother them. In this case, Spence-Chapin had obviously made a good effort to maintain and convey correct information. I cannot know whether Andrew's note at the end reflects what he was actually told, but just thinking that he might have believed I wasn't interested in him brought tears to my eyes, and I called this now grown man immediately to tell him it was not true.

After Andrew got the information from the agency, he put it aside for the next several years. Looking back on his life, Andrew thinks it was good for him to go away to prep school as he did. Although it was hard, he learned to rely on himself, and when he went to college, he was more self-assured and ready to have a good time. But his curiosity had been aroused, and the day would come when he would again wonder about his biological roots and would think more about searching for his birth mother:

> I was very angry about the divorce, but I don't remember being angry about the adoption. I always felt very much a part of my family, so when my parents separated and divorced, I was very upset. With the adoption, I think I just wanted to know who these people were, and get a sense of my roots. You know, I value, and have always valued, my adoptive roots. And they're my real roots . . . but it was the birth roots that I really wanted to know something about. It was just a missing piece of the puzzle really . . . a missing sense of who I was. I didn't really figure out for a while that I couldn't truly know who I was without knowing that a little bit better.

How It Feels to Grow up Adopted

> Of course, no one can fathom what it's like to be adopted except another adoptee—you have to live it to really know it.
>
> From a letter by birth mother Amy Bredes for adoptees in search of their birth mothers, *Pacer Newsletter,* Winter 1996

Adoptees share emotional common ground, but they have not all experienced life in the same way. Yet there is truth to what Amy Bredes writes. The closest we can come to understanding the experience of adoptees is to hear how they perceive themselves and their relationships with others. Adoptee Joyce Maguire Pavao writes in her essay "Thoughts of Adoption by an Adoptee by the Sea" that

> we do have some trauma associated with our first loss and with any other additional moves and losses. Wouldn't you? But the thing that comes along with the loss part is our adaptive quality. We're adopted and we're adaptive. We can get along ANYWHERE as a result of this transplanting and replanting. . . . Place us in a room with junkies and lowlife thieves and we'll be hangin' out and talkin' trash with them in no time. Place us in good schools and we'll either do just fine (aimin' to

please), or we'll be so busy trying to get the social thing down (we *have* to be accepted, after all) that we'll miss our assignments and do rather poorly academically. But we'll be working on something. We just adapt, and adapt, and adapt.

A constant struggle for adoptees, as Pavao illustrates, is the sense of continually striving to belong even though they do not feel as though they really do. Although I am not adopted, I appreciate this experience of adoptees trying to adapt to any situation. As a "military brat," I was in eight different elementary schools. I always felt like I was on the outside looking for a way in, and I learned quickly how to adapt to new people and different cultures. I can well understand the adoptees' struggle to fit in, and the loneliness they sometimes feel.

Joan Cummings describes her childhood as "feeling like a zebra in a herd of giraffes. . . . It was not that I wasn't loved. I just felt separate." Joan believes that some of these feelings arise from the fact that her adoptive parents tried, on a very intellectual level, to be perfect parents. When she and her brother were infants, Joan's adoptive parents were advised to hold the babies and repeat "my beautiful adopted daughter (or son)." Joan saw herself more as an adored possession than as a person because her adoptive parents always described her as a "precious gift." Most adoptive parents are loving and well intentioned, but they do not always understand their children's feelings related to their adoptive status. Adoptee and writer Carol Kaufman elaborates on this in her essay "Is Adoption the Answer to Abortion?":

> We have no bond to our past, so how can we be sure that we'll have one to our future? And without attachments, it's hard to feel responsibilities. Moreover, many adopted children will never identify the source of their inner battles, their ultimate loneliness. I think parents who decide to adopt are special people. But most of these well-meaning individuals are also completely unaware of the issues their child will face.

Parents frequently refer to their children as "miracles" or "gifts," but for an adoptee, the language an adoptive parent uses can mean the difference between feeling like an object and feeling like a person. Abigail Johnson says that she carried an image in her mind that her parents went to pick her out at a department store. She has a vision of herself in a glass case and her parents pointing to her.

It is hard for people to be told they are so special when inside they may not be feeling so wonderful. "If we don't acknowledge the losses," says Marcy Wineman Axness, "the blessings get undercut." Children do not want to be chosen. They just want to be born. Marlou Russell remembers that her parents did give her the "chosen child" story. "When I got older," she says, "I realized that if someone chose me, then someone else had to reject me. And I really got the full picture then." Marlou thinks it is hard for adoptees to take in the good stuff of life and "to celebrate themselves, because their birth is not a celebratory act." Certainly not all adoptees would go so far as to say they cannot celebrate their existence, but the feeling that they were abandoned by their birth parents does affect how they feel about themselves.

Adoptees and Their Rich Fantasy Lives

> Orphaned children contrive images of suffering saints,
> heroes even, who had no choice, even if they did. The
> memory of the long-gone mother collects more gilt
> than dust. That is how much we need our mothers.
>
> Jan Waldron, *Giving Away Simone*

Just as birth parents spend considerable time wondering and fantasizing about their children, so, too, do adoptees daydream about their birth families. Of course any of us might sometimes fantasize that we have other— perhaps "better"—parents, and we may feel that we do not fit in with our families. The difference is that adoptees really do have other parents. Abigail Johnson remembers that she spent many of her childhood years wondering about her birth parents. "I wondered what they looked like, what their lives were like, and if I had any siblings or extended blood relations." In her book *Lost and Found,* Betty Jean Lifton explains that adoptees are often unable to test their fantasies against reality. Lacking any tangible information, many children create two versions of themselves: a surface version they share with the outside world and a hidden version they hold deep within themselves. B. J. Lifton also talks in terms of the "artificial self" that tries to please because she does not want to lose the second set of parents. She may appear cheerful and perfectly adjusted on the outside but feel like an impostor on the inside, where her "forbidden self" resides.

Marlou Russell says she did not think of adoption as an issue or a problem until she was in her twenties. However, she says, "I always had this background thinking and thought process about being an adoptee. I would always wonder Where is my birth mother? and Does she think about me? I would have fantasies about meeting her in a crowd and we'd sort of look across a room and know we belonged to each other." Russell had very romantic ideas about her birth parents until she learned who they were. While finding out about her birth parents was not easy for her, she says, "Having the facts makes it a lot better because I couldn't live in my fantasy world anymore, and a lot of the adoptees I know lead very unhealthy fantasy lives." Many children indulge in what Freud calls the "family romance" theory, where they imagine they belong to a clan with royal ties and great wealth. Adoptees are especially prone to conjuring in their minds either a family of high status or one of utter destitution.

A good number of adoptees, like many birth parents, do not allow themselves to dwell too often on thoughts of adoption. School, romance, social pursuits, and family fill plenty of space in their lives, enabling them to push unresolved feelings of abandonment and loss aside. But that distancing takes energy and reinforces the split between their inner and outer worlds. The internal energy required to navigate between their exposed and hidden selves can cause adoptees to dissociate from situations and people very easily. Marlou Russell feels that "a lot of adoptees are in a daze most of the time. It's somewhat like the hypnotic effect of being in a car on the freeway and you're asking yourself, 'Oh, where is my exit?' And adoptees sort of live in that place. Even now that I'm grown up and have dealt with many issues, I still have to tell my husband that if he wants my attention, he has to really make sure I'm listening. Otherwise, I'm lost after the first few words." Andrew, too, has difficulty with short-term memory, and his attention is often divided. Like Marlou's husband, Andrew's wife, Chloe, has to be sure he is listening or writes things down, or their plans can get very scrambled. I have observed that his mind is always going, thinking of many things at once. While we cannot attribute adoption to every situation, researchers have discerned a number of these common traits.

One of the reasons adoptees retreat into themselves is because they have a difficult time trusting relationships with other people. Erik Erikson says that trust develops during the first year of an infant's life. If one subscribes to the "primal wound" theory, adoptees start life somewhat trust impaired and have to overcome the broken trust of being abandoned by their biological mother. Russell says adoptees sometimes behave like abuse victims, where they trust too much and get hurt. Or, she says, they have a very hard time connecting with others.

Father Tom Brosnan (a Catholic priest) also raises the issue of trust when he describes how his adoptive mother sent him upstairs while she and two Brothers from his Catholic high school discussed his future. "They were talking about *my* life," he says, "and I have nothing to say. And maybe that's very parallel to a lot of issues for adoptees. For me it harkened back to another time when someone was signing the contract of my life over to other people and I had no part of it." For Tom and other adopted people, feeling excluded triggers memories or feelings of abandonment, and so they are cautious about where they place their trust.

When I Was Told

> The child who is born into his family is like a board
> that's nailed down from the start. But the adopted
> child, him the parents have to nail down, otherwise he
> is like a loose board in mid-air.
>
> Peter, an adoptee, quoted by H. David Kirk in *Looking Back, Looking Forward*

Child welfare advocate Kate Burke did not think much about adoption while she was growing up. Like Andrew, she believes this is because as far back as she can remember, she always knew of her adoption.

> I didn't think too much about adoption as a child. I would occasionally ask my parents about it. They introduced it to me in a beautiful manner, and as far as I can remember, I always knew I was adopted. Honestly, I don't think I ever grasped that my parents weren't my biological parents, not until much later. It wasn't until I was in my later teens and early twenties, when I was struggling for an identity, that adoption issues became a big part of my life.

Abigail Johnson also says her parents told her about adoption at a very early age. "I have no memory of reading books about adoption," she says, "it's really just always been inherent to who I am. I don't remember anything formal. Knowing I was adopted was very organic to my relationship with my parents, which I'm thankful to them for."

No one wants to experience the shock of finding out, many years after the fact, that his parents adopted him. The very foundations of an identity can be destroyed, perhaps irreparably, if a person discovers that everything he once thought to be true about relationships and family turns out to be false. As Betty Jean Lifton writes in *Journey of the Adopted Self,* "Children are known to be resilient, to suffer all kinds of early abandonments and other traumas and to recover. But when the adopted child learns that he both is and is not the child of his parents, the shock connects to that earlier preverbal trauma that the baby had at separation from the mother and has retained as an inner experience." By telling him right from the start that he is loved, but that he also has another set of parents who love him, too, parents minimize the damaging effects of their child finding out either by accident or later in life that he is adopted.

Even if an adoptee knows she is adopted and is comfortable with her adoptive parents, it does not mean that their relationship is simple or straightforward. Abigail says, "I grew up knowing and understanding that I was adopted. There wasn't one traumatic moment when I learned my parents were not biologically my own." Nevertheless, she now realizes that there must have been some stigma around talking about adoption with her adoptive parents. She believes that to some degree her adoptive parents did not want to tell her anything that might hurt her, and that by not sharing too much information they felt they were protecting her:

> I suppose I felt I could never ask too many questions because otherwise I would have raised the subject more. It seems natural that I would have, but I guess somewhere in my mind I felt that it was a taboo conversation. I was very attached to my parents and whenever I went somewhere, like sleep-away camp, I was desperately homesick and cried a lot. I was very identified with them and felt it might be some kind of betrayal to tell anyone I was adopted. I would mostly try to keep it private because I was ashamed of it. At school I tried to keep it secret because I just wanted to be like everyone else, to be authentic in every respect.

Sometimes parents feel that if their child is not asking questions, they are not interested, and they should not pressure them. The truth may be different. The adoptee may not ask because she has a lot of guilt about her secret thoughts. She may be afraid to admit to them because she senses her parents are not comfortable talking about adoption issues. Abigail retreated into the safety of her artificial self by trying to insure that no one knew she was adopted. Because she had closed off her inner world for so long, learning how to break free took years of hard emotional work.

How a person is told he is adopted is also important. Every adoptive parent will approach the subject based on their own sensitivity, awareness, and experience, and the adoptee will respond according to her individual psychological makeup. There are some basic do's and don't's, but few absolutes, and what might make one child furious and resentful may create in another a feeling of contentment and safety. David Adler remembers that his parents said more or less what they understood they were supposed to say, although that is not the prevailing wisdom today:

> They said that my birth mother wasn't able to take care of me and she wanted a good home for her child. They said they picked me, they wanted me, and that I was the most wonderful child. I wasn't very comfortable talking about it as a child, because I knew my mother was very frightened of the possibility that someday my birth mother might reappear. My mother never talked to anybody about the adoption, not even within the family. I wasn't afraid of being taken away as a child, but my adoptive mother became very ill when I was young, so I was fearful of her leaving. I didn't have time to worry about being adopted, because I was worried about her. She did die when I was eight and somehow I lived through that.

David's adoptive father was raised in an orphanage, and David, himself, has become an adoptive parent. He has a unique perspective on adoption, one that gives him a multilayered awareness and understanding of adoption issues.

Marcy Wineman Axness was part of an adoption that she terms a "quasi-open adoption." Her adoptive parents and birth mother were introduced through a mutual friend and met on many occasions. In 1956, this prebirth contact was positively groundbreaking and was very much like many of the open adoptions today where the two mothers "bond" before the baby but have little or no contact after the baby is born except perhaps for some letters and photos. Marcy was not told she was adopted until she was seven, a commonly recommended age at that time:

> What I find interesting is that a few years ago I was listening to a tape of Clarissa Pinkola Estes, and she talked about how a key to your inner

life is any books that you loved reading as a child. I realized that mine was *Thumbelina*, which begins "Once there was a woman who wanted a child more than anything in the world, but she had no idea where she was to get it from. At last in loneliness and sorrow she went to a witch and spoke of her desire. The witch gave her some magic seeds to plant in the ground. Up from the ground grew this beautiful flower, and when its petals opened, there, inside, was this perfect little girl." Long before I was ever told that I was adopted, I looked at that book over and over and over. I wanted to crawl into the pictures. I now wonder if my adoptive mother gave me that book with the consciousness that it would give me a context for my situation? I think one of the greatest gifts that any parents can give a child is a context for their experience. My adoptive mother didn't have an easy time talking about adoption, and maybe this was her way of giving me a context. And that's really a wonderful gift.

Once Marcy's adoptive parents told her she was adopted, she became very matter-of-fact about it. Adoption did not play a central role in her conscious thoughts until many years later, after her adoptive mother had died.

Which Am I to Be—the Good Adoptee or the Bad Adoptee?

> Adoptees tend to split the images of good and bad,
> not only for their parents, but for themselves as well.
>
> Nancy Verrier, *The Primal Wound*

The inner conflict of having two sets of parents can manifest in different ways. As we have seen, sometimes an adoptee feels that she has to be perfect so that no one will ever leave her again, or that she will not fail her adoptive parents. Other adoptees take the opposite tack and act out to such an extent that they test the very limits of tolerant behavior.

Joan Cummings spent much of her youth high on drugs, involved in damaging sexual relationships, and listening to a lot of loud rock-and-roll music. Despite the fact that her parents tried to be "perfect" and that she was intensely close to them, Joan always felt disconnected from her adoptive family. On a spiritual level, she says, "I felt like a satellite of my biological family and quite fragmented from my adoptive family." Joan attempted to carve her own identity and gain distance from her adoptive parents by indulging in destructive behavior. Luckily her depression and eating disorders drove her to 12-step programs and therapy.

Adoptees like Joan often believe, on some level, that by acting out and pushing themselves to the limits, someone will finally hear their cries for help. Clinical psychologist John Sebraski describes this type of behavior in an adoptee as "chaotic." At the other end of the spectrum, he says, is the "compliant" child. The chaotic adoptee, he believes, is saying to the world, "I will test to see if anyone will abandon me." The compliant adoptee operates on an opposite tack, when she imagines that "I will be so good no one will abandon me again."

The compliant or "good" adoptee does not act out in the same way that Joan did, but nevertheless, his behavior can be a subtle, yet important warning sign. Adoptees often report having serious intimacy problems. Former football star Tim Green, whose recent book *A Man and His Mother* deals with his search for his birth mother, says that the underlying feeling of abandonment made him cling desperately to girlfriends for fear of losing them. Other adoptees keep a "safe distance," because they are hypervigilant and too frightened to attach with people who might leave them. Getting close is a risk they are not willing to take and will often cut themselves off from profoundly loving relationships. The compliant adoptee might also become a top student or a generally high achiever to get the affirmation she needs. Tim Green says in his book that his quest for praise and his achievements were his way of trying to make himself desirable to the birth mother who, he felt, had abandoned him.

Sometimes children are asked if they feel lucky to have found such a good home to grow up in. Depending on whether their behavior is compliant or chaotic, they respond differently to this question. Adoptees are very adaptable, as Joyce Maguire Pavao reminds us, and can often handle what comes their way by wearing many different masks. But for the most part, children are uncomfortable feeling beholden to their adoptive family. There is no equivalent presumption that children born to their parents should feel beholden or indebted to them.

Adoptees spend a great deal of time trying to figure out how to live in both their real and fantasy worlds. The "good/bad" adoptee syndrome is one that the adopted person must struggle with throughout his or her life. B. J. Lifton writes in *Journey of the Adopted Self,* "Adoptees may go in and out of the Ghost Kingdom as they go back and forth between the Artificial Self and the Forbidden Self at different periods of their lives. For example, they may be compliant as children and then, in an adolescent struggle for authenticity, rebel against the adoptive parents, whom they see as inauthentic and a barrier between them and their authentic self." Of course a shift in behavior at puberty is common to most children, and it may be difficult for parents to pinpoint precisely whether their child's behavior stems from adoption issues or is simply age specific. An adolescent who is not adopted might rebel in similar ways against his parents as he struggles to differentiate himself from them. Andrew followed this pattern to some extent. As a young child, he was relatively stable until his parents divorced. As an adolescent he became increasingly angry, and he had to remove himself from the family to establish his own identity and perhaps to distance himself from a family he could not keep intact.

Since his parents' divorce, Andrew has always been very protective of his mother, and he likes to be in control of what is going on around him. It is not unusual for adoptees to become supervigilant or to try to take care of everyone and everything. For Andrew, the divorce had a destabilizing effect on his life, and that may have compounded any preexisting deeply rooted need to take charge. According to Marcy Wineman Axness, adoptees are taking care of their parents' inability to have biological children and are as a result generally protective of them. "They are the ones who have to come in and fix that part of their parents' lives. They sense that their adoptive parents are not comfortable talking about adoption, so they have to keep quiet, keep things nice, and all the plates spinning at once. After a while it makes you pretty crazy and angry."

Adoptees have to choreograph a complex dance with their parents. The increasing frequency of open adoptions and reunions, where adoptees and birth parents have some form of contact, can make this dance even more challenging for the adopted child or adult.

How Age Matters: Early Childhood

The middle childhood years—approximately ages 7 to 11—are some of the most critical years for children's understanding of adoption. While 5- or 6-year-olds focus on the physical process of adoption, 7- to 11-year-olds struggle to understand why they were placed for adoption and what they have lost as a result.

Lois Ruskai Melina

Most children journey through emotional and psychological developmental stages with fairly clear milestones that adults use to track their progress. Adopted children are no exception, but there are special considerations. Throughout a child's development, he may exhibit all or only some of the behaviors that social workers and psychologists have earmarked as being adoption related. There are so many factors that comprise an individual's personality, both genetic and environmental, that it is impossible to generalize about any two people. Yet there are some identifiable tendencies among adopted children at different stages of their development.

A child's awareness of his adopted status and understanding of what adoption is emerges as his cognitive abilities develop. In the early years, simple straightforward answers to questions generally suffice. Toddlers who know they are adopted may be able to tell people what this means, but their grasp of the concept and all its implications is not yet fully realized. Around the age of five, a child begins to comprehend what it means not to have grown in his mommy's tummy. There may be some noticeable but seemingly unconnected behavioral changes like stealing or hoarding as they unconsciously try to possess and cling to things as a way of controlling their environment. Or they may have a preoccupation or obsession with mothers and their relationships to children. Even nonadopted children are more clingy and exhibit some fear at this age about losing their parents as they begin to learn that people die.

When a five-year-old realizes that she has a different relationship to her parents than her friends have to their parents, she is naturally confused. The authors of *Being Adopted* discuss the idea that when you are born into a family, you have signals and guides in developing a sense of self. You see yourself reflected in parts of your parents and siblings, and generally understand where you belong along life's continuum. Adopted children miss out on those cues. By six or seven, children hold internal images and fantasies about birth families and their pasts. Once these thoughts and ideas are in place, the foundation for conscious grieving is set. If the child does not know his birth parents, then he begins to grieve for the *idea* of his lost family, and some children may seem overly anxious or may have difficulty separating at school.

I attended adoptive parent workshops at Spence-Chapin that brought together groups of parents whose children were eight to ten years old. The parents' concerns and questions largely reflected the issues that commonly arise for their children's age group. Many of these parents wanted their children to talk about adoption-related concerns but found that the children were reluctant and confused. Apparently though, their children liked books that talked about other adoptees and their experiences at school and home. A good number of their children expressed feelings of anger, and some lashed out at their parents with questions and statements like, "How do you know how I feel? You're not adopted," and "I know I'm your second choice." When their children challenge them, it is not necessarily a personal affront but is more a way of expressing their confusion about being adopted.

Adoptee Joyce Maguire Pavao, director of the Center for Family Connections, works extensively with young adoptees and their families. She notes that from a clinical perspective, eight to twelve is a very challenging age. She explained during a workshop at an American Adoption Congress (AAC) conference that "kids are in a latency period at this point. They think very concretely but don't yet have the language to explain how they feel about their thoughts. The best way to get them to express how they are feeling is through art and play. Kids don't always say what is going on inside, but there is often more than you can imagine." Children's inner life revolves around their identity, and it is more of a challenge for adoptees to integrate both their internal and external worlds.

Although children begin to ask questions quite young, according to David Brodzinsky and his coauthors, it is from about age eight that adoptees start to grasp how adoption applies to them. They learned from their interviews with a hundred children in this age group that they also have fears about their place in their adoptive families, and anxiety about their birth parents coming to claim them. After eleven, the fears tend to abate, and children feel more secure about their adoptive situations. Children want permanency in their lives regardless of their age, but it is generally a greater concern for them during the years before adolescence.

An adopted child in her middle childhood years will normally grieve and show sadness, or express some anger. Children in this age range who take part in support groups with other adopted children their age generally like being together as a group. It helps them to recognize that there are other children like them who know just how they feel. Making such groups available, as well as offering special workshops with informed and experienced professionals, is something that many agencies consider fundamental to successful adoptions. "One of the things that we've always tried to make a priority is our expertise and the ability of our staff to understand the breadth and depth of adoption issues," says Kathy Legg, the executive director of Spence-Chapin. "We started the Adoption Resource Center several years ago with the goal that it be an educational forum for the general public, not just for Spence-Chapin adoptive parents, but for everybody."

How Age Matters: Adolescence

> As a teen, I never believed I would ever have a child because I didn't have a mother who had a child.
>
> Pam Hasagawa, adoptee

Gaining independence, establishing an identity, and searching for a sense of self present special challenges for adopted adolescents. Ronny Diamond says that kids around puberty, which is an age of sexual discovery, are much better able to put themselves in their birth parents' position:

> They are beginning to deal with moral and ethical questions about birth control and abortion. Some say they realize that if their birth mother had had an abortion, they wouldn't be here. There are just all these intense questions, and I do think that the issues take a different turn in adolescence. The teens are starting to think about things in a much more significant way.

Adopted adolescents tend to act out, as a group, more than other teens. A great deal of their anger relates to not having answers to their questions, and if parents have been holding on to information "waiting for the proverbial right time," they might definitely consider sharing it with their children now. Another constructive approach is to offer adopted teens a forum for discussing their feelings. Clinical psychologist John Sebraski asks the adopted teens that he works with to make collages as a way of expressing how they feel. Expressing themselves through their artwork channels some of their anger and helps them create a picture of themselves. "Who am I?" is a pressing concern for most teens, and the problem is compounded for adoptees.

Through their teen years, most adolescents transfer their focus and interest on the family to the outside world of friends and school. Being accepted by a social group and appearing sexually attractive are paramount in their concerns and have replaced the priorities of young and middle childhood.

According to the authors of *The Adoption Triangle,* some adopted teens who feel ashamed of their adoptive status distance themselves from others for fear of being exposed. Others they say seek friends from a lower social milieu as a way of associating with a group they feel is identified more closely with their birth heritage.

Adoptee Kate Burke saw adoption become a larger focus in her life during her teen years and wished she had had more information about her birth family. Even the most well adjusted nonadopted child will naturally seek to establish her own identity, distinct from her parents. It is easy to understand how adoptees who have worked hard to blend into their families can suddenly find themselves as adolescents or young adults realizing it is not a perfect fit. When Kate started to try and break away from her family and form her own personality, she found that she was very different from her adoptive parents:

> They're lovely people and I adored them, but I was so wild and artistic, I was into everything. I'm a generalist and they are very specific about things. We're just real opposites, so I think I grew up really disliking parts of myself because there was no one like me. When I hit my late teens, I was just struggling for an identity. I think when adoptees reach this time of life, we have a harder time because we don't have those anchors to grab on to. It would have been helpful at that stage of my life to see that my birth mother, my birth siblings, and I have so much in common. I didn't discover that until much later when I found them.

Andrew has said that he became more curious around the age of fourteen, and that coincided with his choosing to live away from home. By going to a boarding school, he was establishing his independence and seeking an identity of his own. It could not have been easy for him to move out of his familiar world of friends and family, and to fit into a completely new social milieu.

Information about birth families and an ease when sharing it are among the best gifts adoptive parents can offer their teens and ultimately themselves. Lois Ruskai Melina reports in her essay "Adopted Teens Have Positive Identity" that the "stresses adoption may place on identity formation may be offset by the benefits of good family relationships."

In the Best Interest of the Children: Open Adoptions

If you're going to have adoption, it should be open.
The reason it should be open is that the child should
know that although he couldn't be cared for, he was
cared about.

Annette Baran

One of the greatest fears surrounding open adoption is that if adoptees know their biological parents, they will pull away from their adoptive parents. James Gritter has found otherwise. Frequently, adoptees involved in open adoptions feel closer to their adoptive parents, not distanced. In open adoptions, adoptive parents remain the primary caretakers on a day-to-day basis, and the child grows up squarely in that family. She can love her birth parents but understand that it is a different relationship. In time, she usually respects the strength it took for her adoptive parents to allow contact and openness in their relationships.

As a child grows older, some confusion is expected as she sorts out the meaning of the different relationships. But that confusion would exist in any case for an adopted person whether or not she knows or has information about her birth parents. Without information about birth parents, the adoptee lives with the fantasy/ghost parents she has created for herself. The advantage of openness is that the adoptee can replace the fantasy with real people.

Adoptees know that their family is different from that of most of their friends, and their unhappiness about being different from their peers is sometimes turned against the adoptive family. As painful as it is for everyone, it does to some extent come with the territory, and it can be helpful to adoptive parents to understand the underlying reasons for the behavioral problems. Nancy Verrier's growing sense of the differences in the experiences of her biological and adopted daughters—and her experiences with them—led to her research into the primal wound theory.

It is not only the problem of being different from their peers that causes adoptees to act out. The questions about why they were abandoned surface in different ways at different stages of their development. Whether directly posed or left unspoken these questions persist through childhood into adulthood, and they are more troublesome for adoptees who have no contact with their birth family. "Why was I placed for adoption?" "Who are my birth parents?" "Do I have any siblings?" "Are there any diseases in my biological family that I need to know about?" The nagging quality of these unanswered questions often impedes an adoptee's personal growth and can affect future relationships. Their adoptive parents will naturally bear the brunt of their frustration. In her essay "Are Relinquishment and Adoption Really Different?" Connie Dawson, a therapist and consultant to triad members in Evergreen, Colorado, points out that since the adoptee's only conscious experience is with the adoptive family, if he is growing up in a traditional adoption, he cannot resolve his trust issues with a birth parent who is not present. "He can't work it out with the one responsible for the separation, so he is left to work it out with the only family he knows. He can't be mad at a birthmom who exists only in his fantasy, but can certainly be angry at the mom who is in the living room. Anger controls distance effectively. Active anger or passive anger, both work equally well."

In open adoption, adoptees and birth parents have an opportunity to deal with the difficult issues and tough questions directly and to some extent deflect anger away from the adoptive parents. As Annette Baran says, "All adopted kids feel abandoned, rejected, and neglected, but in open adoption they don't feel it the same way." Encouragingly, in a California study of 1,396 adopted children from infancy to sixteen, researchers found that children of open adoptions had better behavior scores (that were rated by their adoptive parents) than children from closed adoptions. The adoptive parents of these children also had a much more positive attitude toward the birth parents.

Statistics on how lack of knowledge about a biological heritage psychologically affects adoptees are controversial, yet we can draw some conclusions. Adopted children in the United States comprise about 2 percent of the population, but they account for about 5 percent of outpatients and nearly 15 percent of inpatients at psychiatric institutions. Studies by psychiatrist Arthur Sorosky and clinical psychologist David Kirschner show that adopted children tend to suffer low self-esteem, be more aggressive, and have a greater risk of developing learning disabilities than their nonadopted counterparts. Proponents of open adoption believe that some of the problems adoptees exhibit relate directly to not having information about their birth families. In open adoption, adoptees, ideally, do not suffer from what British psychiatrist E. Wellisch in 1952 called "genealogical bewilderment." Most of us take our genealogy for granted, but as Wellisch delved further, he found that an adoptee's loss could lead to rebellion specifically against adoptive parents and, in general, against the entire world. Open adoption offers adoptees a remedy for the confusion, if not for the original loss of their birth family.

As a child grows, she should have a voice in determining how much contact she wants herself, and adoptive parents can help their children learn to take responsibility for their relationship with their birth parents. It is natural, though, for children to resist calling and writing letters, and that is not necessarily a sign that they do not want to (or should not) maintain a relationship. In addition, when children are struggling with loyalty issues, they may also exhibit more difficulty with the different relationships. Again, this does not mean that they should drop all contact, and they will need to be helped to understand that they do not need to choose one over the other. Sometimes, too, it is confusing for a child to see a birth parent married with other children and not wonder why she could not care for him too. Situations like these may cause him to withdraw from the birth parent. Adoptive parents can help their children keep the door open for renewed contact by having a positive attitude toward openness. Marcy Wineman Axness says that the mechanics of openness are not the same as the consciousness of openness, and that adoptive parents need to maintain an openness of heart that affirms the adoptee's reality without flinching.

When birth parents are intensely involved in establishing an open plan and then become less available over time, the child is left feeling rejected and hurt. While this is painful, it does not necessarily correlate that it is not beneficial for the child to have had the initial contact. In Ronny Diamond's view, there are complications in any part of life, and we need not avoid doing something because it is potentially painful:

> Part of how an adoptive parent can show his child that the birth parents were not ready to parent is when the birth parent does not follow through with letters and contact. It's part of the whole picture and, yes, it can be hurtful. Adoptive parents have to help their children understand that, and I don't think we need to or should protect kids from that anymore. We've learned we can't protect with secrets. In an effort to protect with our closed system, we've done as much damage as we would have done if we hadn't tried to protect at all. As always, each solution generates its own set of problems. Sometimes we have a difficult situation, where the child is a product of rape or there are other

siblings out there. You don't have to tell a child all at once, but I do think a child is entitled to information about his background. And it can offer some explanation of why the adoption plan made sense, rather than painting this rosy picture that only leaves kids bewildered.

In America, although there has been a strong movement toward open adoption, the majority of adoptions are still closed. Open adoption has been growing steadily, however, since the early 1980s, and there is strong anecdotal evidence that indicates that on the whole it is good for the children. When an adopted person establishes a comfortable place in his evolving family, then his internal struggle will ease, and he will not feel so torn. In creating open adoptions, birth and adoptive parents want adoptees to know that those who gave them life and those who raise them all have love to offer.

Dealing with Adoption at School

> Adoption can impact children at school in two ways: educationally and socially.
>
> Debra G. Smith, director of the National Adoption Information Clearinghouse, "Adoption and School Issues"

Adoptive parents believed for many years that it was better not to tell teachers and school administrators that their child was adopted. Consultants with such programs as Spence-Chapin's Adoption Awareness for Educators or Joyce Pavao's Center for Family Connections in Boston and New York are now doing outreach to schools to educate teachers and administrators about adoption. As they become better informed, they are more able to work constructively with adoptees and their families.

Adoptive parents who choose not to advise teachers their child is adopted are afraid of the negative stereotypes and misconceptions about adoption that influence the way some teachers and schools relate to the children. They also fear that any problem their child may have will be attributed to him being adopted. In the August 1990 issue of the newsletter *Adopted Child*, Lois Ruskai Melina says that adoption should definitely be considered a factor when a student is having difficulties, because it is an influential factor in his life and in his development. However, she says it is important to recognize that other factors may also be contributing to a student's problems.

The issues that arise for a child at school closely relate to how he views himself. A teacher's task is to nurture a healthy sense of self-esteem and to inspire children's natural sense of curiosity and desire to learn. Sometimes teachers are inadvertently insensitive to the special needs of some children. Most adoptees do not have extensive information about their biological family's background, so projects like family trees are difficult for them. Children adopted from abroad may also know little about their cultural heritage. There may be other children with special family situations in the classroom, and although it may not be necessary to pay individual attention to each one, teachers can simply assume there is diversity and develop their lessons with that in mind. They might display different models of families in the classroom showing how some children live with two mothers, others with their grandparents, and some with parents who did not give birth to them. Children will learn quickly that there is no such thing as a "real" family versus a fake one.

Teasing has always been a mainstay of childhood. Other children do not realize how hurtful simple statements like "You don't have a real mother" or "Your parents just gave you away" are. When teachers are able to integrate information about different families into the general curriculum, children are more likely to assimilate the knowledge and to be more understanding.

Each stage of a child's educational development presents new challenges in school. In preschool and kindergarten, adoption issues have not quite taken root for a child, so special attention need not be drawn to the subject. If classmates are curious, and the child is comfortable, then adoptive families can consider making a presentation. Elementary school is a time when children grasp more abstract concepts and ideas, so it is appropriate for adoptive parents to discuss with adoptees how they want to handle their adoptive status in school. Above all, adoptees need to feel that they are accepted and do not stand out because they are adopted. Junior and senior high school present greater worries for educators, adoptees, and adoptive parents. Teens have discovered their sexuality, and the subject becomes a top concern for everyone. Ideally, discussions about adoption are integrated into classes about teenage pregnancy and sexual education. Lois Ruskai Melina suggests that panels of adoptees, adoptive parents, and birth parents would be useful for raising awareness and dispelling myths. This would serve not only to present adoption as one way of handling an untimely pregnancy, but if presented correctly would help adopted teens and their peers gain more awareness of adoption issues and create an opportunity for healthy dialogue.

Having Foreign Roots

> As I have grown, I've come to realize, I was not born an American and I am very much different from the majority of Americans. I am an adopted Jewish Korean. The shape of my eyes has defined my heritage; while the environment that surrounds me has defined my personality. I am adopted, I am Jewish, I am Asian, I am an American, I am Kang Hye Won, and I am Jody Melissa Rubin.
>
> Jody Melissa Rubin, college essay

Once they arrive on these shores adoptees from foreign cultures straddle a cultural fence, and adoptive parents have the task of helping them adjust to life in America. Many form informal groups that meet regularly and give their children a chance to socialize with other children from the same culture. Other initiatives involve camps, classes in the native language, and cultural awareness programs. Parents who make an effort to gather information about their children's birth families also help them develop an individual sense of self.

David Adler and his wife know where they can find their daughter Luisa's birth mother if at some point they feel it is important for her. In the meantime, they keep items around the house from Paraguay to teach her about her heritage. "Sometimes she will look at the Paraguayan things," says David, "and we'll say 'That's from Paraguay, that's where you were born.' So now she says 'That's where I was born, that's where I was born.' I think even though she's young, she's getting a sense of her roots."

Many children adopted from Korea are now in their teens and twenties, and a number have embarked with their families on "motherland" trips, where they meet with the people at the orphanages who arranged their adoptions. One young boy met the policeman who found him and remembered what he had been wearing. Others returning to Korea meet with birth mothers who explain why they relinquished their children. Lately, there are also search groups, both independent and agency supported, that are helping Korean adoptees find their birth families. Friends of mine recently took their ten-year-old and eight-year-old girls back to India. They spent a day at the orphanage with the woman who had cared for them, and they were able to ask questions and to help her in the nursery. Visits to their country of origin help people adopted from abroad reconnect with their cultural heritage. In the process, they gain a deeper understanding of what happened to them and an appreciation for the life they have had.

Eleanor Oakley, who adopted one of her two adopted daughters internationally, says that the two girls approach the idea of finding birth parents in a very different manner. She says her foreign-born daughter is not interested at all in finding her birth parents, because from a very early age she saw it as impossible. "She is the type of person," she says, "who puts things in boxes, and those boxes that can be opened she deals with. The ones she sees as impossibilities, she doesn't give a lot of time to. I have maintained a correspondence with the nun who took care of her in the orphanage, which is a connection to her past, and I believe in some ways that has been reassuring to her. She has let me have the relationship, but I think she draws some comfort from it."

At the end of the Vietnam War, the United States carried out a maneuver called Operation Babylift, which transported orphans from Vietnam for adoption in the United States. These children have now reached young adulthood, and in the May 1, 1995, issue of *People* magazine it was reported that many have begun to explore their Asian heritage. Jennifer, whose Vietnamese name is Nguyen Thi Dai Trang, was adopted by a couple in New York, and was the victim of occasional racial slurs at her predominantly white elementary school. She remembers that when she was young being different was difficult, but now she celebrates her roots by reading Vietnamese literature and learning the language of her ancestors. She hopes to visit the city of her birth sometime in the future. Many of the other Operation Babylift children are happy with their adoptive families, but they, too, would like to learn more about the homeland they had to abandon.

Children adopted from abroad who do not racially resemble their parents have to cope with questions about their origins in ways that children who racially resemble their parents do not. Like children adopted transracially within the United States, they also deal with issues of racism and discrimination. Even when comments are not always intentionally hurtful, they can be upsetting. One teenage Asian adoptee from a large family of adopted and biological children took part in a panel of adopted teens at Spence-Chapin. She said that when she told her mother people say she looks different from her parents and siblings, her mother replied, "I think we all look alike." It was a humorous and affirming way of dealing with a sensitive issue. It is not easy for a child to cope with knowledge that every time someone sees him with his parents, they know immediately he was adopted.

Living with Differences: Transracial Adoption

> For the last 20 years, same-race placement in many states, including New York, was the preference. A new law passed by Congress last month allows race to be considered only if there is more than one qualified family that wants to adopt a child. That new law could mean more transracial adoptions, say experts, and the need for adoptive white parents to understand what it means to rear a black child.
>
> Joanne Wasserman, "Should Families Be Color-Blind?"

Transracial adoptions have always been controversial, and it is ongoing as child welfare and private adoption agencies attempt to place more minority children than ever before. Many people in the African-American community feel that there is little or no possibility that a white parent can prepare a child of a different race to deal with racism in the United States. The transracially adopted child, they feel, will suffer insensitive comments, hurtful epithets, and identity confusion that adoptees who share the same race as their parents will not.

Currently, there are more African-American than Caucasian children in need of homes. There are also more white couples seeking to adopt than there are children who racially match them. Whether African-American children grow up in a home with white or black parents, the fact remains that they need permanent placements. Agencies across the country are focusing on finding African-American parents for these children, and recently, there has been an increase in the number of African-American couples and singles adopting black children. Spence-Chapin started recruiting African-American families directly in the early 1950s, and Mrs. Jackie Robinson was then chair of their home-finding committee. In 1968, the agency founded the Harlem Dowling-Westside Center for Children and Family Services (which subsequently became an independent organization in the late 1970s) to advise, train, and assist black preadoptive parents. Recently, Spence-Chapin has redoubled its efforts, and an active African-American Advisory Committee does outreach to the black community. Gretchen Viederman, the director of domestic adoptions, says they have also recently started a program for Hispanic families. She also points out "that since birth mothers are the driving force in choosing the adoptive family, they seem to be more comfortable selecting families that are similar to themselves."

Another program that has had positive results is the One Church/One Child Minority Adoption Campaign that started in Illinois in 1986 in an unusual alliance between the State Department of Children and Family Services and the state's black churches. The success in Illinois led to the creation of One Church/One Child programs in other states.

A 1991 survey of public and private agencies indicated that of 13,208 placements, 6,347 were black and Hispanic. Of these, 22 percent were transracial adoptions. Nearly three decades have passed since the National Association of Black Social Workers made its much publicized stand opposing transracial adoptions. The group does not support the philosophy of the Multiethnic Placement Act of 1994, which says that any agency receiving federal funds cannot deny a person the opportunity to be an adoptive or foster parent based solely on their race, color, or nationality. That act was amended in 1996 and now prohibits the consideration of race, culture, or ethnicity as even a factor in decisions to delay or deny a foster care or adoptive placement. Despite the opposition, transracial adoptions continue, and most people, both white and black, support them. In *The Case for Transracial Adoption,* Rita J. Simon indicates that "in January 1991, *CBS This Morning* reported the results of a poll it conducted that asked 975 adults the question 'Should race be a factor in adoption?' Seventy percent of white Americans said no, as did seventy-one percent of African-Americans. These percentages are the same as those reported by Gallup in 1971 when it asked a national sample the same question."

Beth Lake has two white adopted sons and one African-American adopted daughter who they are raising in an all-white community. She says that she discusses the issues of race with her daughter, and they know it takes its toll on her. For now, Beth's daughter is a "very present-centered" teenager and does not want to talk too much about being of a different race from the rest of her family. Beth is aware that transracial adoption concerns will arise for her daughter in a more conscious way at some point, but for now sees no reason to pressure her. The Lakes do not have any negative incidents to report about other people's reactions to their daughter, but most parents have some stories, and their children can probably relate incidents they have not necessarily shared with their parents.

Adoption and the Media: A Complicated Relationship

> Responsible movie producers must convey the
> message that children are placed up for adoption for
> many reasons.
>
> Marjorie Wolfe, "The Truth about Birthmothers"

Lately, the subject of adoption is a regular feature of the media. Adoption stories are full of human drama that most audiences easily grasp and identify with on a very basic level. Producers and writers usually focus on more sordid and depressing aspects of adoption because they believe it makes people buy papers, watch TV, and go to the movies. The cost of omitting truthful and balanced information is often paid by adoptees, birth parents, and adoptive parents. The risk in using adoption as a convenient story or plot creates a false public perception of the process.

An adoptive mother in one workshop I attended told the other parents that her eleven-year-old son had watched a dramatic story on television of a destitute birth mother kidnapping her child from his adoptive parents. Her son was anxious for days that he, too, could be taken away. Celebrated court cases like Baby Jessica and Baby Richard exacerbate the fears of adoptees because the media rarely explains the entire story. Sandra Ripberger of Spence-Chapin says, "The cases stimulated a great interest in adoption, and in the relationship among triad members. They also created a lot of misunderstanding, because there really are very few disrupted adoptions."

The cases did bring to light how differently the media portrays each triad member. Jim Gritter notes that the media generally creates a very positive picture of adoptive parents and a dreary one of birth parents—especially birth fathers. "The high-profile cases have really increased the paranoia. The negative attention paid to birth parents insures that many of them keep a pretty low profile. Shame, which they often feel, drives any and all of us to try and be invisible, to try not to draw any attention to ourselves."

Adoption is not an easy subject to comprehend, and that is why quick Movie of the Week attempts can be quite harmful. A TV movie that starred Cheryl Ladd portrayed the birth parents of one little girl as being not only indigent but also baby brokers. They had child after child and then sold them to eager couples. The birth mother ended up having her tubes tied while the barely reformable birth father slunk out of the hospital. The rich, glamorous, and attractive adoptive couple ended up adopting not only the little girl but also the birth parents' last child, a son.

We have seen that adoptees who have no contact with their birth parents have vivid fantasies about them. Movies that continue to portray stereotyped images and to perpetuate myths about adoption feed into their worst fears. Films like *Mighty Aphrodite, Losing Isaiah,* and *Flirting with Disaster* elicited debates and sometimes protests from all sides of the adoption perspective. The award-winning *Secrets and Lies* has come the closest to presenting an authentic picture of the emotional issues of adoption and the cumulative effect of a lifetime of secrecy, and yet even this film once again featured a birth mother eking out a miserable existence.

Kathy Legg feels that the media has improved somewhat. "I think they were really bad during the Jessica days," she says, "but I think they're becoming slightly more aware. Adoption, we have to remember, is not easy to understand in its full ramifications. And people just have a sort of gut reaction that's very often what you see reflected on TV from the producers and reporters. There are so many more elements as you learn, and it's so much more complex. It's not really easily suitable for TV."

Sometimes a film can help children understand more about being adopted. David Adler feels that a movie like *Babe* is a step in the right direction, because the filmmakers handled the material responsibly. "The idea that you have a movie where a pig is adopted by a dog, and where adoption is discussed is such a quantum change from when I was growing up. As far as I'm concerned, just being able to talk about adoption in the open is hugely positive."

Ken Watson writes in his essay "What Adoption Is and What It Isn't" that "each of us has a responsibility to help change the public image of adoption through our everyday contacts with members of the public." Adoption associations, agency outreach programs, legislative initiatives, and the Internet are also educational tools that increase awareness of the complex realities of adoption. An informed public ultimately serves the best interest of the children.

Adoptees and Adoptive Parents Create Families

Adoptive families are made of heart and soul instead of biology and genes.

Randolph Severson, *A Letter to Adoptive Parents on Open Adoption*

We have looked at how a person who is adopted copes with the uncertainties inherent in his adopted status, and integrates his often perplexing experience as he develops his own identity. Father Tom Brosnan says that all the experiences we have along the way make us who we are, and for adoptees, acknowledging the truth of their loss is the only way they can find the peace of forgiveness. Marcy Wineman Axness knows she has become the person she is meant to be, and she is happy with who she is, but she still needed and craved acknowledgment and empathy for her losses. She says adoptive parents can help their children remain connected to their inner truth.

Adopted people are part of many families, as Joyce Maguire Pavao tells us, but the family in which they spend their formative years shapes their worldview. Andrew's parents stood by him and helped him grow into a man they are rightfully proud of. In the next chapter, I will share more of their story and explore how adoptive parents meet the challenges of raising adopted children.

AND I WILL MAKE THEE BEDS OF ROSES

Adoptive Parents Define a Family

The Life of Our Family

> I realized as I sat there on the couch . . . that this adoption had a life of its own. It was an ongoing, endless, dynamic thing that was going to change its shape and its composition constantly. Just when we thought we had gotten a handle on it and understood its complexities, it would change again, expand, and evoke some new emotion. It was a lifetime journey.
>
> Dion Howells, adoptive father and author of *The Story of David: How We Created a Family through Open Adoption*

I CHERISH THE information about Andrew's childhood that I have gathered from conversations with Katherine and Bill. Our conversations have brought me closer to him—and to them, as I learned of the struggles and triumphs of his early years. Katherine and Bill also drew strength from their memories, finding an affirming voice in the words that told the story of their family. Katherine has many happy memories of the two boys as children, including photographs of them during long country summers. She remembers though that life did change for Andrew after they adopted Jason, and she believes he never completely accepted having a second child in the house. "Andrew and Jason have such different personalities. Jason handles things by keeping quiet and shutting down, while Andrew is very extroverted and outgoing. You always knew where he stood all the time. How he felt. He was just all out there."

Sometimes Katherine wondered where his angry feelings came from. Her family kept their feelings to themselves, and it was not always so easy for her to handle Andrew, especially when she was alone after the divorce. "He would blow up over any little thing. He didn't like to be told to do his homework, and he had a strong personality, a strong will. Spence-Chapin had told us that his birth father was German, and I do remember thinking to myself, 'This is where he must be getting this.' Nevertheless, Andrew has always been very protective of me. He has always been very aware of my feelings and would never do anything to hurt me."

Bill also remembers thinking that Andrew's German genes and his military heritage had something to do with his personality. Knowing me now as well, he sees that Andrew has attributes of each of us. "From the point of view of a parent, Andrew has always been a person of very strong views. He's always been very clear on his own agenda. And as a child, you always knew it if he didn't think the parental assessment of crime and punishment was in line. I mean, he didn't much like being told no, if he wanted to do something . . . and so that's still a loving characteristic of the young man."

During the turbulent years of the separation and divorce, Andrew's parents tried to keep as stable a life as they could for the boys, and they arranged it so that Bill would always see them on a regular schedule:

> Katherine and I honored a commitment we had made to each other that we would never let our sons, in any way, become embroiled in any negotiations or divorce settlement. I think that Katherine and I both wanted our sons to be very aware that each of their parents loved them enormously and were going to be there for them. When they came to visit me in a tiny apartment I was sharing with a guy who was out of town on the weekends, they had to make some adjustments. They ate a lot of well-done hamburgers and in a lot of restaurants. But we were together, and that was very important to me.

Divorce is never simple or painless for any family. Katherine and Bill worried that their divorce would hit the boys even harder because they had already lost one set of parents. "Here we were getting a divorce," says Katherine, "and I just felt for both of them, it was a double-whammy situation. I mean, basically, their birth parents gave them up. And now their adoptive father was leaving. They must have been worried that I might too."

"Andrew was very angry," says Bill, "because he did not feel that he had been consulted in making this decision. I don't know if he remembers that, but that's exactly the way he put it. Andrew very much likes to be in control of things, and did as a boy, even before he learned that his mother and I were going to separate."

After their separation, Katherine and Bill each sought support in handling their concerns about their children. There was very little literature available at the time, and although Andrew had refused counseling for himself, Katherine was able to talk with her therapist. Bill was involved in advisory committees at the adoption agency, and that helped him tremendously:

> It was a terrific experience for me. I learned a lot about how things work in an adoption agency and developed a certain sensitivity by listening to people discuss adoption issues. I heard conversations about how adoption was changing during the late 1960s and early 1970s. I was listening to how different things were handled and what was recommended in various circumstances. I was building up a reservoir of helpful information.

Bill's remarriage when Andrew was eleven created a wedge between them for some time. He remembers vividly how he and Andrew struggled on the day of the wedding:

> I have memories of sitting with him on a couch at our friends' home to try to help him get his program together before the actual ceremony. Andrew was very unhappy that I was getting remarried. He didn't want this to happen. He obviously thought that he was going to reengineer his mother and me back together again. I think he sincerely felt that he had the capacity to cause that to happen. If nothing else, this indicates the strength of conviction and sheer will of this young man. It wasn't in the cards. I know it was a long and difficult day for Andrew.

Bill says, "It took many, many years for him to understand, just at a fundamental level, that Sarah, his stepmother, was probably all right." The turning point was when Bill became seriously ill, and Sarah stood by him and nursed him back to health.

Looking back, it strikes me that illness has served as an emissary of renewal and change on more than one occasion in our collective family. It is a terrifying harbinger of our mortality that brings us up short and demands attention. It also offers us a chance to stop and pay attention to the people who matter in our life. For me, it signaled an opportunity for a change of course and reaffirmation. It was a time of emotional healing that set me on my path toward reunion with Andrew. My father's terminal illness united our family and taught us to treasure each moment of his waning life. Andrew's arrival in my life is woven in my heart with the passing of my father. I learned firsthand that from death comes new life. Bill's illness opened the door for Andrew to grow closer to his father and to accept Sarah as part of his life.

The Family Evolves

> When I was a child, I spake as a child, I understood as a child, I thought as a child: but when I became a man, I put away childish things.
>
> I Corinthians 13:11

When Andrew wanted to go away to school, Katherine felt deep down that she could not send him away so early. But Andrew was insistent, and his parents relented. He was a late bloomer physically, and Katherine says, "I remember leaving him at that boarding school, and his clean-shaven roommate was over six feet tall, his voice already changed. I remember crying all the way home. After leaving him there, I thought, 'How could I have done this?' I missed him terribly, especially the first year, because I knew in my gut that he must be having a hellish time, but he never said a word."

After high school, Andrew went to college in the Midwest, and Katherine feels he was comfortable being on his own by then. As hard as it was for her to let go, she recognized his independent spirit. "In the summers," she says, "he would do all sorts of adventurous things. He went off and worked on a fishing boat. He always struck out on his own, and I thought that was really good. I was pleased to see that, but it was hard."

Several years later, Katherine and Bill were thrilled when he married Chloe, who they both feel is like a daughter to them. Although Andrew had always been thoughtful about calling Katherine and letting her know how he was faring, she says that "there were a lot of things that he was keeping inside, that he wasn't able to share with me, which I know that he's able to do with Chloe. She's been the first person who I think he's been able to really, totally trust."

When the grandchildren were born, Katherine says it was an extraordinary feeling for her. Friends had raved when theirs were born, but she says you just don't understand until you see your child with their child:

> He held his baby, Emma, like I held him. It was so natural. He wasn't nervous, he was just so calm. It was like he'd been doing it all his life. It's wonderful he's such a good father. He feels very strongly about family, and I think for him to have his own family is sacred for him, very special. I look at little Emma now, and I see Andrew in so many things that she does and says and the ways she is. She's got the dark hair and the dark eyes, even the cleft in her chin . . . and she's got a wonderful, funny sense of humor. And *very* willful. She's so like her dad. I get such a kick out of watching him try to handle her.

Andrew's ultimate gift to Bill came when he named his newborn son William. A friend suggested to Bill that Andrew's pure gesture of love closed the circle between them. "I guess that's what I feel," says Bill. "If I was hit by a car, and went on to my just rewards, I would feel that my circle with my son was fully closed. I've been saying to friends since that I have drunk deeply from the pool of narcissism, and the water is very good in there."

Katherine and Bill cannot imagine their lives without their children. "The thing that stands out the most to me," says Katherine, "is how lucky I feel to have these two boys. It's just a really special gift."

No family knows what life holds for them. Katherine and Bill carried with them the ghosts of their lost biological children as they started their family life with Andrew and Jason. In raising their sons they did not dwell each day on the fact that the boys were adopted, but they never lost sight of that fundamental truth. Together, the family struggled with the ghost of the disrupted marriage. Now, they have extended themselves again to include me, and they are as much a part of my adoption experience as I am of theirs. Andrew is the unique individual he is because of his own makeup, his upbringing—and his biological heritage. We are who we are because of the life we have been given, the road we have traveled. One without the other would not have made Andrew the caring, independent man he has become.

Discovering My Children

> I feel like it's part of my fate that as an adoptive father
> I can try to guide my child through some of the diffi-
> culties that I went through as an adoptee. I want to
> make it easier for her. Because of what I now know, I
> can help her and myself with issues that perhaps I
> would not be able to if I had had a biological child.
> This is my parenting destiny.
>
> David Adler, adoptive parent and adoptee

When Sharon Rhodes first looked in the nursery window of the hospital, she knew which baby was Jake, her adoptive son. She brought him home the next day when he was just two and a half days old, and she felt she couldn't love him more if he had come from her own body:

> It doesn't make a difference to me. I've heard some other mothers still
> talking about how they wish they could have their own biological chil-
> dren, but that's not there for me. Sometimes, I wish I could have experi-
> enced pregnancy, somebody growing in my body. But Jake feels even
> deeper than from my body, he's from my heart and soul. I think the
> emotional process that led up to him coming into our lives played a big
> part in it for me.

When a child comes to a family through adoption, parents like Sharon Rhodes and Katherine and Bill are ready to assume responsibility for their welfare for their entire lives. Like other parents, they love them uncondition-ally. While it is not hard to love a baby, raising children requires day-by-day, minute-to-minute attention to seize every opportunity to teach them and help them grow, and to be there for them even when they do not think they need it or want it. It is an extraordinary undertaking, and my own heart swells when-ever I think about how Katherine and Bill have been parents to Andrew and Jason and continue to be there to support them as adults and to enjoy their achievements. In meetings at Spence-Chapin, I have been privileged to hear adoptive parents talking about the latest events in their children's lives, their sports activities, or their school plays. Many is the time they have to leave a meeting early to rush home to be there for their child when he gets home from school. This is the ordinary life of any parent, and that is what any birth parent wants for their child. Each and every time I hear a snippet of someone's story, I am filled with renewed respect for the love that adoptive parents bring to their children. There is no doubt for me that they love their adopted child every bit as much as they would their biological child.

Every child comes into this world with some special needs that parents help them resolve. It can be as simple as having difficulty learning to read, or learning how to make choices and decisions, or overcoming shyness. Children may also have other physical or emotional problems that their parents have to help them with. Adoptive parents have the additional responsibility of helping their children understand what it means to be adopted, and they do that in the course of their everyday parenting. While most of that daily job of parenting adopted children has nothing to do with their adopted status, parents always have to be prepared to deal with questions and situations as they come up.

Michael Colberg is an adoptive parent and a therapist associated with Joyce Pavao's Center for Family Connections. In his experience, "things don't manifest in terms of a child coming and saying 'My adoption hurts today.' They will say, 'I feel sad today' or 'Nobody likes me.' Their feelings are no different from those of other people in the population at large, but they come up around issues and at certain times, and you can be expected to look at them, and they might have something to do with their status as part of the triad."

The Growing Years

> In the playgound with other moms, sooner or later the conversation came around to how long the labor was, which hospital the woman was in. . . . I found it uncomfortable to be duplicitous about the experience. I was overjoyed to be a mother. I was perfectly comfortable being an adoptive mother. It was always easier, more natural to disclose up front.
>
> Joanne Carter, adoptive parent

Adoptive parents regularly encounter situations where they are faced with choosing whether or not to acknowledge to others the fact that their children are adopted. By the time her firstborn, Claire, was ready to start elementary school, Joanne was living in a small town where everybody knows one another:

> I went in the first day, and the school nurse asked as usual about the pregnancy and delivery. I said I gather it went well, but I wasn't there for them. We had a great conversation, because as it happens the woman before me made a big deal of not wanting anything in the record that her son was adopted. However, her son was Korean. . . . It was evident to me that early in the elementary years, the teacher did need to know. Around third grade, I felt it became their choice to tell. That made sense to Claire, who doesn't want to share with everybody. She just wants to control who knows, and that's perfectly age appropriate. I don't think my son Rick would dream of telling a friend, but it's important to him to know he has one or two friends who are adopted.

From the moment a child is born, family and friends look to see which parent the baby resembles, and these comparisons continue throughout life. Adoptive families have to create different ways of making members feel connected to one another. They also find ways to celebrate the diversity rather than dwell on the lack of similarities. Rebecca Hunter is the adoptive mother of two children from Korea. Her oldest, Michelle, was born in 1976, and at that time there were not many Korean adoptions in New York. Rebecca says a lot of the issues at first had to do with the fact that her daughter did not look like her and her husband. "It was a very obvious adoption," she says, "not what we sometimes call an 'invisible' adoption. In some ways it made the whole issue of being adopted easier to talk about within the family. It's right out there, and you can't hide. And if you tend to forget about it, which you do, strangers and people on the streets and kids' friends will remind you of it."

Even before Rebecca's daughter Michelle could talk, they told her an adoption bedtime story that always began, "Once upon a time, we wanted a baby, and a baby wasn't growing in my tummy." Although Michelle always knew that, Rebecca remembers one incident when Michelle was five or six, when a child at school had asked why she did not look like her mom:

> She explained that she was adopted, but when we walked home from school she said, "Mommy I just want to look like you." I looked at her and said, "It would really be easier for us wouldn't it if we looked alike —if you looked like me, or if I were Korean and looked like you? But I love you because you're you, just the way you are. If you were like me

you wouldn't be my daughter." She looked up at me and said, "Mommy, I know if there had been a baby in your tummy, it would have been me."

Small children need constant repetition and concrete reinforcement of the truth of their origins. Carey Howells, whose husband, Dion, wrote *The Story of David,* recently told me a story about her son, who is now five years old. Before bed one night, David snuggled with her and talked about how he grew in her tummy. Carey reminded him that he had grown in his Nancy Mom's tummy. "David has always known he came from Nancy's tummy," Carey says, "but he was telling me he wished he had come from mine. I told him I wished that, too, and even though he really did grow in his Nancy Mom's tummy, I was still his Mommy. That seemed to satisfy him."

Parents always have their antennae out, ready to answer their children's questions or to seize an opportunity to teach them something. Good parenting is about paying attention to these daily building blocks, establishing meaningful connections for their children, helping them grow step by step into mature adults. Adoptive parents are no different. Only they have the extra responsibility of helping their children fit the pieces of their adoption story into the context of their lives. Joanne Carter never knew her biological father. As a result, she is keenly aware that adopted children always wonder about their birth parents. She understands that this is an issue that does not go away, and she is attentive to the emotional needs of her children. Her youngest child is only three years old and is not yet asking complex questions, but the two older children express their pain in characteristically different ways:

> Claire is not someone who asks direct questions. She is someone I have to be more attuned to. I just try to make sure I have my ears pinned back to notice signals and opportunities. She seems to be in touch with sorrow and sadness, rather than anger. She has a letter from her birth mother that I shared with her which I know she keeps as a sacred object. I think it's a comfort to her. My son Rick is an entirely different kettle of fish. He doesn't talk about it often, but when he does, it is very high up there on the Richter scale. He can just burst into tears and say, "Why can't I meet my birth mother? I'm hurt in my heart I can't know her."

Joanne says she also has to be watchful outside the home. Recently, in her daughter's school, they were discussing responsible behavior in relation to drugs and alcohol—and sexual behavior. Joanne saw the question coming: "Does this mean my birth mother was irresponsible?" She says she has to anticipate situations to be sure her daughter does not internalize bad feelings about her birth mother or herself. She was able to explain that even very good people are not perfect, and that if they make a mistake, it does not mean they are bad.

Rebecca Hunter also observed that her daughters responded in different ways to their adoption and to their feelings about their birth mothers. She says she always identified strongly with the birth mothers, especially Michelle's, because she came first. Rebecca wanted to let her know she was such a wonderful child, and was healthy and smart. She says:

> I always worried because Michelle has felt very distant from her birth mother. I always tried to get her to work on it. She would say, "I don't want to deal with it; I don't want to talk about it, I'm not interested." I think she is understanding it more but still does not seem to want to think about it too much. My younger daughter, Sherry, was intensely interested. When she was four to five years old, at bedtime every night, she wanted me to read *The Mulberry Bird*. She wanted to know, "Why?" Three years ago, Sherry started to study Korean, because she wants to be able to speak to her mother in Korean. For the time being, that has fallen by the wayside, because she is more interested in being a regular teenager.

We can see from these and other stories that just as nonadopted siblings differ, no two adopted children, even in the same home, deal with their adopted status in the same way. The response naturally varies, depending on individual personality and each child's personal history.

Siblings have an immeasurable influence on each other's lives whether or not they are adopted, and whether or not they become close friends. We all know how parents worry about how their firstborn will deal with the arrival of another baby, and adoptive parents also need to prepare their children for new children in the family. If the older child is adopted, parents like Katherine and Bill explain that they will be going to get another child and usually include them in some way in the process, depending on their age and the circumstances. In Diane Nemes's case, she had a five-year-old biological daughter when she decided to adopt her second child. "I had to explain," says Diane, "why I could not have another biological child, and why my son's birth mother could not keep her baby. I said that the woman who gave birth to him was in Guatemala and that she couldn't afford to take care of the baby. I hope as she gets older she'll have more questions and that she will always love Ted as her brother."

Two of Joanne Carter's children are American born. Three years ago, when the older children were five and eight years old, they adopted a third child from Paraguay, and the whole family went there to pick up Bobby. Recently, her son Rick got obsessed with where he was born. "He was born in Pennsylvania," says Joanne. "He said he should be there, that he didn't belong here or in this family. I had a hunch and said, 'Do you want to go to Pennsylvania?' We went and toured around the state, saw Valley Forge, the Liberty Bell, etc., and had a fine time. That did it for him. He was struggling with the fact that his baby brother was born in a very different place, and he wondered if he came from a different place too. He needed to see if people in Pennsylvania looked like him."

Dealing with their children's angry feelings about their birth parents can be especially difficult for adoptive parents. Sometimes, even if the adoptive mother empathizes with the birth mother and tries her best to convey that the decision to relinquish was a loving choice, the child is unwilling and unable to let go of his anger. Cynthia Beals reports that her oldest son started having a problem when he was about six or seven. "I could remember him coming home very upset," says Cynthia, "saying that the girls at school were teasing him about being adopted. After talking with the parents, I started putting two and two together, and figuring out that my son was actually instigating a lot of it. He was looking for attention. He was looking for answers. And he had, I think, a big resentment against his birth mother." Cynthia, a birth mother as well as an adoptive mother, was devastated by her son's anger. She says, "I didn't want him to feel this way about her. I tried to explain to him that what she did was very loving. No matter what I said or did, I just couldn't seem to touch him the way I had hoped I could. So I finally realized I had to let him go, and let him work this out himself."

The Teen Years

> They sort of close down completely. They don't want to be different. Adoption goes on the back burner. Friendship and personality become more important. It's more about finding your identity. You're trying out all different personas.
>
> Rebecca Hunter

We have seen how adolescence intensifies the adoptee's quest for an individual identity, and how at a time when they are subject to more intense peer pressures, they are often confused and uncertain about who they are. Rebecca Hunter says that most of the situations she deals with are not adoption related, but the adoption part is always back there, and it can come up and surprise you. Sometimes it is as simple as a question about appearance. One day her daughter Sherry did her hair in pigtails and asked her out of the blue if she looked more Asian like that. She told her that she *is* Asian, and she does not look any more or less Asian with a different hair style. Rebecca understood that her daughter was somehow wanting to deny that piece of herself. She wanted to look like all her friends.

On another occasion, Sherry was wondering how she would develop as a woman, what she could anticipate. "Usually you can look at your mom and get an idea," says Rebecca. "I was able to say she might be like me—or like Aunt Judy, and we both came from the same mother! Finally, Sherry said, 'Mom, if I ever met *her,* I'd want to find out how tall she is.' She is short and is dying to be much taller. If you ever wonder if they are thinking about it, it's always there; it comes out in little things like that at any time."

Like all parents, adoptive parents need to keep a level head when their adolescent children act out and distance themselves. Rebecca knows it is part of their growing up and searching for their own identity. Her daughter Sherry is at the stage where she is joined at the hip with her friends and is often defiant:

> She is at the age where she could say, but hasn't quite, "You can't tell me what to do, you're not my real mother!" She wants to make us into horrible people who can't possibly understand her. Fortunately she's the second child, and we know it's a phase, and we're really very close. She's been so good, and now suddenly she's going to be bad. It's more a teen issue than an adoption issue. I think she knows enough to know she can throw words at me, but it's not going to go very far.

Rebecca knows from experience not to be devastated by her second daughter's outbursts. She is "Mom," and that means she is the boss, and she will not let herself be emotionally manipulated.

When Rebecca's teenage daughter Michelle went off to college, it was the conventional wisdom of the school to group students according to their ethnicity, and they housed the Asians in their own dorm. Michelle objected to this because she was different from the Asian foreign students, and she did not want to be identified with them. Rebecca sees how the adoption piece sometimes gets wrapped into the racial identity issue. "These Korean kids," says Rebecca, "who grew up in a white family, are white inside, and they can see racism through white eyes. Michelle sees the stereotypes as a white person." Transracial and many transcultural adoptees cannot hide the fact of their adoption, and although that makes it easier in some ways for parents to talk openly with them, they face their own unique set of problems.

Increasing Our Potential: Adoptive Parents Find Support

> I think that we give the adoptive parents a leg up and
> they, therefore, can give their children a leg up.
>
> Kathy Legg, executive director,
> Spence-Chapin Services to Families and Children

Postadoption services provided by agencies and other adoption organizations were sorely lacking when Andrew was growing up. However, they are now a vital resource for adoptive parents and their children as they confront the complex and multidimensional issues of their adoption experience. Adoptive parents seek support in one another's company and solicit advice from their peers on how to deal with the difficult questions their children pose about why they were relinquished. Ronny Diamond of Spence-Chapin counsels adoptive parents that although they may have information that they can share, that does not necessarily answer the "why"—that essential question that kids have to try and work through. She says, "They have to figure out what makes sense to them."

Kathy Legg says that people who come to the Adoption Resource Center events want to know how to talk to their children about adoption, and they need to know they have resources available to them as their children develop and change. "The parents are completely lost and paralyzed about how to begin having this dialogue. We give our parents the language they need, we do some role-playing, and offer them someone to call when they get stuck. And this isn't just in the first steps of adoption, but all through the child's life because the issues will change as they get older."

We know it is just as important for adopted children to have opportunities to come together with their peers. According to Ronny Diamond, the feedback they got from the children's workshops at Spence-Chapin was that they opened things up for the kids and their families, and that the children seemed to be calmer and were having good discussions with their parents.

"Universally the kids liked being with a group of other adopted kids," says Ronny. "Some of them had never been with another adopted person."

Joanne Carter was happily surprised when her daughter Claire, then ten years old, agreed to come to one of the workshops. "I was amazed, and she loved it," says Joanne. "She said, 'In some ways these kids are better than my best friends, because they really know what this is like.' I didn't participate, but I brought her there, and I think she understands very deeply that I'm very much on her side on this."

When Rebecca Hunter adopted her children from Korea, she found that she needed to connect with other parents who shared her experience. She helped organize G.I.F.T. (Gathering International Families Together), which now has a mailing list of four hundred families in the New York tristate area. While this organization was formed for families with children from Korea, they are now assisting and sharing information with families adopting from China. She says that as these international babies join families here, issues come up and parents want to share, and they want to have culture specific activities for their children. Rebecca says that learning about Korea and its culture has been very important for her, even when her children preferred to concentrate on being like everyone else.

Rebecca made it a point to go to workshops with her older daughter when Michelle was a teenager, even if she literally had to bribe her with a new outfit. After one panel discussion with birth mothers, her daughter announced that she wanted to be on a panel. "She found her voice," says Rebecca. "She realized she had a lot to say, which meant she was thinking about it. Now we do workshops for families who are adopting. We have become the kind of resource I was looking for many years ago. We talk about what life has been like together, and she talks about her experiences from the Korean cultural camp where she has been a counselor." Rebecca says she was overwhelmed when all the parents wanted to hear from Michelle how they could help their children. This was the girl who had stopped going to the G.I.F.T. gatherings! At the workshop Michelle told the parents that it is really important to bring Korean culture into the house. She advised parents not to be surprised, however, if their kids reached an age when they no longer wanted to go to the cultural events or camp. Nevertheless, she encouraged parents to stay involved themselves because, said Michelle, "It meant a lot to me that my mom really loves this part of me, and it was very reassuring."

Joanne Carter thinks it would be very helpful to have adopted teens counsel preteens—to find ways to use kids as resources. She would also love to see the older kids write movie reviews for other families to alert them to movies that might have sensitive material for adopted children. Recently, her children watched the movie *Free Willy 2*, in which the younger brother of the hero of the first movie was dumped on the foster family's doorstep. He had been living with the birth mother, who died. Although it was intense, it was handled fairly well, she thought, but just the same, Rebecca was glad she was there for the ending. "I turned around," she says, "and looked at two little shell-shocked faces. I said, 'Okay, you guys, let's talk about this one.' They just needed to be reassured that this was a little unusual—the way it happened. I try to talk about real people they know and real stories and that not everything they read in the paper or see on T.V. is real. Reviews would help for those times when I can't be there with my kids."

For some families, religion and spirituality can be a stabilizing and comforting force, especially if they do not have postadoption resources available to them. Jack Steadman and his son Caleb reconnected with his Quaker roots to bring some order to their often hectic and disorganized existence. He says, "We had always been Quakers, since Caleb was five. We rejoined the local meeting, because I thought that he and I needed some formal group that would agree to be caretakers for us in some measure. He was raised in the meetings, went to youth groups and camps, and had a rite-of-passage ceremony when he was thirteen. It was an important support system for both of us."

Freedom to Be Themselves

I feel like we're born who we are.

Jack Steadman, adoptive parent

The idea of the perfect child is a concept that parents have to begin to let go of from the moment a real child comes into their life, either through adoption or biologically. Joanne Remy of Spence-Chapin says it is important to "help adoptive parents realize that even if they produce their own biological child, they would not be perfect. We all know many people who have children with learning and behavior problems that appear very early on, and the parents have no idea where the problems came from. I think as an agency we need to begin to think of ways to get adoptive families to think about the adoption process much more objectively." Once parents accept that their children are not going to be improved versions of themselves, they are free to enjoy their children as the individuals they are. In some ways this is easier for parents who have adopted children.

When Beth Lake adopted her three children, she felt that she did not have to exert the same kind of academic pressure on them that her parents placed on her. It was liberating to watch as they discovered their own scholastic strengths, and she enjoys the unique qualities of each of her children:

> My daughter feels different from me, and she *is.* I'm a very domestic person. I cook and am a real homemaker at heart. My daughter hates all of it, she doesn't even know what a rolling pin is. And I think it is not easy for her to be so different from me, but we all have our different interests and strengths in the family. The most I can do for my children is love and enjoy them, and provide them with a safe and happy home. They're each meant to follow their own path.

Jack Steadman saw his son as an individual from the moment he was born. He tried very hard throughout Caleb's life to encourage the differences between father and son without creating too much distance between them:

> I feel having raised an adopted son, that he was who he was early on. There are some ways that one has an effect on someone's upbringing, but there are also a lot of ways that they raise themselves. I feel that the best parent helps that person become the best that they can possibly be. Along the way, Caleb and I had a great many differences. I'm intellectual in one way and he in another. He's a master draftsman, an artist, very skillful at rendering. And I'm not. I can admire it, but I can't do it.

Joanne Carter says it is a joy and privilege watching her children and not knowing the extent of their potential. She feels free of any preconceived notions of whether they should be good singers or scientists. Joanne never played an instrument, but recently her daughter took up the flute. If she were her biological child, Joanne is not sure she would have been so quick to think this might be of interest to her.

As more and more families are benefiting from information and input from birth parents, there are fewer unknowns about their children's heritage. Parents *can* know whether music might naturally be of special interest to their children. They can anticipate what talents they might have and help them develop them. They can also help them recognize those gifts as part of their biological inheritance while they continue to champion their children being uniquely themselves.

Extended Families: Adoptive Parents, Their Children—Birth Parents

> Open adoption is a fluid arrangement that can grow and evolve with the changes in our lives. It feels as natural as birth and life itself. We take pleasure in being part of the transformation of adoption from something austere and incomplete to something warmer and natural.
>
> Adoptive mother
>
> quoted in *Adoption Without Fear,* edited by James Gritter

Many parents raising adopted children naturally resist the idea of open adoption, at least initially. I am uncertain myself how I, as a nineteen-year-old birth mother, would have handled it. Times were so different then. Open adoption was a foreign concept. Katherine says she certainly would not have considered having contact with me when she was raising Andrew. Even, in hindsight, she doubts she would have wanted an open adoption unless she saw as she was raising Andrew that he really wanted it. "I would have gone along with it," she says. "I would have supported him, but I wouldn't have been very happy about it, I don't think. I would have felt threatened. Now, I think things are just opening up so much more, and I think you just realize it's so much better to be open and to have more information. It is the things you don't know that sometimes scare you the most, the hidden things, the things that aren't talked about."

Kathleen Silber says that the people who are the most threatened by open adoption are parents with traditional adoptions because it is hard for them to think about adoption in a different way than how they adopted. She says they also fear that if they admit that open adoption might be good, then maybe they did not do quite right by their child, maybe they did not provide the best upbringing. That is obviously frightening for them, and Kathleen Silber says they convert their own parenting insecurities, or their fear that the birth mother will want her child back, into worries that contact will be harmful for their children:

I hear all the time from adoptive parents that "This is horrible. This is going to be disruptive. It'll confuse the child." Honestly, we find that kids have less confusion in open adoptions, because adoptees have a better handle on their reality. What I have noticed more recently is that the families who do have open relationships tell us that their kids don't talk too much about adoption because they don't need to, it's all right there for them. It's just normal for these kids to have this person, their birth mom, in their life.

By embracing openness from the onset, adoptive parents send a message to their children that they accept not only them but also their birth family.

Many adoptive parents understandably become alarmed when they hear about closed adoptions being opened when the children are still very young, but in some cases it is the children's persistent emotional discomfort that has prompted parents to seek greater openness. Gloria Hochman and Anna Huston of the National Adoption Center have written about one mother who worried about her daughter's state of mind:

> One adoptive mother was so concerned over her five-year-old daughter's obsession with her birthmother that she decided to convert her closed adoption into an open one. "My daughter would go up to total strangers at shopping malls or in parks and ask 'Are you my mother?'" she remembers. Finally I contacted the agency to see if we could get more information about our daughter's birthmother. They contacted the birthmother, and she was just as eager to receive information about the baby she placed for adoption.

Jane Nast is the current president of the American Adoption Congress, an association of members of the adoption triad that advocates for identifying information to be made available to adult adoptees and to birth parents. When she and her husband adopted her son and daughter in the mid-1960s, they were assured that records were "sealed," that the love and security they gave their children would ensure that all their future needs would be met, and they would never be curious about their past. "When the social worker placed seven-day-old David in my arms," says Jane, "in my heart, I wondered how the birth mother could ever forget him. How could she give birth, and then go home and pretend it never happened? I found that hard to believe, but it was an 'easy out' for me to accept it . . . and get on with my life." Jane says their life progressed like other families, and then just two weeks before David's fourteenth birthday, they received a letter with a Maine postmark. They did not know anyone who lived in that state, and so Jane was curious as she opened the envelope and started to read: "Dear Mr. and Mrs. Nast: On April 11, 1966, I gave birth to a child who is your son David . . . and three years after surrendering the baby, I married the birth father." Jane remembers feeling overcome by fear:

> The letter was very nice, but my first thought was, "Will we lose David? Here is a real biological family—he will love them more than us." My husband and I were at a loss to know what to do. This was all so frightening to us, and we had never heard of any adoptive family that had been "found" by a birth mother. We finally decided to write and tell her that we would give her name to David when he was eighteen. But when we talked to our minister, he advised us that if we waited David would ask us why we didn't trust him at age fourteen. The word *trust* kept bouncing around in my mind, and the thought that David might think we did not trust him was what made us change our original decision. We also knew that the trust had to go both ways—we had to trust ourselves enough as parents to do what was in the best interest of our son. We told David and our daughter Karen about the letter, and made arrangements to meet David's birth mother. The moment we met my fears vanished. She was a real person, not a threat to us, and certainly not to our son.

Like Katherine, Jane was initially frightened of the unknown. She worried that David's birth mother would try to reclaim him, but she says that their family life has never been the same since they all met. They searched and found Karen's birth mother, and they have all become active in educating others about how they have benefited from knowing one another and from living lives that are rooted in the truth. "Secrecy and sealed records in adoption help no one," says Jane.

Making room in their hearts and in their lives for a child's birth family can be very difficult for adoptive parents, yet we have seen that some families find it fundamental to their child's well-being. When adoptive parents and birth parents connect to one another through their child, it is almost, in the words of one professional, like a marriage. However, as Kathy Legg of Spence-Chapin points out: "I think that we can't underestimate how complicated these relationships are. You know in your own family, your marriage and whatever, these kinds of human relationships are incredibly complicated, and then when it's around a child, it's even more complicated."

In March 1997, Sharon Kaplan Roszia spoke at the Open Adoption Conference in Traverse City, Michigan. She said that some of the pain of open adoption is a reflection of transformation to a new paradigm in a society that is resisting that shift. It involves a problem of a limited definition of family, and old systems are colliding with the new. "We have an opportunity in open adoption," says Roszia, "to shift away from feelings of isolation which feed the pain." Roszia understands that pain is the gift nobody wants but says that feeling the pain offers the gift of transformation, and that open adoption gives us the chance to experience that process.

Even if parents accept that contact with their child's birth family is important, knowing when and when not to be in touch is not simple. A sense of what is right for everyone in the triad evolves organically over time. When Michael Colberg and his partner adopted their daughter, he says they did not go into the process expecting to be involved with her biological family. From the beginning they had the mother's address and phone number, but they did not disclose their own identifying information. However, after an intense and intimate experience together during a false labor, they realized they should exchange information, that it was not natural not to. After their daughter, Julie, was born, her birth mother, Diane, was a great support to Michael and his partner, Gene, when they faced legal obstacles finalizing the adoption because they are a gay couple. Despite her physical and emotional discomfort, she joined them on several occasions to face judges who demanded her presence. Michael says he started to see that it was hard for her to be around Julie, and looking back he understands the extraordinary love she has always shown both him and Gene, and their daughter:

> She put aside her own needs and came and did it. As I sensed her discomfort, it made sense to me not to have a whole lot of contact, and for the next three years we had no contact together with Julie, although I did see Diane myself for dinner or theater once or twice. Then when Julie was three years old, we joined Diane in Washington at a Reproductive Freedom March. I remember Julie needing to go to the bathroom and her linking hands with her birth mother and walking off, and the variety of emotions I had. It felt to me that this was adding to all our lives. There was a sweetness around it. Also by that time, I had dealt with a colicky baby. I had been thrown up on, I had had a variety of experiences that caused me to know as deep into my soul as I have ever been

that this was the child I was responsible for. I had no questions about ownership or entitlement. And also, because of who she was, even at an early age, it was very clear that this child does not belong to me. She was passing through us. I knew it was an honor to be parenting her.

Michael's experience as a parent and as a professional has taught him about the different needs of each member of the triad. He says that the needs complement one another going into an adoption and produce the kind of intimacy that people experience when they are stuck in an elevator together. After placement, they drift back into their respective lives, and for a time the needs no longer complement one another. Michael says that the tasks of birth parents differ from the tasks of adoptive parents, and it often happens that this is the period of time when things break down:

> People feel letters aren't being answered, and relationships drift away. In fact, birth parents need to make sense of what has happened. They need to engage with their new identity and go forward without the child, and should not be required to stay in touch, because it interferes with their task. Adoptive parents are establishing a family. It is a personal journey for both biological and adoptive parents. Over time, they reintegrate into society. At some point, when people are secure in their new roles, there needs to be a reintroduction of contact, for the sake of the child. Our responsibility as adoptive parents is to help the child value all of their pieces.

Michael Colberg and his family maintain contact with Diane and her family based on what they feel everybody's needs are as they move along. He says they let it be more or less child driven in that as Julie is able to understand more, or has more questions that are appropriately answered by the birth family, they will be in touch with them and will spend time together. When Julie was about six years old, Michael says she went through a period of being depressed. He helped her to connect with her feelings and to acknowledge that she felt very sad. One day Julie finally said that if her birth mother was not able to care for her the way she wanted to, but was doing so well in her life, then she must have been an extremely difficult baby to take care of. "That was quite a piece of language to come out of a six-year-old," says Michael. "She had a deep grief around it. We were able to sit with that and process it, and we were able to include her birth mother in different ways. There are many ups and downs. It's like an onion. You peel one layer, digest it, and sooner or later the next layer emerges."

Michael and Gene have learned from their open adoption how to allow for the relationship they and Julie have with Diane to develop its own rhythm and to change over time. Each family makes its own choices, and the choices differ, depending on the age of the child, and the nature of the people involved. However, there are some key occasions for birth and adoptive parents to cooperate in developing a unified approach for the sake of the child. At the time of the adoptive placement, birth and adoptive parents have a unique opportunity to begin to put together the child's story of adoption. During the toddler years birth parents can help explain who they are in ways that make sense to the child. Adoptive parents can work out mutually agreeable answers to questions with birth parents and deal with how they will explain things like physical resemblance. This is also a time for setting boundaries and determining what is comfortable and appropriate, much in the same way divorced couples do. In the middle years, as children begin to deal with grief issues, they also begin to understand the permanence of adoption. They can see that birth parents come and go but do not take them with them. The reality replaces any fantasy they might otherwise internalize. As they move into their teens and young adulthood, knowing where they come from will provide more answers to questions and help them develop their own identity.

One of the special challenges of open adoption is the way in which children will test their boundaries. All children do this naturally, and in an open adoption children test whether the rules are going to be the same in both houses. "I remember," says Michael Colberg, "Diane was visiting, and Julie was trying on her shoes. I said, 'You should ask if you can do that,' and she replied, 'They're my mom's shoes.' I said, 'That's right, they're not yours, you need to ask.' That was one of the ways she was testing who's in charge and what were the rules and boundaries. We have had a variety of these experiences." Michael also finds that Julie is tested in different ways. She is different not only because she is adopted, but on top of that she has two daddies. Then with open adoption, she has another layer of complexity to deal with.

As Michael Colberg looks forward, he imagines that there will be a time when a lot of anger might emerge, but as he sees things change, he feels Julie has a very solid connection with Diane. Says Michael:

> As my daughter becomes less shy about testing that, I think she'll
> become freer about expressing emotions that have been directed at me,
> because she knows I'm not going to go away. I think she is going to get

to a position where she knows neither is Diane. Over the past few years Diane and I have developed a real intimacy, not that pseudointimacy that people have when they go through the placement experience. I like to think we had angels watching over us. We had the ability to step back and say we respect and trust each other, but we don't know each other. But we do now. It is a special relationship, and I'm grateful we have it.

Sharing the Pain and the Joy

> Adoptive parents can respect a child's birth family involvement by the tone they use, sending cards, and encouraging participation. Most birth parents are afraid of asking too much. The encouragement from the adoptive parents may be the only encouragement they get.
>
> Brenda Romanchik, birth mother, speaking at the Open Adoption Conference, Traverse City, Michigan

In *The Story of David,* Dion Howells illustrates the importance of respectful and loving relationships between adoptive and birth parents. Whenever he discusses Nancy, his son David's birth mother, he expresses a readiness to include her as part of their family. At one point early in the adoption, Nancy loses an infant nephew, and his sudden death catapults her into hysterics about her own son. Nancy felt comfortable calling Dion and Carey to talk about how upset she was and to be reassured everything was all right with David. Dion says they had never anticipated that such a real-life experience would help them learn more about the benefits of openness:

> Because she had been able to contact us directly and immediately, Nancy would not have to go on day after day with the seed of worry planted, wondering if her child, related genetically to her nephew who has died, had succumbed to the same sad syndrome. We realized that there were probably going to be many moments of worry and concern for Nancy, many times when—as a mother—she might need to be reassured that her son was safe and healthy. We loved David with all our hearts, and we could easily put ourselves in her shoes.

Dion's and Carey's feelings about Nancy and her involvement in their life with David provide one example of how communication between triad members can flow freely, and how fear and secrecy need not characterize an adoption.

In *A Letter to Adoptive Parents on Open Adoption*, Randolph Severson reminds us that in order for open adoptions to succeed, three basic principles must be assured: courage, compassion, and common sense. For the sake of the child, he says adoptive parents need to muster all the strength and courage they can and acknowledge the importance of maintaining some form of contact between themselves, the birth parents, and the adoptee. When parents have compassion for birth parents, they are usually prepared to respect their commitment to remain in touch. And finally, Severson says, "An adoptive parent with common sense will recognize and honor the child's need to have a photograph of the birthparents and to talk to them occasionally, so that they hear from those mysterious strangers an occasional word of love."

Eleanor Oakley of Spence-Chapin says it is not always so simple for adoptive parents to comprehend how a birth parent feels. Today's adoptive parents have expectations, and one of them is that the birth parent will stay in touch. She says that lots of times adoptive parents send off a photo and a letter, and they want to hear back right away. "They want to hear immediately that the birth mother was reassured," says Eleanor, "and that she is not going to search out the child now that she sees a picture of him." Eleanor explains that when the parents do not hear back right away, she helps them understand that this is also a process for the birth mother, and that it does not mean she does not care:

> You can't put your expectations on her because you're not where she is. Sometimes it becomes a good guy/bad guy thing, so I think it's very important to encourage adoptive parents to honor their commitment even when they haven't had feedback. You have to help them realize that this is a lifetime process, and if she comes back in thirty years, the pictures they promised should still be there because you must honor the things you said when you met her, whether it's on paper or not.

Sometimes, adoptive parents are truly disappointed when they have no response from a birth parent. In open adoptions, when the birth parents fail to stay in touch, adoptive parents worry about their children feeling rejected again. While nothing really takes the hurt away, they will be better able to help their children if they have a better understanding themselves of what may be going on for the birth parent.

Sharon Kaplan Roszia says that although she is an adoptive parent, she has had an experience akin to that of a birth mother. One of Roszia's adopted children decided as an adolescent that she wanted to return to her family of origin. Her birth mother was dead, and her birth father had disappeared, so she had only her birth grandparents. The birth family asked Roszia and her husband to formally relinquish their daughter:

> We parented her for ten years, and when she was fourteen, after long discussions with her psychiatrist, we decided that if that's what she needed, to be rerooted in that family, then that's what we ought to do. So we signed relinquishment papers. I was shell-shocked when it was over and ultimately it drained the life out of my twenty-seven-year marriage. It gave me a flavor of the birth parent experience and allowed me to be a little bit more sensitized to what birth parents go through. I have worked in the adoption field for over thirty years, and I feel that what happened with my daughter has helped me close some circles and given me a different perspective.

Roszia's situation is an unusual one. Adoptive parents do not need to experience the relinquishment of their children to be able to empathize with birth parents. Often just talking to each other establishes a dialogue that can engender mutual understanding and respect. Jeanne Warren Lindsay, author of *Open Adoption: A Caring Option,* says that the crucial element in open adoptions is "the caring for each other and the trusting." Even in closed and semiopen adoptions, mutual respect is a vital ingredient for the happiness and well-being of the children.

Living Comfortably with Ourselves

In dreams begins responsibility.

William Butler Yeats

By creating families with children whose birth parents are unable to care for them, adoptive parents redefine not only what we call a "family" but also "parenthood." Usually state legislatures and judges make decisions that separate rather than unite families, but occasionally there is an exception that also goes to the heart of the meaning of parenthood. Annette Baran told me of one case where a close friend and colleague of hers was asked to testify on behalf of a child whose birth father was fighting for custody:

> The judge gave a marvelous lecture on the needs of children and roots, connections, and everything else. And this judge came out with a very harmonious decision in a very difficult case where the birth father and foster family both wanted the child. She said, "I'm going to let the foster mother legally adopt the child. The birth father can remain the legal father, and the foster father will be more like a stepfather." The birth mother wasn't around, and the birth father had only recently found out about the child. It was a marvelous decision because the judge knew that the child needed a stable home and that the young birth father couldn't provide that. But she knew that the birth father should be a part of the child's life. He started to visit the home, and now he is like a younger brother to the older adoptive parents. The birth mother was also given visiting rights if she wanted them.

This child will undoubtedly struggle at some point as he tries to sort through his complicated situation. However, he will grow knowing the truth and having an opportunity to have his questions answered by his various parents. Parents cannot protect their children from reality, but they can help them come to grips with it. In spite of their divorce Katherine and Bill provided Andrew with the stability he needed to secure his independence and make his own way in the world.

The adoptive parents' role involves guiding their children in a direction that leads to a healthy and fulfilling life. For many adult and some young adoptees in closed adoptions this means finding the birth relatives they were separated from as infants. In the final section of my book, I will explore how members of the adoption triad redefine their roles and gain a new perspective on the meaning of family as they take the ultimate steps toward discovering a lost identity or finding a child who was raised by other parents.

PART THREE

THE WHEEL IS
COME FULL CIRCLE

WILLIAM SHAKESPEARE

SEVEN

LET THE HEALING FOUNTAIN START

Birth Parents Search and Reunite

I Begin to Make Myself Whole

> Your children are not your children.
> They are the sons and daughters of Life's longing for
>   itself.
> They come through you but not from you,
> And though they are with you, yet they belong not
>   to you.
>
> Kahlil Gibran

WHILE ANDREW WAS growing up, I had virtually no exposure to the world of adoption, no sense of how it was changing through the 1980s into the 1990s. I also had no idea that there was a movement afoot of adoptees seeking more information and contact with their birth families, and I have no recall of seeing any television reunions. And yet, my own gradual awakening was, unbeknownst to me, occurring in step with a surge in the numbers of people wanting to find their biological sons and daughters, mothers and fathers—and siblings.

Sequestered in my own world, some feelings and memories began to stir as I approached my forties. There was no single isolated moment I can remember distinctly, just an emerging tentative but persistent desire to reconnect with that child I had handed over to the care of others, and to know both in my heart and in fact that he existed, and was safe and well. Concurrent with those first tender impulses taking me toward Andrew and the part of myself I had lost with him, was a more pressing sense of being stuck and uncertain about my direction in life. I had pushed hard to establish my literary scouting business, and in the process I had become consumed by it. At thirty-seven, when I had the first bad Pap smear, which propelled me into therapy, I started to explore my feelings surrounding the relinquishment of my child, and after finally submitting to a hysterectomy, I began at last to come to terms with my loss. I could acknowledge out loud to myself that he was alive somewhere, and that I was his birth mother. Those events and that process of self-discovery gradually brought me to the point of looking for him.

Always a fan of astrologers and psychics, I began to inquire: "Was he all right?" "Where was he?" "Would we meet one day?" Answers were mostly vague but encouraging. One woman said he was in school in Connecticut, and I learned later Andrew had been there. Another said we would meet, but not for some years, and that would be best, because he would be more settled in his life. That, too, proved to be true, because we finally met just a few months before his first wedding anniversary. I fantasized about what he might be like, and even imagined worst case scenarios where he would turn up unannounced and full of rage, or pictured him stalking me with an intent to kill. I was that afraid that he would hate me and that I would not be forgiven. Rarely did I visualize a man who might be worried that I would reject him, or one who would actually make space for me in his life. Nevertheless, I tentatively inched forward.

I had little hope that the Spence-Chapin agency would want to help me in any way, but my therapist, Claire Young, encouraged me to contact them to inquire about how to proceed. I was still ignorant of the new openness in adoption practices and was paralyzed by my old memories of the way I had been treated in 1966. Tucked away in my psyche was the teenager who had stepped over the line of acceptable social conduct, and I could not bring myself to call the agency for fear of being rejected out of hand. Months went by before I finally summoned the courage to ask my attorney to call them on my behalf. I was so sure they would be adversarial that I mounted my defenses to prepare for battle. Instead, they were perfectly cordial and suggested to my attorney that I write to them directly to update my file.

By now it was 1990—three years since my surgery. I later discovered that my hesitation, fear, and ambivalence were feelings that I shared with many birth parents. Rendered powerless for decades by a lack of self-entitlement and society's emphasis on secrecy, birth parents, like me, felt we had no right to intrude upon our children's lives. As Betty Jean Lifton says in *Lost and Found*, "The birth mother has a dilemma not experienced by the Adoptee. It was *she* who signed the baby away. And even though she may now feel that she was coerced into it by her family and social worker, she wonders if she is entitled to be the searcher. It is one thing to be searched for, another to search."

I finally wrote a detailed letter to Spence-Chapin updating my file with my current address and indicating that I could be contacted should my son wish to find me. It was important to me that he know I was willing to face him and that I wanted to be available to him. Spence sent a note back informing me that although they would keep the letter on file, they could not give my son the letter until both of us were registered with the New York State Adoption Information Registry. Within a few months I had filed my registration and had also joined the support and search organization Adoptees' Liberty Movement Association (ALMA), which maintained its own list of people searching. A year and a half later, I finally received a notice that the state had processed my registration and would notify me if and when there was a match. I never heard from them again. Meanwhile, I received regular mailings from ALMA about their search and reunion successes, but I never actively participated in any of their programs and eventually let my membership lapse. My attorney suggested I hire a private detective to search for me, but I felt strongly that I could not interfere with my son's life. I carried on with my daily existence, albeit with a low-grade but steady awareness of him as a living, breathing being who despite everything was umbilically connected to me. I never for a minute conceived of the possibility that he might not be alive. Intuitively, I knew he was.

After I received the letter from Spence-Chapin that spring of 1993 informing me that he was interested in contact and had recently registered with the state, I felt a staggering rush of relief and a glimmer of hope that maybe he did not hate me after all, and that knowing me was in some way important to him. I would be given an opportunity to explain myself to him and to confirm that he was all right.

It was not until I returned from my father's funeral that I felt the full impact of everything that was happening to me. A notation in my journal merely says, "Coming home, I suddenly felt lonely and sad. I had a good cry." That simple statement belies an avalanche of feeling that I had held in check for far too long. Although I had shed tears during the previous days and weeks, this was the first time I gave myself to the uninhibited release of pent-up pain, and on the eve of reunion, the memory of an old loss merged with the fresh grief of a life passing on. As the shadowy memory of a child lost became manifest again as an adult man, my father was crossing over to the unmanifest realm. One life, it seemed, was being exchanged for another.

My profound sadness was accompanied by an underlying excitement and elation at the prospect of meeting Andrew. We had rescheduled our meeting, and the days leading up to May 4, 1993, were filled with fierce anticipation. The night before he was to come to my apartment, I was practically bouncing off the walls. In my journal I wrote: "Time has shrunk, and I'm looking at myself through the eyes of a twenty-seven-year-old man who happens to be my son. I will be sharing my story with the only person who really matters. Suddenly my focus is shifting, and a wider angle lense is presenting a whole new picture. How will I inhabit this world?" There were so many questions to ask and so much time to recapture. I desperately wanted to make a good impression, show him that I loved him even though we were "relative strangers." At the same time, I did not want to overwhelm him with a rush of emotion. How I would meet all these expectations and achieve the perfect balance remained to be seen. I know now that in the first flush of a reunion most adoptees and birth parents are not only excited to be reconnected but also report a similar mix of emotions. I was overjoyed to be found, but there was no way to be "prepared" for such an event that by definition contains within it the element of surprise.

As I waited for him in my apartment, I felt like I was about to go on a blind date. We had planned to go out to dinner, and for the last half hour before he arrived all I could do was pace back and forth across the living room. I knew that Andrew was coming from his adoptive father's house to mine and I wondered what his final words to his dad were before he left to meet me, and how he was feeling and what he was thinking as he approached my building. I could only imagine that he was as frightened and hopeful as I, and I was full of admiration for him for the courage it took to face an uncertain outcome. When the doorman buzzed to announce his arrival, my heart jumped into my throat. He was one short elevator ride away, the same elevator where I had stood as I read the letter from Spence-Chapin only a few weeks before. I opened my front door and waited for the elevator doors to part. In those last seconds, I wondered if I was dressed appropriately and if he would like the way I looked, and of course I wondered who he would resemble. And then he was there—a tall handsome young man with my eyes and flowers in his hands.

We were both so nervous and happy at the same time that I am not sure if we hugged or just started talking to each other. I know that I could not take my eyes off him. His coloring and build were so like me and my family, especially my father, and while he has my eyes and smile, he has Tom's nose and a certain look of his that was startling after so many years. All in all, he was a wonderful genetic blend of both of us and our families. I have since noticed that he and his adoptive father also share a similar manner and facial expressions bringing nature and nurture together into an individual whole.

There was an awkwardness as we rushed to fill in the gap in our lives. Andrew had generously thought to bring pictures of his parents, his wedding, and a few childhood photographs, and later I also pulled out albums to introduce him to members of our family. We sat for some time, sharing pictures and stories, looking at each other, trying to absorb every detail as if there were no tomorrow. Every so often I would virtually pinch myself to make sure this was real, and of course I wanted any number of times to reach out and touch him, this grown man who had once been an infant in my arms, but I held back, recognizing the strangeness of our situation.

We eventually went to a small local restaurant for dinner. Andrew wanted to know more about what had happened and if I knew anything of what had become of his birth father. This was my moment of reckoning and my chance to explain myself directly to him—and for me to hear from him face-to-face how he felt about having been placed for adoption. I explained everything I knew about Tom and his family, including the guilt I felt that we had never considered Tom's parents and any desire they might have had to keep him in the family. I offered to help search for Tom if he liked. Andrew thought that at some point he might want to pursue that, but finding me was fine for the time being. He said he had chosen to look for me as opposed to his birth father because he believed his birth mother would be more likely to be interested in him—and I suspect he also meant he felt I would be less likely to reject him.

As we talked more about the intervening years, I could see that Andrew was and is enthusiastic about his life and meets it head-on. I learned then that he had gone to a prep school, that he loved the outdoors, that he had chosen to live in a rural setting, and that he has a strong work ethic and a good head for business combined with an entrepreneurial spirit. As he was in our first telephone conversation, he was most interested in knowing about my business, and we talked easily about it. So often during the course of the evening I wished that my father were alive to meet this young man who in so many ways reminded me of him, and I knew my mother would be even more struck by the resemblance. We had buried Dad just the week before, and I felt his presence at the table with us.

After dinner we went back to my apartment, and as the evening wound down, I got up the nerve to take a few pictures. Andrew also let me keep a wedding picture of him with his family. (Before I met his parents, I would sometimes pull out the picture and study it as a way of getting acquainted with them.) Andrew said he was eager for me to meet his wife, Chloe, and knew that I would love her—as I truly do. When he got up to leave we hugged for real, and I felt the warmth and goodness of this wonderful young man I had given birth to. As he turned into the elevator, he stuck his head back out, and in parting said, "Twenty-seven years is too long!" And then he was gone. I closed the door, went over to the couch, and just sat quietly for a while in the stillness of the night. Some time later, I called my mother and told her that Andrew had the same eyes and dimple as I do, and a cleft in his chin like Dad.

When Mom saw the pictures of Andrew, she was shaken to the core. It was finally real for her, although she had no idea when she would meet him. I learned quickly that like me she was deeply afraid of what he would think of her and worried about how her friends and family would judge her. We had never before talked openly about what happened, and now the burden of silence we had all carried was cracked open. She tearfully apologized for not offering me the chance to keep my baby. It hurt to hear her pain, but in truth I needed to hear her acknowledge her role. Any resentment I had harbored melted as our hearts opened to each other. We were communicating as we never had before. Already Andrew was making a difference in our lives.

I began to tell a few friends about Andrew, but I was not exactly ready to broadcast the news, especially since most people did not even know I had had a child. It was a great story that other people could cry over, but I found myself emotionally tapped out if I talked too much. It was the most powerful and wondrous event of my life, but it was so new, so intense an experience that I was naturally self-protective and needed to hold the feelings close to my own heart lest they be somehow diminished by my inadequate words.

In his enthusiasm, Andrew had told me to feel free to call him anytime and had talked about getting together again soon. I let some time pass before I ventured to call, and when I did I sensed his hesitancy and a need to slow down. Fortunately, the social worker at Spence-Chapin had passed along an informative sheet on reunion dynamics that helped prepare me for the emotional roller coaster that can occur after contact, and I was sensitive to Andrew's need to process his own experience and to handle the new situation within his family. I had told him in our meeting that I did not want to intrude in his life, and I would take my cues from him. I was infinitely happy to know he was alive and well, and despite my impatient nature, I was prepared to give him the space he and his family needed. Although he did not need or want another mother, and I had no intention of trying to insinuate myself into that role, some maternal instinct told me to put his needs first.

I wrote to Andrew within a couple weeks of our meeting to thank him for walking into my life and for inviting me into his. Writing helped me sort out my converging feelings of joy and renewed loss as I thought back on the lost years. At the end of May, I attended the annual American Booksellers Convention and went public with my clients, many of whom are like family to me. Whereas telling the story in the first days and weeks had tired me, sharing my news with my dearest colleagues strengthened me, as each and every one embraced me and expressed their happiness and support.

At the end of June and on the last day of my vacation on Shelter Island with my family, Andrew called me for the first time since our May 4 meeting. It was thrilling for Mom and Laurie and Erin to hear his voice, and for all of us to learn that Chloe was pregnant. I had barely met Andrew, and now I was going to be a grandmother! How odd that sounded. I used to fantasize when I was much younger that I would live to a very old age, and with great-grandchildren around me would reminisce about my life's adventures. I had long ago forsaken that fantasy, but in an instant it was revived and brought a smile to my face.

In that same conversation, Andrew invited me to spend a weekend in his New England home with him and Chloe, and late on the scorching hot evening of July 11, I was settled in their guest room, scribbling in my journal, "I can't believe I'm here!" How had reality shifted so quickly? We spent the Saturday evening watching family films of Andrew's first years and his wedding video. I saw him as a toddler on the beach with his parents, and my heart simultaneously ached for what I did not have myself and filled with love for the family I saw on the screen.

That weekend I began to understand how challenging it would be for me to find my appropriate place within a new family dynamic and how hard it would be for Andrew to fit me into his extended family. I learned that his mother, Katherine, was feeling vulnerable about what felt like my sudden intrusion in their life. She had been supportive of him finding me, but emotionally it was taking a toll. She did not feel able to meet me and would not for three more years. I understood Andrew's uncertainty about how to proceed and realized he was caught in the middle, being completely devoted to his mother and at the same time looking for a way to accommodate our new relationship. Although in my heart I understood Katherine's vulnerability, there was nothing I could do to help, since it was my simple existence that was so unsettling. I knew I did not and could not move in on her son, and I sensed that time would have to show us a way. I hoped she would eventually see that her relationship with Andrew was not in jeopardy.

Each time there is a question about my place or standing, I am in an instant that outcast teenager who has done something society cannot forgive; I feel unworthy asking for something I do not deserve and therefore cannot have. That insidious feeling of shame lies in wait for me and surfaces with the slightest provocation. In these early days of reunion, I was catapulted back in time and relived over and over the weeks and days leading up to the moment I surrendered Andrew—wondering "what if" I had made a different choice. I realize that there are no real answers to this question, and I will never know if I made the "right" decision. I know simply that my baby was adopted by wonderful parents who love him every bit as much as I could have. And now, we were all looking forward to the birth of the first grandchild.

I met Emma when she was about five or six weeks old, and already she looked so much like our side of the family. At some point, Andrew looked over at me and said, "She's one-quarter you." I had purposely avoided any reference to the blood ties, and his gentle acknowledgment of our connection was heartwarming. For now I am "Lynn" to Emma. I am an "aunt" to so many of my friends' children, and I cherish that special relationship with them. But with Emma, the situation is different, and I would prefer not to start off my relationship with her pretending to be something I am not. I know firsthand how harmful secrecy can be. At four, Emma is trying to sort out the various relationships in her family. Recently she asked outright for the first time "Who are you?", and I felt duplicitous avoiding a direct answer. The timing once again is key, and I must defer to Andrew and Chloe. Andrew is juggling so many people, and making room for me—and explaining who I am to Emma and little William without worrying them or other family members—is no easy task.

It is an inherent dilemma of reunions that roles regularly have to be defined and then redefined. Language presents one of the greatest challenges. Andrew's parents are Katherine and Bill. For him, of course, he has only one mother, and it should not be any other way. Nevertheless, I am his birth mother, and although I did not parent him, in my heart he is my son and I refer to him as such when I speak of him to others. Although there is a "family" bond between us, we met as adults, and we are establishing for ourselves a loving friendship that will be the foundation for our relationship. I could I suppose call Andrew my birth son, but for me there is no distinction, and in honoring that part of me, I do not mean to diminish his parents' role. As we tackle the matter of grandparents, this becomes more of an issue, since I know the children from birth. I have to believe though that there is enough love to go around, and that with some help from everyone, the children will come to know and appreciate that they have a lot of grandparents who love them.

As a woman, I am acutely sensitive to Katherine's feelings about my relationship to Andrew and the children. We met for the first time just two years ago, and I do not doubt that were I in her shoes, I would find it just as difficult to make room for the woman who gave birth to her son, and to have her thinking of him also as her son. At the same time, we like each other, and we are beginning to establish our own relationship. Once again time will be the stabilizing factor. Bill very kindly refers to Andrew as "our son," and that young girl in me whose self-esteem suffered a tremendous blow is touched beyond belief by Bill's generosity. As the birth mother in this equation, entering into a relationship with Andrew and his family, I am careful not to overstep. If we are all so careful, I realize that things may go unsaid that need to be expressed, and in some way this book is allowing us room to address our concerns from our individual perspectives. As we become more comfortable with one another, and the years provide a basis for trust and intimacy, our interaction will be less inhibited, and with mutual respect and friendship, we will be much like any other family. This can only happen over time, and I keep reminding myself that only a few years have passed since we met. For now, I am a part of Andrew's family no matter what I am called by his children.

My mother and sister have also welcomed Andrew into their lives. Laurie says, "It's like a fairy tale for us. Now we have Andrew in our family, and I can't imagine not knowing his wife and kids, and not having them be a part of our lives. I think finding him, building a relationship and having it continue to grow, has made a part of you that was in pieces complete." For my mother, welcoming Andrew back into our lives relieves many decades of guilt that she felt about letting him go. "I feel we have been blessed," she told me, "to have a second chance at having this young man and his whole family be a part of us. He's so wonderful and such a joy. I will always have a certain amount of guilt about the lost years, but you have been very generous in not judging me too harshly." After years of silence, my mother now shares the news of her grandson and great grandchildren with pride and satisfaction.

Andrew has from time to time expressed an interest in meeting his birth father, and I have made some attempts to find him. He does not appear that easy to locate, and my efforts have waned as Andrew has expressed more ambivalence about "opening that can of worms." Neither of us knows how Tom would receive the news, and Andrew has a lot on his plate now, caring for his family and adjusting to me. Perhaps, like everything, it is a matter of timing, and he will one day wish to pursue the search more aggressively. Knowing what it meant for Andrew to see himself in my face, and to know more about our family, it may someday be just as important for him to complete the picture by finding Tom.

In essence, my reunion experience with Andrew is an adoption that has been opened. There are several parties involved, all striving to do their best for the child they mutually love. Andrew's adoptive parents and I have begun to develop our own relationships, and I think of Katherine and Bill as part of my extended family. After so many years of feeling alone, I feel sustained by the support of caring arms extending through generations. I am keenly aware, as Betty Jean Lifton writes in *Journey of the Adopted Self,* that in reunion, a birth mother's "joy is bittersweet, tempered by the realization that she can never fully have her child back. The adoptee has been nourished by the love and culture of the adoptive home, and some part of her will always belong to that world." I can live with that truth, but I do not want to lose any more years. Search and reunion cannot change the events of thirty years or a lifetime. What they can do is begin to heal wounds and build foundations for the future.

What It Means to Search

Go in peace
My son, grow in grace, swim in seas, dance
through years—Child I should have known,
Child of strangers, morning star, child
of patient, all-enduring love
I will wait
for you.

Mary Anne Manning Cohen, from "Search Day"

Searching for our children is one way for birth parents to reconcile a part of our lives that was lost to us. Nevertheless, arriving at the decision to search is never simple, and like most aspects of adoption, search and reunion are not isolated events. They are part of a complex process of rejoining and extending families, creating new relationships, and putting to rest some of the ghosts of the past. Timing is also a critical consideration in any search. When Andrew found me, he was comfortable and secure in his adult life, and I had also thought considerably about searching. We were both ready. Search and reunion take an enormous amount of emotional energy and are best undertaken when people are not overly taxed by other life events. An adopted colleague of mine has a library of books on adoption that sit undisturbed on her bookshelf waiting for a time when she might be ready to consider a search. For now, she prefers to live and work and develop her career without stirring up ghosts that she is not emotionally prepared to deal with. Searching is not for everyone, and many people lead perfectly harmonious lives without any apparent need for more information. On the other hand, people may feel for years they have no interest in searching. Then one day they wake up with a compelling desire to know more, or *they* are found, and they realize that deep down they *did* want to meet their child or birth parent after all.

Search and reunion statistics are as difficult to verify as any other adoption numbers, but there is little doubt that more and more birth parents and adoptees are seeking each other out. During the 1980s thousands of adult adoptees sought and reunited with their birth parents. In its seventeen-year history alone, ALMA, the largest national organization devoted to search, has reunited over thirty thousand people. The reality, as demonstrated by the plethora of talk show reunions, is that the desire to search has become acceptable to the general public.

At the 1997 AAC conference, Sharon Kaplan Roszia explained that a number of factors, including underlying issues of identity and possible tensions related to a person's status in the adoption triad, give impetus to people's decision to search. A significant event in a person's life (e.g., marriage, death, or birth) may then strip layers of inhibition and trigger the decision to act. Searchers cite a variety of reasons for commencing their journey, including the need to convey pertinent medical information, sharing family history, satisfying curiosity, regaining control of their lives, knowing that their children are well, validating the original adoption plan, and healing unresolved issues of loss and grief. Being clear about why one is searching is essential and is part of the preparation for facing the challenges along the way.

Birth parents commonly feel, as I did, that it would be wrong to intrude upon the lives of their children. Judy Greene of Spence-Chapin says too that many more adoptees search than birth mothers because a lot of birth mothers don't feel entitled to search. This is especially true, she says, of birth mothers of my generation who feel they are the ones who caused all this pain. They are afraid their child is angry with them, hates them, and does not want to see them, so they do not want to go and find out. Judy Greene suggests, though, that if the adopted person is afraid to intrude on her birth family or is also afraid of rejection, and the birth mother feels she has no right to search, they might never connect despite their mutual desire to meet. For those birth mothers who do initiate their own search, the need to know outweighs the fear.

Many women of my generation did not search for their children earlier because they did not know that it was even an option. Mary Anne Manning Cohen, a birth mother, poet, and editor of the newsletter *Origins*, remembers feeling shocked the first time she heard at a support group that adoptees were searching for their birth parents. It had never occurred to her that an adoptee would want to find a birth mother. Search and reunion were new concepts in the early 1970s, and birth parents like Cohen were just beginning to attend support groups. Cohen wanted to find her son from the moment she heard about the possibility of searching. "I had to know if he was dead or alive," she remembers. "I wanted to see him and tell him that I loved him."

Jane Leeds first realized adoptees and birth parents *could* find each other when she met an adopted woman and her birth mother at a party. "This was unbelievable to me," she says of the surprise encounter. "I didn't think it was even possible, that you could find your birth mother. I didn't openly question them because I still hadn't told many people and didn't want to give myself away, but I was very curious."

Bonnie Bis thought about finding her two relinquished children long before she actually searched for them, but without help from her husband she held off looking for many years. "My husband had always been my supporter in so many ways," Bonnie told me. "When he wouldn't support me, I just told myself I couldn't do it. It wasn't until eight years later, when we were divorced, that an Oprah Winfrey show reunion got me going. I remember the adult adoptee saying that she really wanted to know her birth mother. I started crying and thinking that maybe my kids wanted to know me." Bonnie's next step was to join a search and support group. She was sure that the members would accuse her of being a horrible person, but instead they were wonderful, and she feels that she could not have searched without their encouragement.

Some birth parents never let go of mourning their lost child, and this can be especially true for birth parents who have married each other. The child they relinquished leaves a hole in their lives that they cannot reconcile. This was the case for Jane Leeds, who eventually married her son's birth father. They had another child together, a daughter, and tried unsuccessfully to bury the past. In the rare instances they discussed their son, they felt guilty for not getting married when he was born. After Jane's husband died, she felt she could no longer hide the secrets of her past. She confessed to her daughter, who had suspected something her entire life. "Yes," she said, "there is a secret and the secret is that you have a brother." Her daughter urged her to begin searching immediately, and Jane soon joined a local ALMA chapter where she, like Bonnie Bis, was amazed at how supportive the groups were for both birth parents and adoptees.

Jon Ryan and his wife also never recovered from relinquishing their daughter. They were married for ten difficult years before they finally sought marriage counseling. Jon says, "It was the first time we ever, I ever, talked about our daughter. My wife just couldn't deal with it, and we got divorced shortly thereafter. I immediately started searching for my daughter."

Support When We Need It Most

> Since it is impossible to control access to information,
> adoptees and birth parents are increasingly locating
> one another, often in the absence of preparation and
> guidance.
>
> Ronny Diamond, Director of Post-Adoption Services, Spence-Chapin

People are often unable to cope on their own with the complicated emotional issues raised by search and reunion. Bonnie Bis and Jane Leeds both joined support groups when they needed help dealing with the feelings that threatened to overwhelm them as they took their first steps. Those already engaged in the process are excellent models for those just beginning to search, and they are often an excellent resource for search tips. There are times, though, when additional help is useful. Mary Anne Manning Cohen strongly recommends, however, that if a searcher needs individual therapy that she choose a therapist familiar with adoption issues. Too often people go to therapists for years who refuse to discuss adoption because they do not consider it relevant.

People tend to become completely preoccupied by their search. In *Adoption Wisdom*, Marlou Russell says, "Many who search seem obsessed and driven in their pursuit of finding people and information. The activities of searching, writing letters, making phone calls, and going to meetings, are a way to manage the feelings that surface during a search." In the middle of all of this activity, relationships can suffer, and it is not unusual for family members to feel fearful or jealous when attention is diverted from them. Others find that the excitement and intensity actually bring them closer together. When birth and adoptive mother Cynthia Beals finally decided to search for her daughter, she was thrilled that her husband supported her efforts. Cynthia also wanted her adopted children to accept what she was doing but felt she needed to understand more about how adoptees feel about searching. She attended several triad support meetings, and as she listened to adopted adults express their thoughts and concerns about birth parents, she learned that adoptees were just as fearful of intruding upon others' lives as were birth parents. This gave her greater insight into her children's feelings and encouraged her to proceed with her own search.

In the last ten to fifteen years, just as birth parents have pressed for more openness in adoption placements, they have also begun to reclaim through search and reunion what they feel was lost to them when they relinquished their child. What many birth parents find in support groups, whether in a national organization like ALMA and CUB or a local group like Mary Anne Manning Cohen's, is the empathy they need to move forward. Family therapist and author Ken Watson believes that the healing process in adoption has two phases: empathy and empowerment. He writes in his essay "What Adoption Is and What It Isn't" that "people cannot recover from the pain of their past until they have faced it, and they can be helped to do this in an empathetic relationship or environment. In order to lead more satisfying lives and to achieve their optimum potential, however, people must move beyond the empathy phase and become empowered to change. The energy formerly needed to deny their pain is now available to them to make choices and to take action to reach desired goals."

While I tried to imagine what my reunion with Andrew might be like, I could not know how I would feel until we actually met. It is never certain where anyone's search will lead. Just as it is very different to be pregnant and then have a child, so is the idea of a reunion different from the real thing. Feelings stir that have lain dormant for years, and no one knows how they will react—or who they will find at the "end of the rainbow."

To Seek and to Find

> Does the road wind up-hill all the
>   way?
> Yes, to the very end.
> Will the day's journey take the whole long day?
> From morn to night, my friend.

Christina Georgina Rossetti

Once a birth parent initiates a search, there is often a sense of predetermination, of "no turning back" no matter what obstacles they might encounter. Searchers can become mired in endless bureaucratic delays when agencies, often restricted by law, refuse to release information. If the state has a passive registry, as New York State does, then a birth parent or adoptee must wait until both parties register before the state will release identifying information. With an active registry, like the one in Missouri, an intermediary is allowed to search for a birth parent or adoptee without their prior consent. There are also private registries that are not governed by the rules and laws of states. Perhaps the best known of these is the International Soundex Reunion Registry in Carson City, Nevada. This registry is completely confidential and matches relatives who have registered by computer. If two people have corresponding information, then Soundex notifies them. No intermediaries are required, and it is understood that people register because they want to be found.

There are other ways of finding birth relatives, including hiring a private investigator or an independent search consultant, or sometimes just getting on the Internet directly. Dozens of sites on the World Wide Web have sprung up across the country. Over one nine-month period, Shea Grimm's Seattle-based Web site, "An Adoptee's Right to Know," had over twenty thousand visits. "The number of people who are hooking up for adoption-related searching has grown exponentially," she reported to *Self* magazine in December 1996. All people have to do is log on and begin looking. Sometimes that can be too easy, and people can reunite before they are fully prepared. If they are not also connected to some support services, they may not know what to do if something unexpected happens. A rough start can adversely affect the chances of a positive long-term reunion. Personally, I was glad to have the guidance of a social worker at the agency to facilitate my first contact with Andrew. Having exchanged identifying information through that intermediary, we knew more about the kind of person we might meet, and as dramatic as it still was, our first contact was less of a shock.

Bonnie Bis hired a private searcher, but it still took two years because she searched in "fits and starts." She says, "It was very scary, and I couldn't handle it all at once. But then the searcher found both their addresses within days of each other." It is very common to take a few steps forward and then stop, sometimes for a prolonged period. The intensity of feeling or the fear of getting close to the goal too quickly can be overwhelming. A person may need to step back and regroup. Readiness itself is a process, and while a person may be ready to begin a search, they may not be ready to find that quickly. Feelings may come up unexpectedly that they need to integrate before moving forward.

Once Bonnie did locate her children, she discovered that both of them had been raised in suburbs close to where she lived. She chose to contact her daughter first by writing a letter, and when her daughter called, they arranged a time to meet:

Her husband was working so it was going to just be me, her, and her two children. She opened the door to her apartment and we just went into each other's arms. It was amazing. Neither one of us is terribly demonstrative by nature so we couldn't have planned the outpouring of emotion. It just felt so right. We spent the entire evening together talking and staring at each other. She was just so wonderful and understanding.

Bonnie could not have predicted the close relationship that she and her daughter now have. Conversely, she could not have known how negatively her son would respond when she contacted him. After an initial meeting that seemed to go well enough, he cut off communication with her completely, and she has not heard from him in over five years. When Bonnie thinks back on their meeting, she realizes how angry he is. "He said things to me like 'What took you so long?' and 'Why didn't you come for me when I was eighteen?' Basically, I know he wonders if he can trust me, and of course he can, but I can't change the past." Bonnie hopes that in the future his anger will cool and that they will have a relationship.

Jane Leeds contacted the agency where she relinquished her son, but they were unable to disclose any identifying information. At ALMA, she was advised to write letters and get her name on lists. They also told her to try and get information from the hospital where her son was born. To her surprise, the hospital sent Jane his birth records. Suddenly seeing his tiny footprint made him real to her for the first time. "It was an unbelievable revelation because somehow, after all that time, he didn't seem truly real in my mind, or I hadn't allowed him to be." Jane continued her efforts for two more years until the adoption agency actually called her to say that her son was in touch and wanted to meet her. Instead of waiting for a letter, he telephoned directly. "I was so thrilled when I heard his voice on the message tape. All of my children called that day, and I still have that tape with all their voices. When I first met my son, I played it for him. We all laughed when he said, 'Well, this is Michael. I'm the missing link.' When I spoke with him, he told me that we might as well take the bull by the horns and that I should come down to his home directly."

Jane remembers driving up and seeing Michael standing in the doorway of his house. From the car, she remembers saying, "Oh my god, you look just like your father." After that, she says, "My throat got too tight to talk and I had to wait a minute." She recalls that one of her first impulses was to cradle him like a baby, and she says, "When I finally got out of the car, I went up to the door and we just hugged and hugged. Then we started nervously talking just as fast and furious as we could. I just wanted to hold him the whole time and never let go. I was never going to leave him again. We've now gotten to the point where he's just like one of the family. Michael told me that when he met me and his siblings, he felt that for the first time in his life he was standing on both legs." Jane, too, has the sense that her family and her life are finally grounded and complete.

Once Cynthia Beals overcame her fear that her daughter would not want to be found, she realized she had nothing to lose. She says, "I became comfortable with the reality that if she didn't want to be a part of my life, I could live with and accept that fact." Cynthia was close friends with a couple who were part of an open adoption and was able to observe firsthand how well triad members could coexist. Seeing this very positive and loving open adoption inspired her to keep going with her search. When she received her daughter's name and phone number, she grew afraid again. She prayed and asked for guidance and finally decided her daughter was no longer a child and it would be all right for her to call.

Three days before she actually contacted her daughter, Rebecca, Cynthia walked through an outdoor shrine in her town, enjoying the peace that the natural beauty brought her. "I got all the answers I needed by walking through the shrine," she told me. "I remember God speaking to my heart and saying 'I give good gifts to my children. This is my gift to you.' And it was at that point that I knew it would be a good reunion."

After a number of attempts, Cynthia was finally able to reach Rebecca from the lunchroom phone at her office. She asked Rebecca a few identifying questions before revealing that she was her birth mother. "All I could hear on the other end of the phone was this scream. She was so excited," Cynthia recalls. "I just felt this overwhelming sense of relief. Rebecca told me that she had done a little searching herself, and we talked for a good forty-five minutes. I was able to tell her how I felt, that I didn't want to interfere with her family, that I didn't want to hurt her adoptive mother, that I wasn't trying to replace her." Cynthia stressed this point, because as the mother of two adopted boys, she knew how frightening it might be for Rebecca's adoptive mother.

They set a date to meet two weeks hence to give themselves time to digest what was happening and to prepare for the reunion. The next day, however, Rebecca called back, saying she could not wait. She wanted to come that very day to Cynthia's house with her husband:

So she arrived, we hugged, and she gave me a big kiss. She's just such an open person. I didn't cry that day because I think I had spent so many years crying that I only had joy. My husband finally came home and we all went out to dinner. We discussed Rebecca's children and that she didn't want to bring them into the relationship just yet, but after the second or third meeting, she brought them. The older one knew who I was right away, but out of respect for Rebecca's adoptive mother, I'm still called "Cynthia." For now I'm okay with not being "Grandma." I just want to keep the relationships honest because from my experience, I realize you have to be honest with children.

She also realizes that she cannot change what has happened in her life, nor does she want to. Trusting her daughter's judgment—and her own—as they go about their life now is what guides Cynthia. There is no room for regret.

Cynthia also recognizes the role grace has played in her life, and she looked to God for guidance as she took the final steps toward reunion with Rebecca. When I was about to meet Andrew, I found it helpful to remember that I did not have to figure everything out alone. My close friend Pastor Bill Grimbol reminded me that God is present and has a hand in what is happening, and once I let my faith take hold, I felt immediate relief. LaVonne H. Stiffler believes that search and reunion can also help restore faith to those who feel that God has rejected them. In her essay "Adoption's Impact on Birthmothers: 'Can a Mother Forget Her Child?'" she says that if "the day comes when she is finally reunited with her child, it is to her a miracle of the highest order. It may have the power of her original encounter with God, like being born again. . . . She may feel that the authentic self she acquired in her original salvation experience was lost at relinquishment and restored after reunion with her child." Stiffler couches her spirituality in terms of God and religion, but others interpret their experiences as a renewed trust in a higher power or natural order. However it is expressed, the faith we may have lost in ourselves and in our God is often restored when we see our children again.

Birth Fathers in Search and Reunion

> Birthfathers are in even deeper closets than
> birthmothers.
>
> Judith S. Gediman and Linda P. Brown, *Birthbond*

Many birth fathers fail to search for their children simply because they were unaware of their existence in the first place. Others were aware of the pregnancy and adoption but may have been disconnected from what was happening either by choice or involuntarily. As a result, they often remain isolated and do not think of searching. Some men have maintained an emotional connection with their child but do not know where, or how, to start looking. Many men are, however, happy to be found, and some do decide to search.

Birth father reunions are also affected by the relationship they have or once had with the birth mother, who may have a difficult time emotionally dealing with renewed contact with a man she may not have seen since she found out she was pregnant. Sometimes, too, she might resist providing the information an adoptee needs to find her birth father, or he needs to find his child.

Roger Hanson always thought about his daughter, and he told friends and relatives that someday he would find her. He began his search when his daughter was eighteen, and it took him six years to locate her. It was especially difficult because his name was not in the adoption records, and he first had to find the birth mother to solicit her help with the search. He got some assistance from her, but in the end he had to find his daughter on his own. It was a painstaking endeavor, tracking down one name after another, and it took weeks and months to get responses to his queries. When he finally found her, she was surprised, but not unwilling to meet him. Her adoptive mother had encouraged her to search when she turned eighteen and has continued to be supportive of the reunion. Roger has since attended his daughter's college graduation and has an ongoing open and honest relationship with her. On the first anniversary of their reunion, he told her: "You know, I got up the other day, on a Saturday, and realized that I didn't have to search. I could actually do something else on a Saturday. I got up and I realized the search was over. It took me about a year for it to sink in."

When Jon Ryan decided to search for his daughter he was not sure how to proceed. "I saw a *Donahue* show that featured a few members from Concerned United Birthparents (CUB) and got involved with them," he says. "One person just led to another and eventually someone showed me how I could get information on my own. So that's what I did. I'd say to people just starting out that searching is a matter of trying different options until you find the right resources." When Jon finally located his daughter, five years after beginning his search, he decided to write to her adoptive parents and to connect with them first. "At that point," he says, "I didn't even know if she was still alive or not. Unfortunately, my daughter intercepted the letter. It didn't have a return address on it, so she just assumed it was something for her and opened it. She read it and from that point on the cat was out of the bag."

When Paul Adams's daughter sought him out, he was relieved not to have to wonder about his child anymore. As far as he is concerned, the reunion was a healthy experience for both of them because it cleared up pressing questions they both needed to answer. He feels comfortable though that his daughter is not trying to replace her adoptive father. "My daughter knows that the man who raised her is her father, even though he and her adoptive mother have had a hard time with the reunion. Unfortunately, there's bad blood between all of them." While Adams is pleased to have met his daughter, he is honest about what it represents for him. "It just took something that was in the closet and brought it out into the open," he says, "and there were no ill effects from it. I never had high expectations, and she was smart enough to know that she couldn't replace the people who raised her with someone who had basically donated genetic material and then walked away. I don't think you can justify replacing a parent with a sperm donor. You just can't do that. And I think she understood that." Paul and his daughter have remained in sporadic contact since their initial meeting, but he feels a vital link has been forged in both their lives no matter how infrequently they talk.

Not All Reunions Are Happy

> Glimmers of hope
> Then hope died.
> Then, so did She.
>
> Mirah Riben, from "A cold stove and a flickering candle"

Birth parents tell themselves that all they want is to know that their child is alive and well, but it is very difficult to hold back greater expectations. When they find children who reject them, refuse to acknowledge them, or simply do not want them in their lives, the disappointment adds another layer to the pain they have endured since the relinquishment. Sometimes, too, the guilt and shame they still harbor make this rejection by their child seem a fitting punishment for having surrendered. This is what they "deserve."

Bonnie Bis's son distanced himself after their one-time reunion, but she still writes to him. When Mary Anne Manning Cohen first approached her son's family, they were not pleased. "I was told to back off, and I did," she recalls. "Three years later, when he was sixteen, I contacted him directly. He was very polite and pleasant but essentially said he was not interested in knowing me. It was not something he cared about at that point. That was the only time I ever spoke to him in person." Mary Anne has struggled with the ongoing rejection and has continued her attempts to maintain contact. While she is still not in touch with him, Mary Anne and his adoptive mother have developed a mutually supportive relationship with each other, and in some small measure, she is a part of her relinquished child's life and family.

Mary Anne has not given up hope that she and her son will one day communicate. "I hope he works through whatever he needs to relating to the adoption and all of his parents. He's really hurt and it's very difficult for him to deal with it." In spite of her own experience, she remains firm in her belief that searching is fundamentally beneficial for all those involved. "No matter what you find," she says, "it's worth it because then you know. Prepare yourself for the worst possible outcome and then act." There is a qualitative difference between searching and being found. The birth mother who searches has worked through her fears, her guilt, her inhibitions, and has moved toward her goal. The adoptee she finds may not be prepared for a reunion. Readiness and the complexity of family relationships are among the factors that strongly influence the initial and even extended outcome of reunions.

The cruelest discovery for a birth mother is to find out that a child is no longer living. In her twenty years of working with birth parents involved in search and reunion, Mary Anne has known several women in her local support group who found that their children had died. Having endured the years of not knowing their child, the pain of learning they will never have a chance to see them is almost unbearable. And yet in the end, the finality of knowing puts to rest the anguish of not knowing.

There are no guarantees that searching will bring happiness to the seeker, only answers to long-standing questions. Although relatively rare, birth parents sometimes find that their children were neglected or abused by their adoptive families, while others ended up in foster homes and institutions. Some find emotionally disturbed adult children who disrupt the stability of their families. No one wants to think that they will find out something terrible has happened to their child, but sometimes they do. It is important for people who decide to search to do their best to prepare themselves for any eventuality.

We have so far focused on search and reunion from the perspective of birth parents who search or who have consciously thought about or hoped for a reunion. There are of course birth mothers and fathers who decide not to search because they do not want to open themselves to the wounds of the past. Others are afraid of disrupting the stability of their marriages or their relationships with other children. (Both Carol Schaefer and Bonnie Bis struggled with husbands who did not support their efforts, and eventually their marriages collapsed.) When birth parents who had chosen not to search or who are simply not prepared are found by the adoptee, the reunion outcome may be uncertain, at least initially.

I was also surprised and disturbed to learn of another situation that can seriously disrupt a reunion and harm the people concerned. Apparently, natural and perfectly understandable inclinations to hold one's baby again or to dress to impress the adult child or birth parent can evolve into inappropriate sexual encounters between birth parent and adoptee. This phenomenon is known in adoption circles as genetic sexual attraction, and unfortunately it occurs more often than we would like to think, especially when people have had no guidance and do not know how to handle the intensity of feeling that surrounds the initial reunion experience. When birth parent and adoptee finally meet, there is a powerful drive for connectedness and intimacy that can be sadly misinterpreted and played out sexually. Sometimes the newness of the experience feels like a courtship or the beginning of a romantic relationship. In *Journey of the Adopted Self,* B. J. Lifton says, "I think we can begin to understand the libidinal pull that parents and children have toward each other if we see it on the far end of a continuum of repressed longing that has accrued over the years since separation and builds up during search and reunion. The touching and holding that they were denied with that separation can become eroticized when they return to each other emotionally regressed but in adult bodies." Whether the birth mother may be overtaken by her desire to hold the baby boy or girl she had lost, or the birth father may be rekindling the love he felt for the birth mother, the adoptee is once again the baby looking for maternal nurturing or paternal love.

The magnitude of the experience can overwhelm people's normal boundaries, and their lives can be irreparably and unnecessarily damaged. Lifton writes extensively on this issue and cautions people to learn about the dangers of genetic sexual attraction before they proceed with a reunion. She points out that the natural desire to touch and to hold does not usually lead to breaking of healthy taboos, but cautions that if there is a hint of danger, people must get help to avoid the tragic pitfalls of acting out their feelings. While one need not be overly afraid of what feelings may arise, it is important to be forewarned so that both birth parent and adoptee can act responsibly and the reunion relationship can have a chance to grow.

When Children Are Young

I had to grow old to learn what I wanted to know, and I should need to be young to say well what I know.

Joseph Joubert

One topic that always instigates debate in the adoption community is that of birth parents searching for minors, and people are confused about what is even legal. Jon Ryan says a good number "of people will tell you 'Wait until they're eighteen. Wait until they're twenty-one. Wait until they're twenty-five.' Some people say it's illegal to search for minors. The fact is, it's not illegal to search for minors. It's not illegal to search for anybody in this country." Jon followed his own instincts and eventually located his daughter just before her fifteenth birthday.

According to the law in any state where identifying records remain sealed, it is just as improper, though not illegal, for a ninety-year-old birth mother to look for her seventy-year-old child as it is for a thirty-year-old birth mother to search for a fifteen-year-old child. "The right age," believes Mary Anne Manning Cohen, "is when you feel you need to do it and have considered everything that you can. Eighteen or twenty-one is a legal age that someone arbitrarily created. It has nothing to do with the heart and soul."

Locating children is also not the same as actually making contact with them. Once Mary Anne Manning Cohen found out she could search for her son, she did, and although she discovered his whereabouts when he was eight years old, she did nothing about it for several years. Searching for minors was generally unheard of during the mid-1970s, and Mary Anne says that most groups and professionals advised waiting until the adoptees were older. Nevertheless, when she and several other birth mothers began their local support group, Origins, most of the women had searched and found their relinquished children when the children were under eighteen, and the results for each depended on their individual circumstances.

Several of the women in Cohen's group found children in difficult situations and were able to step in and help them. One woman discovered that after her son's adoptive mother died, his adoptive father had placed him in a boarding school and had not seen him for years. The birth mother took legal action to reclaim her twelve-year-old son and raised him in her family. If she had not searched for him, he very well might have spent the rest of his youth languishing in boarding schools and other institutions. Instead, he was able to find the love he needed with his birth family. Although most adopted children grow up in loving adoptive families, there are times when an early reunion is without a doubt in the best interest of the child.

Even when the child is not in a dire situation in her adoptive family, it can be beneficial for her to be in touch with her birth parent, just as children in open adoptions are benefiting from having an ongoing relationship with their birth parents. Some adoptive parents in closed adoptions, like Jane Nast, who accepted her son's birth mother and then searched for her daughter's birth mother, have recognized the importance of the birth family connection for their young children.

The stories vary. Sometimes birth parents have a strong hunch something is wrong, and when they search, they find they were right. At other times, while nothing may be wrong, the timing may be right, and the adoptive family may truly welcome hearing from them. And there are times when the adoptive parents will resist contact because they are afraid, or because it simply is not an appropriate time for that child. Whenever a birth parent decides to search for a young child or teenager, there is even more uncertainty about the immediate outcome than when searching for an adult, and when a child is found, both birth parents and adoptive parents must consider what is in the child's best interest at that time.

Life in Reunion

> When a parent-child reunion occurs, the initial task is
> the connection and repair of the broken Gestalt . . .
> Then follows the post-reunion period, in which the

significant task is the development or limitation of a
relationship.

LaVonne H. Stiffler, *Synchronicity & Reunion*

After an often protracted and arduous search, birth parents usually want to
establish a relationship with their children as soon as possible. Searching is
all about finding a lost child or parent, but once a reunion takes place,
energy needs to be refocused on the relationship. Because postreunion goals
and expectations are often ambiguous, triad members tend to tiptoe around
one another. Figuring out how to incorporate all the new family members
into one's already full life can be a formidable task for even the most
grounded of individuals. From the moment I met Andrew I wanted to be a
part of his life, but I knew that finding him did not instantly resolve the loss
of twenty-seven years or make up for the time we had not shared. Nor did
it miraculously restore my self-esteem or absolve my burden of guilt. We
needed to create a new foundation, and that would require more time,
energy, and patience.

Triad members can prepare themselves for a postreunion relationship by
learning what factors have been found to influence and shape the experience. Communication between the parties, geography, individual schedules,
attitude of the adoptive parents, characteristics of sex, age, and familial
identification, and whether there is mutual consent or general readiness all
play a role in the dynamic of life in reunion.

Lillian Blaine lives across the country from the daughter she has been
reunited with for over fourteen years, and geography has contributed significantly to the slow but steady pace of their relationship. She says, "The
distance has allowed us to give each other space, and we have been very
conscious of the boundaries that are inherent to both of us. The slow pace
has helped us to establish a relationship based on trust." Recently reunited
birth mother Karen Logan also admits that the three thousand miles that
separate her and her son "contribute to not having to juggle family members all the time." She says, "I don't feel like I'm interfering in his life, and
his adoptive parents are less threatened." Logan acknowledges that the distance is also hard because she misses her son more intensely when they are
apart now after being separated from him for so long.

The attitudes and feelings of adoptive parents also strongly influence the
course of birth parent and adoptee relationships. After meeting her son's

entire extended family on the West Coast, Karen Logan realized that at first his adoptive parents had a difficult time accepting her presence. She says, "His adoptive mother made several comments about how my son was really more interested in finding his birth father and not me. More recently, however, her letters have become much kinder, and whenever I'm out there they are always pleasant. My relationship with them has evolved very slowly."

Carol Schaefer found that she "had to go through issues of trust with Jack's adoptive mother, because she was very much involved and very influential with Jack's feelings." She says, "I went through a long period of walking on eggshells where I felt I was starting to lose my own identity again because I couldn't be true to myself."

In spite of the many issues and conflicting emotions in postreunion relationships, it has been found that most people value the connection. A 1981 study conducted by the Triadoption Library found that of 533 reunited persons who responded, 90.8 percent rated their experience favorably. While I have not found any more recent hard statistics, registrar Anthony Vilardi at the International Soundex Reunion Registry concurs that in their experience most birth parents report that the experience has been positive for them, even if the actual outcome was not picture-perfect. Birth parents' reactions to reunions range from extreme happiness to feeling palpable discomfort about the meeting, and many report a combination of emotions in a constant state of flux.

Since my reunion with Andrew, I have frequently referred to the sheet Spence-Chapin provided that outlines the Relational Stages after Contact. Not everyone experiences all of the phases described on the handout or goes through them in the exact order listed, but the key developmental stages of reunion are indicated. The *honeymoon* stage occurs in the first days, weeks, or months of reunion and is characterized by euphoria, joy, and a rush of emotions. Carol Schaefer says she felt that way the first time she talked to her son, and she likens this ecstatic experience to the euphoria of giving birth and becoming a mother. Reunion is in a sense a kind of "rebirth." As Carol says, "Giving birth is a profound experience, and just hearing Jack's voice took me back to when I gave birth to him. I didn't feel the ground beneath my feet. We didn't actually meet until six months after we talked, but each time he called I was thrust back into this euphoria."

During this honeymoon phase, birth parent and adoptee share stories about their lives and often discover unusual and uncanny coincidences. This phenomenon of adoptive synchronicity is widespread, and some believe that it is linked to the prenatal and genetic bond. I knew for instance that Andrew had been adopted in New York City, but I had understood from the agency that the family planned to move out of the city soon after the adoption. When I met Andrew, I learned he had spent his first thirteen years just a few blocks from where I lived when I moved to New York three years after his birth. I had also visited the small town where he attended prep school. This synchronicity can also occur between birth parent, and adoptive parent as it has for me and Katherine. On our first meeting in New York I chose the restaurant where we would meet, and it turned out to be the same one she had thought of suggesting. We also discovered that my friend singer/songwriter Beth Nielsen Chapman was one of her favorite artists. And when I received Andrew's identifying information, I soon realized that his adoptive father lived virtually around the corner from where I had lived until that year.

Karen Logan discovered that her son and uncle shared an enthusiasm for the sport of curling and that they lived in the same area of the country. When she called her uncle, she learned he had once traveled to Canada with her son's adoptive parents to attend a curling event.

Lillian Blaine and her daughter found they have the same funny taste. She once wanted to buy some decorative wooden trees for her brother as a wedding gift, but her husband dissuaded her. When she visited her daughter sometime later, she says, "I walked into her house, and she had three of these trees. It was bizarre." Lillian says they have had a lot of experiences like that. "We both love to go grocery shopping, we go down every aisle. We both love the same Chinese food. We pick off of people's plates in restaurants. She has the same way about her."

Jane Leeds and her son, Michael, realized an amazing coincidence while looking through piles of old photographs. Michael recognized a house in one of the pictures as the first call he responded to as a fireman, and Jane told him it was the former home of his paternal grandfather.

It is not clear what synchronicity tells us about biological families who have been separated. But if we assume as LaVonne H. Stiffler suggests in *Synchronicity & Reunion* that families are joined on more than just a physical level, then perhaps these accounts of synchronicity help reconnect a "broken" Gestalt.

Early in a reunion, a birth mother's feelings of happiness and renewal are often accompanied by bouts of depression and grief related to the original separation between mother and child. When Cynthia Beals reunited with her daughter, she was very eager to see all the baby and early childhood pictures of Rebecca. She did not reckon, however, with the feelings these pictures would arouse of the original pain and loss of relinquishment:

> I had to mourn all over again that I was not a part of her younger life. Thankfully, it did not last as long as the initial depression when I gave her up. I think what finally put my depression to rest after reunion was forgiveness. I forgave my father, I forgave the boy who raped me, I forgave society, and more than anyone else, I had to forgive myself. It didn't happen overnight, but through the process of forgiveness, I became a whole person again.

Karen Logan found that she, too, had to grieve the original loss of her son that she had buried and postponed until the moment of reunion. Coming home from their meeting, she started crying hysterically. "It felt like I was losing him again," she says. "Even after I was home for several days, I was still crying. I sought a therapist to help me figure out what was happening, and I'm pretty sure I was going through the grieving that I had never allowed myself to go through when I first said good-bye to him."

After the initial rush of emotions, which can be both ecstatic and mournful, either adoptee or birth parent can begin to feel like they are *left hanging*. They find issues are left unspoken whenever they meet. One person usually pulls back, generally the adoptee, leaving the birth parent confused and frustrated. Carol Schaefer points out that it is a very common experience for adoptees not to return calls after the reunion, leaving the birth parents to wonder if they did the right thing by making contact in the first place. Sometimes birth parents push too hard or overreact and the relationship can suffer. Carol encourages birth parents who do not hear back from their children to keep the lines of communication open and to allow time to help rebuild the relationship:

> The way I handle it with Jack is that I just call. If I need to call just to reconnect, to make sure everything is fine, I do. I advise keeping it light if you can. They need to know, and this contact allows for it, that you aren't going to abandon them again just because they aren't doing what you need them to do. This is a really hard period, but it often reinforces for the mothers what their role is with the child. If you hang in there in a light way, just call or drop a note, then the time will pass and you will reconnect again on a deeper level. If you don't stay in touch then the

odds of a really deep relationship emerging are diminished because that sense of trust hasn't evolved from these messages and calls.

In their 1996 AAC workshop, Rocky Road or Smooth Sailing: Paths to Healing in Reunion, birth mothers Margaret McMorrow, a regional director for CUB, and Ann Hughes also address abandonment issues. Eventually, both sides come to realize that this time no one is leaving; no one will be abandoned again. However, this trust does not just happen because we *say* we are not leaving again; there is no instant intimacy. The kind of relationship we want can take years to build, and people need to allow for that to happen. In the meantime, there is a certain amount of walking on eggs and being extra careful of people's feelings. It is a delicate process, and working out the timing and approach that work best depends on each family situation.

One of the big issues faced in reunion involves how and when to tell the grandchildren the truth about birth parents and what kind of relationship they will have with their birth grandparents. Karen Logan's grandchildren know who she is and seem comfortable with her. She says, "Once when I called my son's home after our reunion, his six-year-old answered the phone and said, 'Dad, it's your birth mother.' My son is quite open about who I am with his children." Carol Schaefer's young grandchildren understand she is their dad's birth mother, and after some family negotiation, they now call her "Grandma." However, they have had questions about their father's relinquishment that she has had to answer for them. Once when she was baby-sitting all four grandchildren, they sat propped in their beds asking her why she did not keep their father. Schaefer says she tried to explain the situation to them, but they kept insisting she really could have kept him. She says, "Finally, I said to them, 'You know I could have kept him, but I didn't know it at the time.' They were okay after that, but I hadn't realized how much they were impacted by the adoption. It's another generation, but it's part of their story too."

How birth parents and their families fit into their children's extended family and how they are identified can be an awkward and uncomfortable dilemma. If there is too much pressure to establish roles or to identify one's place, this can result in a *slowing down* of the pace of the relationship. Carol Schaefer says, "Whenever I did assert my needs to Jack, the relationship would suffer, and I wouldn't hear from him for a while. I had to deal with my feelings in my support group and with my friends. I was the mother and I could be patient." This slowing down can also be a natural part of developing a relationship. The adopted person may simply need to take more time to integrate all the new people in his life. It is important for the birth parent to have other emotional outlets and not to feel like everything has to be expressed or worked out directly with their children. Like Carol Schaefer, many find that friends in their support group are the most helpful because they understand best one another's experience.

I am very aware of the need to allow Andrew to determine for himself how much contact is comfortable, and when and how he will tell his children who I really am, or whether he can fit in a visit with my mother or sister. After five years we can explain ourselves and our views to each other, but we are still very careful, and not everything is verbally or directly communicated. Birth parents can sabotage future relations with their children and risk a *disengagement* process if they choose to confront them or press them aggressively to meet *their* needs.

In time, if handled with care, birth parents and their children *solidify* the terms of their relationship and learn to weather the painful times and celebrate the joyful ones. Ann Hughes recalls not being invited to her daughter's wedding as one of the most excruciating moments of their reunion. She did send candles for her daughter to light at the altar, and in that way she was there in spirit. She now believes that gesture was critical for them because her daughter realized that her birth mother "put her first." Ann says, "I came close to not being able to keep my cool, but I did, and our relationship has only benefited from the crisis."

Since their reunion, Lillian Blaine and her daughter have not felt the need to confront each other about the past. They discuss instead how their relationship will progress in the future, and Lillian cannot remember any pulling back on her daughter's part. She says, "Our relationship has grown beautifully over the years, but I wouldn't say it's exactly one of mother/daughter. I don't even think there's a name for how we're connected. It is very intense. Even though we call each other by our first names, she recently gave me a nightshirt that said THE WORLD'S GREATEST MOTHER as a belated Mother's Day gift."

Many birth mothers report that their depression and sadness lift as their relationship grows. As a therapist, Lillian Blaine believes that her experience has enabled her to "understand on a profound level other people without judging them." She says, "I now have a hopeful view of life, and my relationship with my daughter has helped immeasurably with that." Karen

Logan feels that her search and reunion process has made her a much more grounded person. "I don't fly off the handle like I used to," she says. " I'm generally more patient, and I'm able to let go of things that I've held on to for a very long time." For years, Logan saved every report and piece of research she had collected from her various jobs, but she no longer needs that clutter to fill the hole that her son's absence had created in her life.

Patience is certainly something that I, and many of the birth parents I spoke with, strive for as we follow our children's cues. Sometimes we have to bend in directions that are unfamiliar or uncomfortable for us, but ultimately we realize that the spiritual ties we have to each other outweigh our fears. As Ann Hughes says, "Somehow we're all in the flow of life together and if you're open, listening, paying attention, and asking questions, rather than ramming your way through the reunion, trying to make it go your way, then you will be guided on this journey. . . . My search and reunion have taught me that."

I too am willing to be guided, and trust between Andrew and me is building slowly but surely as we spend more time together and learn more about each other.

Learning to Live with the Past

Teach me to hear mermaids singing.

John Donne

When birth parents find their relinquished child, they find that living without the onus of secrecy and denial is the key to self-forgiveness and a new appreciation for life's blessings. My reunion with Andrew reawakened so many feelings I had thought buried or lost and uncovered layers of myself I did not know existed. As I admire the photographs I display in my home and office of Andrew, Chloe, and their children, I marvel each day at the remarkable stroke of luck that brought them into my life.

In the following chapter, I will explore how it feels for adoptees to get a second chance at knowing their birth parents and reclaiming their genetic heritage.

EIGHT

AND I SHALL HAVE SOME PEACE THERE

Adoptees Search for What Has Been Hidden

I Just Want to Know

I always knew that I could never go on with my life
and have my own children without completing the
circle, without looking into the eyes of the person
who had given birth to me.

Abigail Stone, an adoptee

WHEN ANDREW BEGAN to search for me, he was motivated in good part by
his curiosity about his biological background. At the very least a meeting
between us would provide answers to a number of questions that were on his
mind when he and Chloe married and discussed having children. Although
he may not have realized it, he was among a substantial group of adoptees
who step up their search efforts during or after a significant life event that
adds fuel to their curiosity about their blood relatives.

When I get together now with Andrew and Chloe, our conversations
tend more to the quotidian, a comfortable and familiar place for all of us.
Nevertheless, while we never find it easy to broach the more sensitive sub-
jects, we usually manage in time to discuss anything really important. Early

in our reunion, he told me what he remembers about how he came to search for me and how he actually found me:

> I don't have the greatest memory about all the search details, but I do know that once I began to really put my mind to it, I found all the information I needed pretty quickly. I had collected some stuff about my birth parents before I met Chloe and had registered with a few groups when I was younger, but nothing added up to much. I was always very curious, but I never talked about it with friends. I just didn't talk about that kind of stuff. I think people look and go through this for different reasons. I never got too wrapped up in it, just periodically, I would try something new. There just came a point when my curiosity got the better of me, and I decided I really wanted to do this. It was either just before or after Chloe and I got married. We were thinking about having kids, and Chloe had asked me about medical records. Of course I didn't have any. That wasn't the most important thing for me though, and I think people say that's what they want because that's comfortable for . them. Chloe was a support for me, but really, these kinds of things I typically internalize and figure out myself.
>
> Someone pointed me in the direction of a support group that also helps with searches. It wasn't my thing to go to support meetings, but I wanted some help on how to go about searching myself. The first thing I had to do was find my original birth certificate, and I learned there was a way I could do that by correlating numbers on my amended birth certificate with the birth records in the archives at the public library.

Andrew's search tactics are particular to New York, where agencies' hands are absolutely tied unless there is a match with the state registry. Since there had been no match with the private registries he had tried, Andrew felt he had to search on his own and did not bother at that time with the state registry. Sometime prior to his twenty-seventh birthday, Andrew and Chloe visited Bill in New York. Armed with his own plan of attack, he decided to make a side trip to the library to look up the birth records for 1966:

> I hadn't really told my dad much about my search, but by announcing that I was going to the library, I was able to let him know what I was looking for. He actually came and hung out with us for a while, but I think it quickly became too tedious for him.

My parents were always outwardly supportive of the idea of me searching. I don't think they thought it was a good idea, but if I wanted to do it, then that was okay with them. I mean, it was my life and if I wanted to open this Pandora's box, then I should be sure I would be comfortable with the consequences. My dad was worried about what kind of person we would find and what kind of state you would be in. He believed that once we met you, if you weren't doing well, then we would have to help you. We couldn't just turn our back on you. My mom was concerned, obviously, that she'd become number two or something. Chloe was afraid you'd want to keep me and told me, "If she wants your organs, no way!" All these things made me wonder all the more, why bother? Still, I felt if you go slowly enough then no one is going to be shocked or hurt by it. I wasn't doing this in any kind of malicious way because of any kind of unhappiness in my life that made me want to shift gears here. I just had the feeling I wanted to know.

Handling adoptive parents' feelings, as Andrew has described, is not easy. Andrew has clearly defined for himself the difference between his mother and the woman who gave birth to him. He says he understands that although I would naturally think of him as my son, he could not think of me as his mother. While we do not have a parenting bond, he accepts that our bond is real, and it is lifelong. In *Lost and Found*, B. J. Lifton writes that an inherent ambiguity almost always remains deep within the adoptee's psyche. She says that the great paradox for many adoptees, whether conscious or not, is of "having not one mother, but two—and often feeling one has none. After reunion, there is the task of separating out one's feelings for the birth mother from those for the adoptive mother. There are times when the two merge into each other." Andrew seemed clear from the outset about his different feelings for each of us, and yet there remained the task of finding this "woman who gave birth" to him.

The prospect of finding his birth record was exciting, but it also turned out to be quite daunting. There were massive volumes of records at the library, and Andrew was shocked by how many there were just for the year of his birth:

> They were so dense and filled with so many names that I was over-whelmed even before we started. I wasn't even sure if it was worth it to me at that point, but I have the kind of character where if I start some-thing, I have to finish it. After completing one section in the books, I

began thinking that time didn't matter that much. I was in no hurry and could come back in a month or a year. It was just fun to make a little progress. The books were arranged in alphabetical order, and Chloe and I picked letters at random that we thought were the most common. It was like *Wheel of Fortune. F* was our twenty-third choice, and we didn't come across the magic number until our second day in the library. There's a point where you've gone through so many letters, that you just know someone has missed the number. You're sure of it, because these are long numbers, and after hours of looking, there's a real chance that you're not going to see it or be able to stop on it. Suddenly though, there it was. The record had the last name "Franklin" and the first and middle names that you gave me, but not your name. It was fun to find that number and at least have a name associated with it.

It turned out that I didn't need to go back to the search consultant to find out what to do next because my dad suggested then that I call Spence-Chapin and ask if my birth mother had been in touch. At that time apparently the agency directors thought they could legally reveal first names, and although they had me register with the state, we got the name "Lynn" from them. We wondered if you were still in New York, and Chloe remembers that we were sitting on the couch in my dad's apartment when she found the name in the phone book. Then we called, and we both got on the line. When a woman answered the phone, we hung up, and when we checked the address I thought, "My god, that's so close to where my dad lives. . . ." We spent that night going through all kinds of scenarios about how you and Dad probably had passed so many times on the sidewalk and didn't even know it.

I was feeling a little scared at this point, thinking, "If I did meet this woman, what next?" I wasn't sure if I was doing the right thing, or if this was something I could turn on and turn off. I mean we're talking about human beings. You can't just pull open the curtain, see who's there, and then be able to shut it again. I don't know what exactly was moving me forward, but I had come this far and wasn't going to stop now.

Once I registered with the state, I guess someone from Spence-Chapin wrote to you. I know I waited quite awhile before they got back to me. In the end though they set up our first phone call. As I got closer to making actual contact, I became more and more nervous, but in the end despite feeling very awkward, I thought it went really well. Then when we met at your apartment, it was a great time. It was really fun to see how we looked alike and to learn about what happened. It was interesting, too, to learn how our families were different and how they were the same.

I'm happy now with what I know and happy with the way my life turned out. I have never been angry about what happened, never at all. I think birth mothers suffer a lot more than anyone else. If a birth mother is mature enough to understand all the implications of her decision, then she suffers even more, mourning the loss. But for me, I can't see obsessing about the situation or being angry about it, unless life with my adoptive parents had been miserable. If that were the case, then I might take it out on my birth parents because they had given me up. That would be easy to do. But I think if you've had a good life with your adoptive parents, then I can't see why there's a real reason to be angry. And I just don't want to be an angry person. I'd be miserable dwelling on the negative things.

Although Andrew has had his share of personal difficulties, for the most part he feels his childhood and young adulthood have been happy. He knows he has had many advantages, and he holds no apparent grudge against me. Anecdotal evidence indicates that adoptees who have had a more troubled home life bring that emotional baggage into the reunion and may expect more from a birth mother than an adoptee like Andrew, whose home environment was so nurturing. It seems that Andrew, however, was more worried about whether I might want something from him that he could not give me:

Honestly, I was afraid you would want to be my mother again. But you haven't, and as a result we've become closer friends. I think that we have a strong and growing friendship and that if there's anything between family and friends, then you fall somewhere in there. Where the relationship becomes tricky is with all my other family members. Chloe has certainly been affected by all this, but she has been very sensitive, first seeing how I handled everything and then giving her reaction. She's been very good about letting me figure out how I want to handle the situation with my parents and children.

It has always been important to me that my mom know she doesn't have to get more involved than she wants to, that she can go at her own speed. Since day one, my dad said, "Let's have her over for dinner." My feeling is that visits are great. We can schedule weekends, we can go places, even take trips together, but when it comes to holidays and all the stress there, I don't want to generate any jealousy and get mixed up with all the feelings that sharing holidays can cause. It's a real challenge to try and juggle all the different family members, including my step-mother, and my dad's "sort of" adopted side of the family, who took him in at the age of sixteen when both his parents died. Sometimes I don't know where my family ends. The numbers are enormous!

Figuring out how to share the truth with my kids has been one of the hardest parts of this whole thing. Emma is now at the age where she's very curious about who's who and how everyone's related to one another. Since we have such an extended family, she wants to know who is *really* an aunt and who isn't. For now, I've told her you're an aunt, and even though it feels sneaky I think it's right. I don't want Emma and William growing up thinking that they might be abandoned or adopted just because Dad and I went through it. I want them to know this will not happen to them. They have to be old enough to understand that, and right now I think the whole thing is just confusing for them. It's going to be a few more years before I tell them who every-one really is and how we're all related. I think my experiences have made me a more careful parent than some. Perhaps I'm being overpro-tective, but I feel that there are a few early years in a kid's life where you have to be extra careful.

Having this conversation with Andrew has helped us understand each other better. Initially, I know he was worried that if Emma were told now, she is so young she could easily say something that could upset his parents. Now I also understand his feelings for Emma's emotional stability. She is just beginning to understand that people and animals die, and she already worries about what might happen if her mother dies. Although Andrew feels he was comfortable knowing he was adopted, he cannot help but be especially sensitive about this issue in regards to his children. He is a wonderful and unusually attentive father. I know he has thought deeply about this, and of course we will wait for a time he feels is more appropri-ate. In the meantime, I will try to answer Emma's questions when they come as honestly as I can without getting caught up in whether or not I am an "aunt."

Andrew has had to deal with not only fitting me into his life but has also had to consider whether to include other members of my family. He has generously extended himself to them, but he admits it is not that easy, and he needs to control the pace of the relationship:

> Your mother and sister and niece are always welcome in our lives. Terry is a strong formal British woman, and I identify somehow with her. And I like Laurie and Erin a lot. Sometimes, though, I feel like it's all too close too fast. In a way they consider me like a *cousin* they don't get to see very often, whereas I feel like they're good *friends* I don't see very often. There are different emotions, and they don't always meet in the middle. At times, I can feel guilty that I haven't made enough time for everyone or haven't reacted exactly as you or they would like. At other times, I feel good that I've done a lot to accommodate everybody, and I've really enjoyed the time we've spent together. I want our relationships to grow, but if I push it, then it might get uncomfortable. I just don't want to have any regrets, because I like where I am. Maybe I'm the one slowing things down right now, but I like the pace of it.
>
> Years tend to grow their own roots as far as I'm concerned, so if you go slowly for a few years, then feelings get stronger over time. At the end of the day, or in twenty years' time, the bonds that we have might be indiscernible from any other family bonds. Right now, there is a difference. I certainly have no regrets. The relationship has grown more than I thought it would, because I was unrealistic in thinking that I would meet you all and then see you a couple seasons later. I never had any issues of wondering if you, Lynn, would stay interested. I knew you would always be interested.

Andrew and I also spoke again about finding his birth father, and he says he is definitely not interested right now. I knew he was ambivalent before, but I was not completely clear about his underlying concerns. I knew he was less certain about how he would be received. The men I have spoken to have reunited with daughters, and I do not know if many birth fathers feel differently about being reunited with a son. It turns out that apart from any anxiety he had about being rejected, Andrew thought I was more interested in actively searching for my own reasons, and he feels he could be caught in the middle of a volatile situation that he wants no part of. He says, "I don't want anything to do with a reunion until I've seen how you and Tom might work things out together, and even then I might say 'no thanks.'" I was curious before, but I have enough going on in my life right now without opening myself and my family to another set of people."

It has helped Andrew and me to clear the air between us, and I have no doubt we will have many more opportunities to clarify our feelings as time passes. We each have our own perspective, and unless we talk, we might not realize that the other person is approaching a situation from a completely different angle. I know I was surprised to hear Andrew's concerns about me and Tom, but when I thought about it later, I could well understand why he might feel the way he does. As Marlou Russell so aptly says in *Adoption Wisdom,* "Navigating the reunion relationship takes time, patience, and practice. There are ups and downs, times of feeling close and distant, and moments of clarity and misunderstanding. The relationship will have a life of its own and will need nurturing."

Adoptees in Search of Themselves

> Raise the stone, and thou shalt find me;
> cleave the wood and there am I.
>
> Henry Van Dyke

Despite the risks and unknowns, more adoptees than ever are searching for that piece of themselves lost when their birth parents relinquished them. In "Adoptees in Search in the United States," former AAC president L. Anne Babb estimates that as many as eighty-eight thousand adoptees search each year, and supporting that figure is a mass of literature indicating that anywhere from 60 to 90 percent of adoptees have some interest in being able to get identifying information about their birth families. Nevertheless, not everyone chooses to search. Many adoptees say they have absolutely no desire to know more, and others may admit to being curious but prefer not to make waves in their families and in their own lives.

For those adoptees who do decide to search there is a sometimes confusing array of resources available to help them devise an approach that will work best for them, including registries, intermediaries, support groups, television, and the Internet. Along with the logistics of search, adoptees are also dealing with the emotional implications of their decision. Adoptees, like birth parents, need to be ready; they need support during the process; and they need to be prepared for any outcome. Betty Jean Lifton recommends that adoptees use the time it takes to find their birth families to become warriors, to strengthen and fortify themselves for the realities ahead. She says that adoptees who search have to be prepared to dismantle the fantasies and let go of the ghost birth parents they have created for themselves, and that is risky business. They have to replace fantasies with real people. In the process, they risk being rejected by the birth parent—and alienating their adoptive parents. That would be a tough order for anyone. On top of that they are very vulnerable during search and reunion and may feel until they reach some kind of closure that they have lost the person they were before they searched.

As Andrew indicated, the reasons adoptees choose to search ranges from the desire to know more about their medical and genealogical history to gaining a more complete sense of self. Father Tom Brosnan says he first thought of searching when he noticed how the son of a man he was counseling looked and acted just like his father. He says, "Maybe for other people it's a matter of fact, but for me, it was a revelation. It made me think about genetic connections and how much I don't know about myself. Consciously, I had not really thought about it when I was growing up, but later as I have reinterpreted my life, I always felt somewhere inside that I was missing something, and that I needed to find out what that was."

Kate Burke thought about searching for many years, buying books and absorbing bits of information about adoption issues here and there, before she began in earnest. She somehow always knew that she would track her birth mother down but felt that she "needed a blending of the right time, the right place, and the right state of mind" before she could put her heart into it. Joan Cummings spent much of her adolescence rebelling against her adoptive family, but at the same time she felt overly attached to them as she moved toward young adulthood. Searching for her birth family was both an attempt to deal with her relationship to her adoptive family and a way to establish an identity for herself as an adult.

Searching for birth relations affords adoptees an opportunity to meet people who resemble them physically and who are connected by blood. "Because my children are adopted," remarks adoptee Kimberly Nelson, "I had never met anyone before my reunion who looked anything like me or who shared my blood." Abigail Stone was never comfortable growing up with everyone noticing that she did not look Jewish like her parents. "It made me aware of missing that physical connection and likeness to someone." Alexandra Burton has significantly different values and sensibilities from her birth family, but she appreciates the physical similarities. "I had always felt different from my adoptive family in terms of certain things and I now realize, after meeting my birth family, that the differences were biological. I feel like I belong more, like I have a place, and wasn't a test-tube baby."

Adoptees who have dissimilar personalities or interests from their adoptive families sometimes feel as though they live among strangers in their own homes. When they finally get more information about a member of their birth family, or actually have some contact, they sense immediately they have connected with someone with whom they share innate characteristics and traits. In her early twenties, Kate Burke went back to Chicago, the city of her birth, and secured from the Children's Home Society some information about her birth mother. After hearing about her, she says, "I sat in my Volkswagen bus and dissolved in tears because the person they described was exactly like me." It was not until nearly a decade later, when Kate finally met her birth mother, that she learned how similar they really were. "It's like we're carbon copies. After we spent some time together, we realized we both love art, hate math, create things in our heads and then write them down and fill in the blanks as we go along."

Alexandra Burton discovered that even her eating habits were the same as her birth mother's and brothers'. "We like the same bland food. I never eat all of my food at the same time and my birth mom kept saying that I had a great uncle with the same habit." Marlou Russell also feels at home with her extended birth family. "They are my people," she says, "just down-to-earth, down-home folks. I feel like them." Discovering these similarities in habit and temperament is very important for adoptees who were raised in a closed adoption and who have been wondering their whole life about where they came from and who they really are.

Although adoptees search in greater numbers than birth parents, who feel more inhibited about whether they have a right to search, many adoptees feel that they were abandoned once and that if their birth mother wants to know them, she should find them and prove her love. They wear their protective armor and are not prepared to risk a second rejection. They may wait a lifetime for a birth mother who does not come looking for them, because she, too, is afraid of rejection. Even when a birth mother does come looking, an adoptee (like Bonnie Bis's son) may not be prepared to trust that she cares, or may wish to punish the birth mother for having relinquished her in the first place. Betty Jean Lifton believes that when a child's biological connections are severed, he begins to lead a double life, where one self grows and the other remains infantilized as an abandoned baby. When an adoptee searches, or is found, he finds that baby frozen in time and must begin to bring the two halves of himself back together.

Being aware of a sense of loss, or incompleteness, as Andrew might say, is the first step on the search continuum. However, the literature indicates that, generally, males are *less* in touch with their loss than their female counterparts, and certainly fewer men actually do search. On a subconscious level, it seems the male adoptee may experience his relinquishment differently from his female counterpart. According to Jean A. S. Strauss, the "birthmother was the first woman who ever 'rejected' him. The decision to look can take great courage, for the risk of rejection by the birthmother carries an enormous weight for a man. To search might place his ego, his sexuality, and his very being at risk." Male adoptees may also have particularly strong emotional attachments to their adoptive mothers and feel that searching for the birth mother poses too great a risk to the relationship they have with the mother who raised them. And like many men, they may simply be less introspective and prefer to just "get on" with their lives.

Adoptees commonly begin their search sometime between the ages of eighteen and twenty-one as they begin to think about where they want their lives to go. Betsie Norris says, "I started coming to a place where the search issue was the last thing of my childhood that I needed to deal with, to put to rest, in order to move forward and become an adult. At about the same time, I found the book *The Adoption Triangle* in a bookstore. I read it straight through and was just so enthused and alive afterward. I couldn't believe that people had actually felt these things that I'd felt and never even put into words to somebody else, much less even to myself." Alexandra Burton decided that finding her birth mother before she went off to college was the best thing she could do for herself. She says that the summer before her senior year of high school she had been upset because, like Abigail Stone, she grew up looking so different from her Jewish parents. "I always felt like I stuck out," she says, "and people were asking me about it. So I let my mom know how uncomfortable I felt about religion and Judaism. At that point she realized why I felt no connection, and she wanted to help me find my roots."

Although many adoptees start their search earlier, the average age at the time of reunion with birth parents is actually twenty-seven, exactly the age Andrew was when he found me. Abigail Stone was twenty-eight when she first made contact with her birth mother, though she had thought about it for years and had always known that her life could not be complete until she found her. At eighteen, she had written to the adoption agency asking for some information about her background, but she says, "I wasn't quite ready or mature enough in myself and didn't have my own life apart from my parents to take it the next step."

Support groups offer adoptees one way of handling feelings throughout the course of the search and reunion. Adoptee and adoptive mother Kimberly Nelson mustered the strength she needed to begin her search by joining a triad support group in her area, and she says that being in the group enabled her to see that birth mothers did want to have contact with their babies. "When I started the process of searching, the most I thought I would ever find was some information. I never thought I could find people." Betsie Norris sought advice during her search but was really out there on her own most of the time. "I just kept thinking how great it would be to have the support of people who were involved in adoption directly. A lot of people were supportive of me, but I think if you haven't been through it, you just don't get it in the same way. And I really longed for people who got it." After her reunion, she formed her own organization, Adoption Network Cleveland (ANC), which runs support groups for members, provides search assistance, and generally advocates for open records. Adoption agencies in Cleveland regularly refer their prospective adoptive parents to ANC to sit in on triad groups as part of their preadoption program.

Marlou Russell's search was "very on and off." She says, "It was real important for me to be with the search when I could and then let go of it when I needed a break, because it's so intensive and so obsessive." Kate Burke says she fell into a mania of search where it was all she could talk or think about. She believes people search so intensely because it becomes a primal urge, and she recognizes the need to allow for emotional time-outs:

> There's such a compunction that it has to happen, that people completely lose their grip and believe everything must focus on this one goal. Some people are able to let their searches cool down. It all depends on the situation. If you have a long, difficult search, then you have to let it go at certain points because the compulsion will make you crazy and send you over the edge. You need to take a rest from it.

Although Andrew would not characterize his search as obsessive, he too made several preliminary forays into the field and ultimately gave it his full attention when he was sure he was ready.

Betsie Norris's search took her in many directions and was sometimes uncomfortable, but she was intent on her goal and was determined to weather the difficulties:

> Each stage, as you can probably imagine, was so emotional. Going to the bank to get a document notarized brought joy and exhilaration, but also shame. I was scared to death to call the agency to get my nonidentifying information. I can't tell you how many times I opened the book, looked at their number, and shut the book again, thinking, They're going to judge me. They are going to think something is wrong with me or my family. And it wasn't about that. It was so intimidating. But I was bound and determined to do this myself and I didn't care how much it would cost or how long it would take.

The journey is as much an inner experience as an outer search, and aspects of the experience touch on triad members' vulnerability around issues of trust and self-esteem. Many adoptees, for instance, have difficulty trusting their own instincts. Marlou Russell says that just allowing herself to be her own guide while searching helped her overcome many emotional blocks. She now counsels other searching adoptees to listen to their inner intuition, to "go with their gut" because that inner trust is what has been missing for them, and is what they need most to reclaim for themselves. Adoptees can also feel intimidated and demeaned by having to beg for information about their identity, and their sense of self-worth is constantly challenged.

Part of deciding to search involves whether or not to involve the adoptive parents. There is still a lingering misconception in the public mind that adoptees who search for birth relatives do so as an act of betrayal or vengeance against their adoptive parents. If anything, most adoptees are wracked with guilt and take great pains to protect, shelter, and reassure their adoptive relations. Sometimes the fear of disrupting the family equilibrium is so powerful that they wait until their adoptive parents have passed away before initiating their search, only to find that their birth parents have also died. This happened to Kimberly Nelson, who felt too guilty even to entertain the *thought* of searching while her adoptive parents were alive. "It [searching] would have qualified as a treacherous act against my adoptive parents," she says. "Whenever thoughts of my birth family occurred to me, I felt guilt-ridden and dismissed them." Kimberly did not search until her adoptive daughter had a reunion with her birth mother, and by then only her birth siblings were still living.

No parent really wants their child to feel so afraid or guilty, but adoptive parents' underlying vulnerability can inhibit their children's desire to search. Their fear is real and perfectly understandable, but it need not be unresolvable. A parent at a recent workshop at Spence-Chapin voiced this question of betrayal and asked the panel of adoptees if they gave any thought to how searching might be a breach of trust with their parents. In fact, several of the panelists had held off searching until one or both of their parents had died precisely because they were afraid of hurting them. One panelist, who searched after both his parents had died, addressed the question by making a distinction between being a caretaker and being a parent. He argued gently that adoptive parents are not simply caretakers; they *are* "real" parents, and that place in their child's heart is reserved for them, regardless of whether he feels he needs to find his birth family.

Instead of actually waiting for parents to die before searching, many adoptees just keep their adoptive parents in the dark, refusing to disclose any information about their attempts to reconnect with their lost families. Others may share their intention of searching for birth relatives with their adoptive parents but make it clear that the search is something they need to do on their own. "My parents were very supportive," Betsie Norris recalls. "I think they saw the search as my right. It was my information, and I deserved to know it. My mom went through periods where she felt threatened and needed a lot of reassurance, but I told both my parents everything I was doing and kept them up-to-date. My dad really wanted to help, but I had to let him know that it was just something I needed to do myself. It was important for me to work independently."

Abigail Stone also felt she had to pursue her quest on her own terms: "I needed to answer the question 'Who am I?', and I don't think I could have done that if my parents had been involved. The journey you go through when you search is so full of complex emotions that I didn't feel I could take responsibility for anyone else's feelings but my own. I love my parents too much to include them when I don't even know what the journey means to me." Abigail has a loving and open relationship with her parents except when it comes to talking about her birth family. Sensing all her life their discomfort about discussing adoption, she could not tell them she was searching, because she feared they would be upset. She knew she could not handle all the emotions at once.

When Marlou Russell asked her adoptive parents for information about her birth mother, she says, "My father got up out of his chair and left the room, saying, 'Don't you think we took care of you?' And my mother started crying. They just couldn't handle it at all. My mother later told me that my father had a picture of my birth mother that he tore up. My adoptive parents were very threatened by the fact that I wanted to search. I ended up waiting until my adoptive father died, because I felt I could deal with my adoptive mother more easily on her own."

When adoptive parents have trouble dealing with their child's search the adoptee is burdened with having to accommodate everyone's needs. Kate Burke knows from her own experience that it can be very difficult "for adoptees to achieve a balance between their birth and adoptive families, but then again, so many are used to juggling the relationships in their lives. When you do try and bring your birth and adoptive family together, you're in the middle again, trying to find that balance and protecting everyone at the same time."

Accepting Where the Road Leads

> I'm going to be sixty in a couple of years and I'm faced
> with what looks like leaving this world without ever
> knowing how I got here. It's incredibly painful for me.
>
> Joe Soll, an adoptee

Adoptees generally reason that struggling through the logistical and emotional challenges and setbacks will be worth it once they meet the people who are responsible for their existence. But when adoptees reach the end of their search only to find that a birth parent has died, they feel a bitter despair. In *Searching for a Past,* author Jayne Schooler says that it is truly the death of the dream to hear the words that your birth mother or father has passed away. Somehow, as they grieve what is forever lost to them, adoptees whose hopes have been dashed must find a way "to redefine their dreams, to redefine their hope" and in some way "rewrite the script." In the end, the process of searching and dealing with the outcome becomes the heart of the journey. As sad as it is to lose an opportunity to know one's birth parent, the adoptee may at least gain more information about her family and may find joy in relationships with other birth relatives. Betty Jean Lifton even suggests that, paradoxically, when an adoptee finds a birth mother who is deceased or institutionalized, it establishes quite fundamentally the limits of the relationship. The adoptee is spared having to work through the uncomfortable and unsettling emotions that arise in an open-ended relationship. However, I think it is fair to say that most adoptees would choose to have that opportunity, even if the relationship took some work.

The private investigator who searched for Kimberly Nelson's family called her one Sunday with good news—and bad news. "He told me that he had found a man who was probably my half-brother. We shared a mother. The man had told the investigator that my birth mother had been deceased for ten years. I wanted to find my birth mother so badly and was devastated by the news of her death. For me, she died that day. She was gone and that was it." Kimberly learned that same day that she had several siblings, but it took her months of grieving her birth mother's death before she could think about contacting them.

Adoptees who search but never find a birth parent also have to find some way to live with their disappointment. Around the time David Adler was trying to adopt his first child, he tried to find information about his birth mother. Going through the process of deciding to adopt made him curious about his roots. He says, "There has been work done on how adoptees fantasize about their birth families, and as an adoptee, I'll have fantasies about who they were, where they came from. . . . This was a person from a rural background who came to Chicago, or—this was a person who grew up in Chicago. You just don't know. A lot of things go through your mind, and they lead to an eagerness to find out about it." David hired a private detective who managed to get the records from the hospital and actually talked to the doctor who arranged the adoption. He got a name, and it meant something to him to see the records, but he could never find a trace of a person with that name. He was disappointed but says, "It wasn't crushing. We had so much else going on. When it seemed something might happen, I would start to become preoccupied with it, but I was actually concerned about that potential to be so preoccupied. I really didn't want that to happen to me—and it didn't." David's experience was a letdown, but in his own way, he managed to get a grip and move on with his life. He had, at least, the small satisfaction of knowing he had tried.

Pam Hasegawa lost her adoptive mother when she was very young, and by her early thirties she had also lost her adoptive father. Pam set about searching for her family of origin in 1975, a time when it was almost impossible to search. After intense investigation, Pam eventually contacted a woman who she believed to be her birth mother, a cellist named Signe Sandstrom, who had been raised in Hampden County, Massachusetts. Pam's surname at birth had been Hampden, and she was given the names Rolande *Sygne,* although *Sygne* was sometimes spelled Signe on the various documents. When Pam called the woman, she brushed Pam off and abruptly hung up the phone. Pam thought surely this was her mother because, she says, "no one had ever spoken to me in that tone except my adoptive mother." For fifteen years, Pam pursued Signe and even established a relationship with some of her family members. Pam finally met Signe in 1992, only a few months before she died, and discovered she had kept all her letters. She visited her again on her deathbed and stroked her and told her she loved her. Following her death, with the permission of Signe's family, Pam had a DNA test performed to put the matter finally to rest. When the results arrived, she was devastated to learn that she and Signe were *not* mother and daughter.

To this day Pam does not know why there was such an uncanny synchronicity with Signe, but she believes that somehow she and her mother knew each other. "I still have trouble figuring out why the Lord let me find the wrong woman," Pam says. "All I can conclude is that God knew how desperately I needed to *believe* I had found my birth family, and so God allowed me to find the wrong woman. I have told God many times that I trust the path he has given me, and even though I was heartbroken, I would keep on trusting until I reached heaven and could ask, face-to-face, 'Why did you do it that way?'" The years keep rolling by without any more news for Pam. When I asked her how she feels today, her instantaneous tearful response—"When is it going to be my turn?"—pierced my own heart. Pam is still searching for the truth, just wanting to know where she fits on the human continuum.

It is also painful for adoptees when birth parents refuse contact. This confirms, at least in their own minds, their worst fear that their birth parents did not and do not care about them. Maybe, they think, it is true after all that they are unlovable. In some instances, the birth mother is simply emotionally incapable of integrating her birth child into the family and life she has created since the relinquishment. She may not have told her husband or children, and at least on first contact she cannot cope. The same may be true for the birth father who might not even have known of his child's existence. Sometimes, an adoptee's phone call or letter is inadvertently intercepted by a child or spouse, and the unexpected news rips through a family and tears them apart emotionally. It is very important to learn how to approach the birth family to minimize the possibility of rejection.

Nevertheless, even when every effort has been made to handle the approach with care, some birth parents will still refuse to engage in any kind of relationship, and somehow the adoptee has to come to terms with that and recognize that it has nothing to do with them being "unlovable." In other cases, an initial rejection may lead to a change of heart. Regardless of how it turns out, Betsie Norris counsels adoptees who meet with rejection that their birth parents are not rejecting them *per se*, but rather all of the conflicting emotions that suddenly bombard them.

Dee Davis, an adoptee and professional searcher, presented a workshop on search at the 1997 AAC conference in Dallas. She began searching for her birth mother after both her adoptive mother and father committed suicide. Her birth mother refused to recognize her existence and gave no indication that she would ever change her mind. Dee's birth siblings have also ignored her overtures. Yet somehow Dee has been able to adjust her expectations, and in a fundamental sense she is satisfied, because she searched and found the truth.

Kate Burke did not know how to handle her birth mother's initial rejection after contact. She wanted to reverse all that she had done and pretend that she had never begun her search in the first place, because she felt she had caused her birth mother pain. Fortunately, she and her birth mother later developed a sustainable relationship.

When Abigail Stone contacted her birth mother she told Abigail that she was so shocked and confused that she would need a great deal of time to work through the situation. "All she kept saying was how much time she needed, and it was very sad to me," recalls Abigail, "because I felt like I took her totally off guard, as if she had never thought it would be possible. I later found out that my birth mother had been counseled when she relinquished me that it would never be a possibility to get in touch." Abigail decided to move slowly, did not do anything impulsive, and gave her birth mother time to work through her feelings. She sent a letter, letting her birth mother know how much she had always meant to her and that she was glad to have a chance to say thank you. Since then, her birth mother has written her several times and feels grateful that Abigail found her. As of this writing, the two have not yet met, but Abigail remains hopeful that when the time and place are right, they will. This is another example of how readiness affects the outcome of a reunion. Abigail's birth mother was not expecting to hear from her daughter, and she was not prepared for a reunion. Even though it was painful for Abigail to feel rejected, she knew it was important to proceed carefully and to give her birth mother time to adjust to her.

Most of the stories in this chapter describe reunions with birth mothers, usually the first port of call when an adoptee searches. Not only do adoptees seem to feel more compelled to find their "first" mother, but, like Andrew, they also feel they have a better chance of receiving a warm reception from the birth mother. They do not know if the father knew about the pregnancy, whether he was around, or whether he was ambivalent or was marginalized by the birth mother. In Andrew's case, having found me, and having realized how complex a reunion can be, he is in no hurry to proceed with his quest to find his birth father, especially not knowing how Tom and I would deal with it ourselves. Others who learn that the birth father abandoned their mother may feel protective of her and may feel resentment toward him. In cases where the reunion with the birth mother has been disappointing, the adoptee may be more inclined to continue the search in the hope that she will have more luck with her father.

Adoptee and adoption reform pioneer Jean Paton probably best epitomizes the healing potential and power of search regardless of the outcome. Now well into her eighties, Jean searched for her birth family long before most people realized it was even possible to do so. Jean never knew or felt the loving embrace of either her birth mother or birth father, but in her soul she most assuredly "found" them when she sat beneath the portrait of her grandfather and summoned his spirit. In her classic book *Orphan Voyage,* she briefly and eloquently conjures her father and addresses him about that time she sat with that old painting:

> Well, father, my childlessness has broken your line, insofar as it descended into me. Had I known whose it was, perhaps I would have been less careless. Perhaps I would have had a child, or children; and at least I would have recognized these Celtic stirrings as matters to be known and dealt with, plumbed and lived. I talked with my friends, told them the pieces, and they said: "Why, His father must have been so-and-so!" . . . Of course I could not speak to him any more than to you. But his traces were clear and solid. It was not necessary to scrape around in directories and employment lists to find him. No, he left epitaphs, his self, his things, his expressiveness—all where anyone could see them if they but came. . . . I went to the Northwest and I looked at

them. I put my hands upon his old office table, scrutinized with understanding the titles in his library, and I looked straight behind his portrait eyes. And perhaps he knew I had come, in my name and in the
name of my father—after eighty years.

Jean found a way to connect with her birth parents even though she never
saw or spoke to them. Perhaps adoptees who undertake the enormity of a
search can expect some measure of a connection, whether an embrace, a
phone conversation, or a good look into the eyes of a long-dead, but somehow present relation. At the very least, like David Adler, or Pam Hasegawa,
they know they have done their best, and in the process, they have found
something more of themselves.

Now That We Have Met

> The bond between parent and child creates a base on
> which to build a lasting relationship. Sometimes this
> bond feels tenuous and held together by a thread,
> while other times it can feel indestructible.
>
> Marlou Russell, *Adoption Wisdom*

Reunion has a lasting impact on adoptees and their families. As Andrew
wisely noted, you cannot just open a curtain, take a look inside, and forget
that you ever met your birth family. It is simply not possible on any level—
emotional, psychological, or spiritual. Reunion is bound to elicit an array of
intense responses and feelings, and in the first phase those feelings depend
largely on the reception the adoptee receives from the birth parent.

When a birth parent responds ecstatically, the adoptee is naturally eu-
phoric. Betsie Norris first reached her birth mother by phone, and before she
finished introducing herself, her mother exclaimed, "Oh, my God, I've been
praying for this call for twenty-six years!" Betsie remembers she felt like she
was having an out-of-body experience watching herself dial and then speak to
the woman she had wanted to meet all her life. She says, "The adrenaline was
tremendous, and then when there was immediate acceptance—especially
because I had probably overprepared myself for rejection—the acceptance
was incredible. I remember literally standing up, because I couldn't contain
myself—and I could have shot through the ceiling!" When she found her birth
mother, she soon learned she had also found her birth father, because her

parents had married after her birth and subsequently had three more children! After the euphoria of first contact, they settled into learning about each other. In the beginning, the excitement everyone feels is almost "too good to be true." Eventually there is a return to normalcy, and at times some pulling back to reassess and regroup. In Betsie's birth family, the oldest boy realized he was no longer the firstborn, and although he did not hold it against Betsie, he had to work that out for himself. Betsie had to adjust to having a ready-made family of birth parents and full siblings.

Fear of rejection by the birth family or fear of not fitting in with them are in the forefront of an adopted person's mind. Joan Cummings says, "I felt very self-conscious when I met them [birth mother and siblings], because I didn't feel comfortable being myself. It really mattered to me what they thought then." Joan's discomfort is typical for both birth parents and adoptees, because there is no societal code or precedent on which to base their behavior. "At the moment the birthmother and children first meet," write the authors of *BirthBond*, "they meet as roles: abandoning birthmother (the woman who gave me up), rejected adoptee (the baby I gave away)—but these are roles for which no models or guidelines exist. More importantly, no one wants them anyway. Once post-reunion begins, these labels cease to fit in any case, and the individuals look to traditional roles (child, friend, aunt, sister, etc.) for guidance, but they have only limited appropriateness for these 'funny mothers' and 'funny children.'"

After Kimberly Nelson dealt with the grief of learning her birth mother had died by the time she traced her, she decided to invite her sister to visit her. She says, "It was the scariest time of my life. I couldn't believe she was real. It was so exciting, but also so frightening. I wanted her here, but I was afraid. I came up with a hundred good reasons not to have her come. My sister said she understood everything and that we could slow down if I needed to. I thought about it for maybe a minute and told her to come. She told me not to be terrified and that when I met her, I would see how down-to-earth she really was, and she is."

Beyond the first wave of feelings, the postreunion relationship develops at its own pace for each family. For some this means the easy excitement felt in the beginning can slip away as memories of buried pain and loss surface. Marcy Wineman Axness was adopted in the 1950s, and although it was unusual practice for the times, her parents met and even developed a relationship with her birth mother. Marcy knew nothing about that early "openness" until she was in her twenties. After the death of her adoptive mother, her father took her to lunch one day and asked if she wanted to meet her birth mother:

> I never went through the search process the way most adoptees who aren't involved in open adoptions do. It was not very hard to find her and we had a "fairy tale" reunion. We seemed alike and resonated with each other. Our minds work in similar ways. It was incredible to meet this person who I clicked with in so many ways. It wasn't until years later in the reunion that I realized how out of touch and hurt I was because of the adoption. My birth mother had put her feelings in a very neat little spot and believed that she was carrying me for my adoptive parents. It was a dispassionate place and to me it felt like a rejection. We've had to work very hard to establish boundaries that are good for both of us. It has taken years, but now I can say things are nice between us.

Like B. J. Lifton, Marcy thinks searching serves a useful purpose, one that she was denied. She would not exchange places with anyone who had to search unhappily for a long time, and politically, she certainly thinks people should not have to fight to get access to their identifying information, but still she feels search provides an opportunity to sort out some issues before the reunion occurs. "You know, I was so asleep," she says, "and I was just given this name . . . given this reunion . . . without ever having examined what adoption meant in my life, or what not knowing my birth mother meant to me. I hadn't asked myself any of those questions, so I was a sitting duck for the feelings that took me by surprise."

Marcy counsels people to be careful not to expect reunion to be the ultimate panacea. The moment of actual reunion is gone in the "blink of an eye," but like adoption itself, reunion is a lifelong experience. "Even so," says Marcy, "it is only one of the many roads on the journey toward wholeness, and it is secondary to what I call the 'inner reunion' of reuniting with the piece of myself that I separated from at the time of my relinquishment. For me, inner reunion is about traveling back to find my own inner essence of who I was. Part of that was having a reunion with my birth mother and with my family."

In addition to the psychotherapeutic work she has done, Marcy's pathway to inner reunion has included actively participating in organizations promoting adoption reform, and doing postgraduate studies in perinatology. Spiritually, too, she has come to a place where she can honestly say she is happy with the person she has become, and she knows she would not be the same person were it not for the experiences she has had. Not long ago, when she took her children to meet her birth mother for the first time, Marcy realized she had healed some of the pain and feelings of rejection that had adversely affected their relationship. They all met in the Child's Play Park at Golden Gate Park, where she and her birth mother talked for a while before Marcy and the children went over to the merry-go-round:

> My mother couldn't get on because she had her dog, but the kids and I each found a horse to ride. Our horses weren't close together and I noticed that each time I came around, my mother had her camera trained on me and was taking pictures. I was thinking she should be taking pictures of the kids, not me, and then it just hit me how right it was for my mother to be taking pictures of me on the merry-go-round. I just let that flow over me and fill me up. I'd just come around and I'd smile and she'd take another picture. It was really a wonderful moment. The healing had truly begun.

Kate Burke's work with triad members in reunion has given her a healthy perspective on the process. She says she has many good friends who are at their birth mother's house all the time, and she understands that can be wonderful. If Joan Cummings's early reunion experience is indicative of how things will evolve in her relationship, she seems to be on her way to developing the kind of close ties with her birth family that Kate Burke has described: "They're my family," Joan says. "That's how I feel. I now feel that my physical being is connected to these people. I see parts of me, like the little crease in my nose, that is similar to one my brother has. It's almost as if all the information is starting finally to settle in a little bit. I feel like I found my family, and it has turned everything in my life a different color." Kate also says, however, that there are other kinds of reunions more like her own, where adoptee and birth family are in touch and part of each other's lives, but it is not as intense as for some people, and that works fine too:

> It's important to realize that reunions develop differently, depending on the people. I think we tend to look at reunion one way and send a message that if you're not at your birth mother's house every week, then there's something wrong. And it's not. I gained from my search an identity that I love and a comfortableness with my self. The reunion is integrated well into my life now, but it's no longer the main cornerstone of my existence. It's just one facet of who I am.

Five years have passed since Alexandra Burton met her birth mother, and time has changed her perspective of reunion. She is presently experiencing a need to pull back from the intensity of the relationship and the pressure she feels from her birth family to spend time with them. The stage was set for her on her first visit when her entire birth family threw her a birthday party and welcomed her wholeheartedly into their clan. Since then, she has gone to see them once a year. On her most recent trip, Alexandra found that she was feeling depressed:

> I couldn't eat or sleep. I felt for the first time like I was being manipulated by my birth mother into coming out to visit them. The entire family was putting pressure on me to come out more often. My birth family is very different from my adoptive family, and meeting them gave me an opportunity to reevaluate my relationship with my adoptive family. I think that alone was almost as important as meeting my birth mother, but I wasn't looking for a new family. I started to feel like I had to be daughter, sister, and granddaughter to my birth family, and it just wore me out. I think they expect me to be an integrated member of their family and there's no way that's going to happen. I can't really see them again for a while.

Alexandra's withdrawal from her birth family is a normal response to the conflicting emotions that can surface at any time. It does not mean that she will not one day redefine her terms with her birth family and again feel comfortable visiting with them. On the other hand, Andrew has pointed out to me that an adoptee may not always be inclined to want to develop a close relationship. He feels that while he is pleased that we have a relationship, the adoptee who chooses not to stay in close touch with the birth family is not necessarily in the wrong, and that choice also needs to be respected. Although the birth parent may feel it as a rejection, it may have more to do with the adoptee having satisfied his basic need for information with the initial contact.

Like Alexandra, Joan Cummings also feels more settled in her adoptive family, and they are all more relaxed. She says she is glad things went the way they did and that although she has a strong bond with her birth mother, she knows her mother is the woman who raised her. She also has a clearer sense of who she is. She says, "There's me—and the stuff I've gotten from everybody." Many adoptees report that their relationship with their adoptive parents improves or grows closer as a result of reunion. They may pass through a rocky stretch, but once the immediate euphoria of reunion passes, they realize their questions have been answered, and they are better able to appreciate their parents' role in their lives.

In reunion new fantasies often emerge, and lurking in the adoptee's heart may be the hope that one day his birth and adoptive families will somehow merge into one. In Betsie Norris's case, the fantasy may be close to reality. She says, "The first time my birth parents came to Cleveland, they met my mom. She showed them home movies and updated them on everything in our lives. As an adoptee, it was a wonderful thing to see my birth mother and my adoptive mother come together and hug. It was probably the first time I could say I felt whole. Witnessing them both crying and thanking each other for the piece of my life that they had that the other one would have given almost anything to have shared in was an incredible experience." When I met Betsie, she was about to get married, and birth parents, adoptive parents, and stepmother were all planning to attend the wedding.

Kate Burke feels her two families are as integrated as she would like them to be at this point. She says, "I love my birth mother and sisters. I love my adoptive mother. We all get along quite well, though we're not involved in one another's everyday lives." As of now, Andrew also seems happy enough for us to visit on a semiregular basis and yet preserve some distance so that his family relationship remains as much as possible as it was before we met. I sense, though, that there is less strain for everyone now that Katherine and I have met.

Sometimes the adopted person's spouse has difficulty adjusting to yet another set of "parents" in the husband or wife's life, especially if their mate needs time and space to sort through new and unexpected feelings surrounding the whole adoption experience. As Andrew has said, Chloe has definitely been affected by our reunion, but as long as he is happy with it, she is fully supportive of my having a place in their family. In fact, she has helped us all bridge the uncertainties and awkwardness that sometimes arise. Now with the children, everyone wants to be a part of their lives, and Chloe is a solid presence as the extended assembly, including Andrew, his parents, my family, and I, work out how we will handle the challenges that arise for us.

Ultimately, reunions are about healing, and for Kimberly Nelson meeting her sister was a seminal event in her life. When her sister first arrived, she says, "It was both scary and wonderful. I was shaking from head to foot and wondered if I was ever going to calm down." Her sister was more than willing to pace herself with Kimberly and even joined her at a support meeting and graciously answered everyone's questions. She stayed with Kimberly and her family for many days, and Kimberly said that although she desperately wanted to hug her and tell her how much she meant to her, she was unable to break through her own fear and her sister's natural reserve. As the day of her departure grew near, she and Kimberly went shopping together at the mall:

> She told me that she wanted us to buy something very special and personal for each other, and it would be our way of never separating again. We went to a jewelry store and she bought us two heart necklaces. I was shaking so much I couldn't put mine on, so she said, "It appears my little sister is so nervous that she can't even dress herself, so I'm going to put this on for her." And I just felt so loved and so wonderful, like a child. This was a turning point. When she left and returned home, I felt terrible. The night before her departure, I hugged and hugged her, but I still didn't tell her that I loved her. I spent the next three nights in the bed she had slept in, and I cried and cried. It had just been my time with my sister. The first birth relative I had ever met.

Not long after her sister's visit, Kimberly and her family traveled to Canada to the small town where she had been born and where she had been confined to a notoriously negligent and corrupt maternity home. She, and all her siblings with her, participated in a memorial weekend honoring the survivors of the home. It was the first time she met her three brothers, and she was immediately overcome by their warmth and love for her.

When Kimberly returned from Canada, many of her friends and family expected her to be riding high from her experience, but instead she crashed from the emotional overload as soon as she reached home. Like many adoptees, she was overjoyed to connect with her birth family, but she also needed time to grieve and to heal the loss of so many years. She had the additional trauma of learning about the home that had mistreated her and so many other babies, and about the lies her adoptive parents told her. "It's so hard to integrate it all," she says. "I feel like a hand in a glove in my newfound family. I fit so wonderfully. When I first met them, I thought we had nothing in common but our blood. I now know that isn't true. There's a heart connection, and for me it's very strong. As far as my sister is concerned, there are aspects of my experience that I can only discuss with her. She is truly a gift from God. I think we have a great future together."

When Marlou Russell contacted her birth mother, she discovered her suffering from multiple sclerosis and living in a rundown facility. When they met, she was in a wheelchair and her entire right side was paralyzed. "You couldn't understand what she was saying," says Marlou, "because her throat was affected by the MS. A year and a half after our reunion, she moved into a nicer facility, was walking with a cane, her right side had regained feeling, and you can now understand everything she says. The reunion has really helped her to heal physically in miraculous ways." Marlou says her birth mother was sixteen when she was born, and she handled the pregnancy and relinquishment on her own without anyone knowing, and she kept the secret from everyone, except her husband, until the reunion. She says, "I think that over the years she just sort of closed down with her secret. She says that from the moment I called she started getting better. She also finally told all of her brothers and sisters, and they have been really supportive."

The ground is always shifting for families in postreunion relationships, but regardless of the various outcomes, search and reunion help adoptees resolve their inner need to understand who they are and to achieve a sense of wholeness and a measure of self-acceptance that have eluded them no matter how well adjusted they are in their adoptive families. Some even feel that the search and reunion experience is intimately tied to the fundamental spiritual question of one's purpose and place in the world. Father Tom Brosnan says that although he considers that he has just set foot on the road toward making his own peace with himself, the searching experience "has to hit on those spiritual issues, even if people don't come from a religious background." As an adoptee who has searched, he also feels strongly that despite any legal arguments to the contrary, it was "spiritually essential" for him to know the facts about his background.

What Is Rightfully Ours

These other two and I
all found the ones we dreamed.
We found out where they were.
And you will too.

Penny Callan Partridge, from "For Larry,
who just dreamed about his birth family"

The majority of adoptees overwhelmingly believe they should have the right to seek and obtain their birth records. For some adoptees (and birth families) the medical records are essential to preserve life, but although there are provisions in most existing statutes that allow access for "good cause" or for medical emergencies, the time it takes to cut through the red tape often results in tragedy.

Adult adoptees' access to identifying information is currently denied or substantially restricted in all but three states. Records in Alaska and Kansas have never been sealed, and a new law (currently under appeal) was recently passed in Tennessee. Another law recently passed in Ohio grants access to records from 1996 forward. Prior to 1964, records were already open, but records between 1964 and 1996 remain sealed. (The Ohio law also specifies that open adoption exists, and requires agencies to inform prospective birth mothers of that option.) Most of the proposals submitted to state legislatures also allow for access by birth parents under specific conditions. The battle to make available an adult adoptee's records is ongoing in almost every other state, with members of groups on national and grassroots levels fighting for this most basic civil and human right.

The United States sadly lags behind many countries in its continued insistence on closed records. Scotland's records have been open for adult adoptees since 1935, England's since 1975, and other countries from Norway to New Zealand allow adoptees to gather the information they need to piece together the facts of their biological heritage. Fighting to ensure that all *adult* adoptees have equal access to their identifying information is at the heart of the national adoption reform movement, which presumes that knowlege of one's heritage is an inalienable right. Advocates believe that adult adoptees and birth parents should be able to decide for themselves if they want to establish a relationship. They do not, however, suggest that records should be open to the general public or to minors, and no one is suggesting that people should just barge into people's lives. It is equally important for birth parents and adoptees to be considerate of the families they want to meet, and special care should be taken to protect unsuspecting minors in both families.

Adoption reform advocacy groups around the country have joined forces to wage a legislative battle against groups like the National Council for Adoption. Lobbyists for the council are pushing for passage of the Uniform Adoption Act, which would seal records for ninety-nine years, and would in some cases make it a criminal offense for adoptees to contact their birth parents. They and groups including members of the Christian right purport that if records are opened, adoptions will decrease, abortions will increase, and a birth parent's guaranteed right to privacy will be violated. Adoptions are declining for a host of reasons already discussed in this book, none of which have anything to do with opening records. Interestingly, the National Center for Court Statistics shows that adoption rates are actually *higher* in the two states with open records, and abortions are not statistically greater. In Great Britain, where records have been open for over a decade, there is also no evidence of greater numbers of abortions. If anything, the rate has *decreased*.

Efforts by conservative forces wanting to maintain sealed records rely substantially on scare tactics in the court of public opinion. Their unsubstantiated arguments suggesting that breaking the promise of confidentiality to birth parents will encourage women to abort or abandon their babies are intended to introduce fear in the public mind. To the extent they can reach a poorly informed mass audience, they can in fact influence public opinion with well-calculated sound bites. Any implied threat to "family values" is sure to win supporters in this highly politicized climate.

When birth parents relinquish a child, they sign no documents ensuring their privacy. That so-called guarantee or expectation of confidentiality was, if anything, forced on birth parents of my generation. Adoptees had no involvement in the adoption plan, and they claim records were sealed without their consent. The current president of the American Adoption Congress, adoptive mother Jane Nast, wrote an opposing view to a *USA TODAY* editorial entitled "Sealed Adoption Records Protect Everyone's Privacy," which supports the adoptees' position that their rights are being violated: "Adoptees had no say in the decision-making process of their adoptions. Part of protecting their rights is honoring their need to know the names they were given at birth, their ethnic and religious backgrounds, updated medical history of their birth families and whatever else is available to them in the records or through contact with their families." The confidentiality argument for maintaining sealed records has thus far been shown to have no acceptable basis under Constitutional law, and neither has it succeeded under general contract law. Adoption professionals also largely support adoptees seeking access to identifying information, and statistical surveys of triad members indicate that the majority of all members, including adoptive parents, favor making the records available.

One particularly vocal adoptee advocacy organization on the adoption reform scene, Bastard Nation, is fighting for adoptees to have access to birth records and accompanying identifying information. Bastard Nation grew from a grassroots, Internet-based group to become a national organization, and since its official debut on January 3, 1997, it has gained a reputation for bold and attention-grabbing tactics. Cofounder of the group and outspoken open-records proponent Damsel Plum told the *San Francisco Chronicle* that "our organization has a shocking name, but if you don't shock people into really thinking about what's going on, they're just going to sit back and not ask any questions." Sealed records did not stand in the way of Plum finding her birth parents, who attended her wedding along with her adoptive parents.

Bastard Nation has focused its efforts on such high-profile events as staging a peaceful black-tie rally at the 1997 Academy Awards to take advantage of the popularity of Mike Leigh's film *Secrets and Lies* to draw attention to the campaign for open records, and to point out that, unlike in England where the film was shot, adoptees across America do not have the right to see their birth records when they turn eighteen. In addition, they help sponsor Reg Day, an event born on the Internet by adoptees and birth parents with the goal of having everyone register with the no-cost, nonprofit Soundex (ISSR) registry. One coordinator of the November 16, 1996, event reported that triad members at over forty-one sites in sixteen states observed the second annual Reg Day.

Adoptee Pam Hasegawa, who continues her valiant search for information about her birth family, feels hurt and abused by the system, which questions her right to know who she is. She says, "If someone wants to push me over the edge, all they have to do is say, 'What right do you have?' That questions brings up in my heart and mind all the anger and frustration I had to bury when I was first searching. People would say to me, 'What right do you have to your birth certificate?' or 'What right do you have to your court papers?'" In addition to proceeding with her personal search, Pam tirelessly lobbies the New Jersey legislature to open the records and is hopeful that a law will soon be enacted. Though she knows she may never succeed in her own search, she can help change the system for others.

* * *

Putting the Pieces Together

Who sees Me in all,
And sees all in Me,
For him I am not lost,
And he is not lost for Me

Bhagavad Gita

While the debate over access to adoption records continues, Andrew and I continue our reunion journey. We may not know what our future holds, but we move forward, placing one foot in front of the other, each of us respecting and caring for the other. We both took the paths that life laid before us, and coming together again is a new and wonderful twist in our individual lives. Katherine's and Bill's experiences are no less a part of the journey. Their own account of their feelings about Andrew's search and reunion, as well as the stories of other adoptive parents, will complete the chronicle of adoption I have sought to relate in this book.

NINE

WHAT'S TO COME IS STILL UNSURE

Search, Reunion, and Adoptive Parents

Making Room in Our Hearts

It all comes down to trust—trust in the bonds that
time and love and common experience make.

Jean A. S. Strauss, *Birthright*

JUST WHEN WE think all the ghosts have been exorcised and that life will proceed relatively smoothly, something comes along to throw us off balance. Like relinquishment itself, reunions are notorious for upsetting the equilibrium in the lives of triad members, and this can be especially true for adoptive parents. They are not the ones who search, they cannot go looking for the child they never had, and many are left feeling betrayed, abandoned, and confused when an adoptee and birth parent reunite. Although, in principle, both Katherine and Bill supported Andrew's efforts to find me, they had very different reactions to the actual experience, and they generously offer in these pages a candid recollection of their concerns, questions, and personal feelings regarding his search and reunion with me.

Katherine had gladly helped Andrew get his nonidentifying information from Spence-Chapin and had even volunteered to get forms to register him with some private search lists, but she had never really prepared herself emotionally for the possibility of Andrew actually searching for and finding me. When Andrew told her of his plans, her first thoughts were, "Now wait a second. I don't know if I think this is really so great. It's funny when reality hits, and all of a sudden the things I was so supportive of seemed like less than a great idea. I felt that especially when Andrew was going to meet you."

Katherine never tried to dissuade Andrew from his involvement with me because she sensed how fundamentally important it was to him. She was not comfortable with the reunion at first, but as his mother, she knew instinctively what was best for him. When Andrew telephoned to tell her that he and I had set a time for our first meeting, she says, "I was very nervous and felt very threatened. I didn't really tell Andrew how I was feeling, but I did talk to a few friends about how afraid I was. One of my biggest fears was that he would really like you, and although I knew my relationship with him was good, I didn't want to share him. I kept thinking, 'Now we're going to have to share Christmas and Thanksgiving with her each year. She's going to become part of this family.' And I wasn't happy with that."

Now that I have had a chance to speak with other adoptive mothers, I understand that Katherine's initial reaction was completely normal and even typical. It is natural for adoptive parents to be fearful in the early stages of search and reunion, and those feelings need to be acknowledged and respected. Adoptive mothers have particular difficulty accepting the biological mother. Bill, on the other hand, was more comfortable with the whole idea of reunion. Perhaps, as a father, he did not feel threatened by "another mother" coming on the scene. When I spoke with him, he enthusiastically began to tell me about how Andrew had disclosed that he was looking for me:

> It's quite a wonderful story. Andrew and I have a semiregular birthday and Christmas ritual where we go over to Brooks Brothers in New York City and find him a new sports jacket and a pair of slacks. It was fun to be there once again with him and with Chloe helping to pick out something for him. As we were leaving the store, he said, "Dad, aren't we near the public library?" I said yes and made some joke about how pleased I was that he was interested in going to the library, because he never seemed that keen when he was in college. He let me know then that he had something serious to tell me, and that basically led to him

informing me that he was looking for his birth records. I was surprised at that moment, but I had prepared myself for this. I had thought about it a great deal. I was immediately supportive. I always knew I must support my sons in this search, and I had thought about it for several years. It was just a surprise to hear about it as we were coming off a fun experience that had become a habit of buying Andrew a new set of duds. . . . He had done all the preliminary leg work before telling me.

When adoptees inform their adoptive parents that they are planning to search, they are in effect asking for their blessing. Adoptees are saying that they have faith in the relationship and that they love and trust their adoptive parents enough to share this most intimate journey with them. Bill had practical concerns about his son's search, and about whether Andrew would be prepared for what he might find, but that did not sway his feeling that the search was important:

"I felt that for my boys to be truly healthy people, in the final analysis they would have to conduct this search. I felt that if I had been adopted, I would have had to do it. I had talked by then to a number of people who had been adopted many years before Andrew who were never able to complete their search, and they were very troubled by it . . . and so I knew that I would be supportive."

Bill helped Andrew and Chloe for a while as they flipped through the records at the library, but he soon realized they did not really need him. When they found the record of Andrew's birth, Bill says it meant a lot to all of them that I had given Andrew a name:

> It was very significant, because I'd seen that first day at the library that a great many of the records referred to "Anonymous Baby" or "Anonymous Baby Smith" or "Jones." Seeing this very specific name was very moving. It told us there was a serious person involved who probably someday wanted to be found. It was probably impossible for you to have been thinking that as you gave him a real name on his birth record, but these many years later, we took it as very good news, and we were reassured that we would find you somehow.

When just a few weeks later Andrew came to meet me, he was consciously or unconsciously beginning the voyage toward extending his family boundaries. Bill told me that he has a very distinct memory of Andrew leaving for our first meeting:

> I think he was excited when he left the house, and I think that he was perplexed, as he returned . . . in the sense that obviously he too had his own sea of imagination of who you might be and what you might be like. At the same time, he seemed very content and had a certain peace of mind. He had done something that obviously he had been thinking about for some time. I think Chloe was very supportive of him and probably helped move him forward when he wanted to stop. She grew up in a medical family, and she would have known the significance of the genetic contribution, and naturally would have wanted to know what she could know about her own child.

Andrew is by nature and design a private person who does not share personal experiences freely. Bill remembers that he was careful not to pry too deeply into Andrew's feelings when he got home. He was very anxious though to meet me himself—the next day if possible, to give me a hug that he felt had been a long time coming:

> Andrew never told me anything about the specifics of your conversation that night. I didn't ask because I felt it was his experience and he should savor it and think about it and feel it before he ever had to talk to anybody about it. I was very respectful of his reactions and his feelings. But that then started three years of waiting, which I had never anticipated. It was very frustrating for me to wait several years to meet you, but I waited out of love for Andrew and out of a desire to let him manage this process himself. I also knew he was waiting for his mother to resolve her feelings.

Katherine had much less involvement in Andrew's search than Bill did, partly, she thinks, because he was being protective of her. Sensing her ambivalence and fear, Andrew did not share much with Katherine about having met me or about how our relationship was progressing. "It is very difficult," writes Betty Jean Lifton in *Journey of the Adopted Self*, "for adoptees to respond to a birth mother when their adoptive parents feel threatened. They move into a protective mode—especially some boys, who have a hard time dealing with emotional conflict." Andrew told me that his mother might never want to meet me, and I know he was careful not to tell her about our early visits. At some point, he said Katherine was willing for me to write to her. I had been waiting for an opportunity to tell her how thankful I was that Andrew had such loving parents, and I let her know in the letter that I had no intention of disrupting their family or of trying to take over Andrew's affection from her. In retrospect, I can see that simply being more tangibly in the picture could feel disruptive. Although Katherine remembers my letter as being "very nice," she says she just was not ready to meet me:

"I think, looking back on it, that it was a wise decision on my part, because I needed to see where your relationship with Andrew went and to feel less threatened about the whole thing. Your reunion also coincided with a time in my life when I was feeling a little insecure myself. I had just moved from the city to the country and was feeling fragile and unsure about my own abilities. I needed time to settle into this new place and phase of my life."

Not surprisingly, there were times when Katherine was resentful of my involvement in Andrew's and Chloe's lives. At one point, she remembers, "I felt really angry because I thought you were coming on really strong and wanted to see him all the time. And I remember thinking to myself, 'God, who does she think she is?' I saw it as all of a sudden you came into his life and then boom. When I would talk with Andrew and Chloe about you, to me, it felt like you were taking over."

It was difficult for me to hear Katherine's words, especially since I felt I had tried very hard to pace myself and to be sensitive to her, even though I knew she did not want to meet me. I appreciated how difficult it must be for her, and I tried to keep a healthy perspective on her inability to accept me. Just as Katherine intellectually accepted Andrew's need to search, I intellectually accepted that she had a legitimate right to keep her distance. The reunion, after all, was about Andrew and me. I said I could live with her choice not to meet me, although in my heart I hoped she would change her mind. I even defended her to others around me who sometimes voiced their frustration for me. It was tough, too, because I was so prepared to judge myself harshly and to agree that I had no right to be involved in Andrew's life. I *thought* I was proceeding very slowly and had been careful not to press for more than anyone was comfortable with. On the other hand, I could not help my eagerness in responding to any overture to spend some time with Andrew.

It is always interesting to hear the other side of a story, especially one where you have played a major role, and I understand how from Katherine's standpoint everything was happening too fast. Even Bill has commented that while the feedback he got from Andrew was positive about his experience of getting to know me, the relationship was progressing more quickly than he had anticipated.

Waiting to see where our reunion would lead gave Katherine a chance to absorb and consider everything that was happening in her and Andrew's lives. After several years of uncertainty, she decided that she was ready to meet me:

> All of a sudden, I just said to myself, "This is kind of silly." And I knew that I really would like to meet you. Andrew and Chloe both assured me that I would really like you and that we had so much in common. When we actually made our plan to meet, I was very nervous, as no doubt you were, too, but I think we both felt really good about it. We just seemed to click. It was like having made a new friend. I saw that you were just a regular person who happened to be Andrew's birth mother. I feel very comfortable with the whole situation right now, and that's nice for all of us.

As we talked, I felt that we were linking pieces of a lifelong puzzle together, from the schism that occurred in my life when I relinquished Andrew to the closing of an aching gap in Katherine's understanding about how that came to pass. She says that hearing about my experience helped her understand what I went through:

> It was very helpful for me to understand the whole process when we talked about it. I now understand why you did what you did, whereas when Andrew was young, so often I would think, "Oh, how could anybody have done that? I never would have been able to give up a baby." But you know, you do understand as you get older and do appreciate the situations people are in, and I came to understand how terribly difficult it was for you. After our meeting, I would try to put myself in your shoes, and I thought if I had had to do the same thing I would certainly want to find out where my baby was and what kind of life he was leading. I gained a perspective that made the whole situation much easier to handle.

In addition, when a close friend's daughter got pregnant and carried her baby to term, Katherine unexpectedly gained an even deeper understanding of how birth families struggle with the decision to relinquish:

> I really saw it from the other side, because the father and mother decided to relinquish the child after going through a lot of anguish. At

one point the mother was going to keep the child, and everyone became very emotional about how she was going to manage to take care of the baby. Most of us felt, intellectually, that the best thing for the baby was for him to be adopted because no one could figure out how she was going to raise him, and the father really didn't want the responsibility. Once all of us actually saw the baby, it became that much harder to imagine him leaving her family. The baby went into foster care until she made her decision. I followed what was happening very closely and felt a lot of empathy for the birth mother.

Katherine was also able to empathize with the birth mother because it brought to mind her own memories of past losses. Birth parents and adoptive parents can share an understanding of one another's loss because they have both grieved and mourned for a child they could not have—or keep. Although the perspective is different, the feelings of loss are similar. At the time of search and reunion, it can be healing to consider one another's experience of past hurts.

I did not meet Bill any sooner than I met Katherine, but he says he was always happy to hear from Andrew and Chloe that our relationship was growing. He feels the reunion has been greater than he had ever hoped. He also believes that Emma's birth truly cemented all the intergenerational bonds, and that her existence, and now baby William's, have brought everyone together:

> The feedback that I got from Andrew and Chloe told me that there was a very loving person who wanted not only to give them love, but also to share presents and to find opportunities to be supportive in ways that Andrew could accept. I think that at the end of the day, Andrew was very careful in what he told me. He didn't ever want to hurt my feelings or cause me to feel like I was in some kind of different position in his life or in my relationship with him. You know we talk about this very lovable man, but we don't often talk about this sensitive, careful side of him that is very, very protective of the people he loves. He never wants to do anything that diminishes his sense of responsibility to them.

I have no way of predicting where my relationships with Bill and Katherine will lead, but I can only feel optimistic that we will continue to grow closer with time. We are still figuring out who we are to each other, and I suppose in some ways we are not unlike new in-laws who are tentative with each other at first but whose love for their children connects them. There is no doubt that families living in reunion are dealing with complex emotional circumstances, and once again there is no charted course. Ronny Diamond, the director of Post-Adoption Services at Spence-Chapin, says "I used to think stepfamilies were one of the most complicated family forms, and they are, but now I think reunions are far more complicated."

Though Katherine first worried about my involvement in family gatherings, she has recently indicated that is no longer a problem for her, and I did get together with Bill and Chloe's family right after William was born. We may not spend Thanksgiving or Christmas together anytime soon, but that is truly not an issue, and I understand and welcome the spirit of her message. Every family has its own style, and Andrew likes thinking of us as different families. The degree of "togetherness" we have is not a yardstick for how we are doing.

Coping with Our Worst Fears

Emotion is the chief source of all becoming conscious.
There can be no transforming of darkness into light
and of apathy into movement without emotion.

Carl Gustav Jung

The words "I want to search for my birth parents" are anticipated with dread by many adoptive parents. Even though parents readily tell their children about adoption, they are not always prepared for them to want to search. This is especially true of those parents of my generation who raised their children in completely closed adoptions and for whom the prospect of reunion did not exist at the time they adopted. If their children want to search, they often feel like they have failed as parents. Other adoptive parents view search and reunion as acts of betrayal because they cannot understand how their child or children could love two sets of parents. If they manage to accept intellectually that it is somehow possible, the reality of reunion can be overwhelming emotionally. In her article "The Fears of Knowing," adoptive mother Joyce Greer says that she became increasingly frightened of losing her daughter as she grew closer to her birth mother. She says, "The thought absolutely terrified me. For a while, I could not control my jealousy. I pictured having to share my beautiful child with someone else whom I didn't know. But this 'someone else' had a connection to her that I could never have—the physical resemblance, the shared personality traits and family heredity. I could not compete with this. There was nothing I could do about it."

For decades adoption professionals counseled adoptive parents that they were the "real" parents of their adopted children, and that if their children did not know anything about their birth family, they would feel more like *theirs*. "Accepting and dealing with the birthfamily," writes Jean A. S. Strauss in *Birthright*, "means confronting a reality the adoptive parents have long been encouraged to ignore—this child is not completely their own." Now, when the children are grown, search and reunion all too readily remind them of the period before their child entered their lives when they struggled with infertility and loss. In *Thoughts to Consider for Newly Searching Adoptees*, social worker and birth mother Carole J. Anderson writes, "Most adoptive parents know why they are who they are, but the sorrow of knowing that their genetic line stops with them can make it hard for some to see why the children they adopted need to know what came before adoption." Their own pain can interfere with their ability to understand and accept openheartedly what is going on for their children.

Prospective adoptive parents coming into adoption today are counseled to acknowledge their children's biological heritage, and if they are in fully disclosed and open adoptions, they are dealing from day one with any issues regarding their role as parents and the place birth parents have in their family. Instead of having fantasies of what they may be like, they also know the birth parents as real people. Nevertheless, the majority of adoptions are still closed or only semiopen, and if the parents have not had the benefit of good pre- and postadoption counseling, they are in the same boat emotionally with regard to search and reunion as the parents of previous generations, except that if they adopted domestically they know that reunion is on the horizon. Even for parents of international children, the prospect of search and reunion is not out of the question. The fear is the same for everyone and is simply confronted at different stages, depending on the time of placement and the type of adoption.

Kimberly Nelson felt like a failure as a mother because her daughter wanted to find her birth mother. When Kimberly was adopted, search was unheard of. It was also not an issue when she adopted her two children. She says that she now knows that being so closed herself to any mention of birth parents made her son feel abnormal for wondering about his own. "I did him a great disservice that I didn't even realize at the time. Fortunately, my kids spoke to each other about their concerns and curiosity and were their own built-in support systems."

It is not surprising that when her daughter, Janet, first told her she was going to search, Kimberly was terrified and thought her daughter was walking out on her life. She was so certain a search would mean the "end of her baby" that she denied having any information about her birth parents.

> I told her you just don't know what you might find or what the people would be like. I was giving her all the cons and none of the pros because I felt like such a failure as a mother. I told her I didn't have the answers to her questions, but I really did. After we hung up, I told my husband everything and he told me I had to call her back and tell her all that I knew. He said we couldn't live with me lying to her, and he was right. So, I called her back, told her everything I knew, and we cried a lot about it. She told me she loved me and would protect herself. After Janet found her birth mom, I was very upset and I think she knew it. She kept trying to reassure me, but now I understand there is no explanation good enough to erase the fear. It is a fear that an adoptive parent always has, even though we're not talking about stealing an infant from a crib. Even when they're adults, there is this fear. It never goes away.

Perhaps most frightening to adoptive parents is the looming question of whether they will now be forsaken, replaced by the child's birth parents who were not there to raise the child. Jack Steadman was apprehensive about his teenage son's reunion with his birth mother, but he knew that it was something that needed to happen in order for them to get on with their lives. He says, "Caleb was calling me the entire time he was visiting his birth mom to make sure that I was okay. He was more worried about me than he was about himself. And, of course, I had been afraid that once he met her, he would have some big revelation, that if only he had been with her, then everything in his life would have been perfect. You can imagine the thoughts that went through my mind that I would never see him again." For Jack and Caleb, the reunion not only answered many lingering questions in both their minds but actually brought them closer together as father and son. Experience has now shown that even when adoptees develop close ties with their birth mother or father, the love they may feel for them does not diminish their love for their adoptive parents. Simply put, there is love enough for everyone in open relationships.

Cynthia Beals remembers that when her son first wanted to search for his birth mother, she felt intimidated. "Our relationship wasn't real secure at the time," she recalls, "and it wasn't a healthy time in either of our lives. My son was a very rebellious teenager." Cynthia decided to learn more about search and reunion, and she discovered that adoptive parents who are comfortable and confident in their relationship with their children have less of a problem with them finding their birth parents. Cynthia's relationship with her son was actually strengthened by him learning more about his birth mother. Although he chose not to contact her, he learned that she was only fifteen when he was born, and that answered for him the nagging question about why he was relinquished and helped him understand that he was not really abandoned. He was much happier afterward and more at ease in his adoptive home.

Today, many adoption social workers try to deemphasize the "us" and "them" mentality that can make adversaries of triad members. Instead they attempt to foster a working relationship between the two sets of parents. Adoptive mother and social worker Eleanor Oakley says that what she tries to convey to adoptive parents is the importance of separating their needs from their child's. "I think a key piece to searching," she says, "is realizing your child's need to do this. You have to ask yourself as a parent, 'Can I take risks because my child needs to do this?' I think when you're a parent, whether biological or adoptive, you're doing this all the time."

It is no easy task for adoptive parents to work through the raw and often overwhelming emotions that search and reunion pose for them. More attention is being given to the concerns of adoptive parents, and professionals are beginning to address the serious question of how they can help parents deal with their fears and adjust to the profound changes in their family life. Once adoptive parents understand themselves that their child's need to search is not about trying to find *real* or *better* parents, they are able to assume more comfortably their regular role as Mom and Dad and to be there for their children, as always.

How to Give of Ourselves

> The mind of man is capable of anything—because everything is in it, all the past as well as all the future.
>
> Joseph Conrad

In their workshop at the 1997 AAC Conference in Dallas, Texas, Sharon Kaplan Roszia and Dee Davis offered some helpful advice for adoptive parents dealing with search and reunion. One important recommendation encourages adoptive parents to work through their fears without encumbering their children. If they can spare their children the additional stress of their apprehension, adoptees have an easier time sorting out their own emotions during search and reunion. This is not to say that the involved parties should not discuss how they are feeling, but if adoptive parents, like birth parents, can find another outlet like therapy or a support group, they will be better able to handle the experience themselves and will not place undue stress on their children, who are always trying to balance their concern for their adoptive family with their need to search.

Kimberly Nelson went to a support group right after her daughter started her search. As an adoptee who had repressed any inkling of a desire to know more about her own birth family, she had a particularly difficult time working through her feelings. She says, "I went to a support group that really represented each side of the triad, and I got a chance to meet birth mothers, adoptive parents, and adoptees. Because I wear two hats, my head and my heart were always at war with each other." Her daughter's reunion and her work in the support group helped her accept that searching was normal.

As we have seen, although reunions often begin as private affairs between adoptee and birth parent, adoptive parents influence the whole process—even if they do not know their child is searching. Once there is a reunion, parents deal with their own questions about whether or not they want to meet the birth parent. Although Katherine needed to keep a safe distance, Bill was eager to meet me immediately but had to wait until Andrew was ready. Betty Jean Lifton says in *Journey of the Adopted Self* that it can be very hard for some adoptive parents to remain on the outside. They want to meet the birth mother immediately and can feel rejected if they are not included in the reunion from the start. Eleanor Oakley often has to remind herself that her daughter's search is her own. "I found myself wanting to get in there and make things happen," she says. "I wanted to get the answers for her and present it to her, but I couldn't do that. I had to be supportive of her, but not do it for her. It had to be her timetable."

In the hope of averting a search, some adoptive parents warn their children that searching for birth parents can be dangerous and unrewarding. In addition to any fears they have for themselves, they are genuinely worried for their children and do not want to see them hurt. We know there are no

guarantees about the outcome of search. Some situations are richly rewarding; others are tragic; some are just fraught. Either way, instead of trying to
prevent a search, adoptive parents have an opportunity to help their adult
children cope with the real situations and people they find in reunion. They
can constructively help prepare their children as well as themselves for
whatever they may encounter, and in so doing help them feel secure enough
to face any outcome. Bill was concerned that I might not be financially self-
sufficient. He wanted Andrew to be prepared to face that possibility, but he
had no desire to deter him from his endeavor.

Just because adult adoptees may not talk to their parents about their
desire to search does not mean they are not interested in knowing more.
Not asking questions is their way of protecting their parents. Parents who
try to discourage questions in the hope that they can make the birth parents
disappear may effectively discourage or stall a search indefinitely. When
adoptees wait until their adoptive parents die, they run a greater risk of
finding that their birth parents are also deceased. Adoptive parents like
Katherine and Bill, who talk to their children honestly about their birth parents and share what they know, have learned from their experience that
they will never lose their children. Standing by their children shows them
once again that they can be counted on.

Adoptive parents who have another connection to adoption—either
through their own experience, or through family or friends—are often more
attuned to the realities of adoption and have a better perspective of search
and reunion. Being a birth mother helped Cynthia Beals understand what
her own children might be wondering when they had questions about their
birth mothers. As an adoptive parent, she also feared losing her children if
they searched. She came to understand, however, that most children "are
loyal to their parents, even abused children." She says, "I know the daughter I relinquished is very loyal to her adoptive parents and very conscious of
their feelings. I know that my children are too. They were very concerned
about our feelings and about expressing an interest in finding their birth
families, because they thought it would hurt us." Once her older son
searched for and located his birth mother, Cynthia decided it was time to
tell her children about her daughter. Her reunion with her daughter
prompted her younger son then to express an interest in searching. "He
knows he has our support," she says, "and he knows I am not intimidated,
and that our relationship won't change because of him searching. Our love
for him won't change, or his for us."

Support for Search and Reunion

> You are the bows from which your children as living
> arrows are sent forth.
>
> Kahlil Gibran, *The Prophet*

Search and reunion are a watershed experience for an adoptive family. As we have seen, adoptees generally choose to search during or after a significant life change. A wedding or a new baby offers families an opportunity to rejoice together. Likewise, according to Marlou Russell in *Adoption Wisdom*, "The time of search and reunion can also be an opportunity for the adoptive family to come together around a topic that is important to all family members. Embracing the inevitable—that an adoptee has two families—can lead to closer relationships for everyone." Adoptive parents who readily accept the need for their children to discover the missing pieces to their individual puzzles tend to be secure and at the same time flexible in relationship to each other. Like Bill, they welcome, and even celebrate, the possibility of widening the circle of love for their child.

Susan and Alexandra Burton have always had a close mother/daughter relationship, and it only seemed logical to Susan that Alexandra would one day want to find her birth mother:

> I never had a problem empathizing with Alexandra. Having all those unanswered questions would probably drive me crazy and be intriguing at the same time. I felt that, particularly as a woman, as Alexandra approached child-bearing age, not knowing her genetic history would certainly make her uncomfortable. When she expressed a desire to search just before her eighteenth birthday, I encouraged her to act on it. When she decided to go forward, I got my hands on as much material as I could to understand more about the process. Eventually, I contacted a support group that was close to us and they were very helpful and encouraging. They also gave us the name of the private investigator who found Alexandra's birth mother. He was very kind and sensitive throughout the process, and we really learned an enormous amount about searching from him.

For some, sharing the search experience can be very rewarding—as long as limits are set and everyone is comfortable with the process. Eleanor Oakley believes that the positive aspects of her relationship with her daughter have been enhanced since her daughter began looking for her birth mother. Eleanor welcomes the fact that her daughter is searching and looks forward to meeting her birth mother. She says, "I know that what I have with my daughter is truly out of a lifetime of parenting." She says, "I'm very pleased that we have such a wonderful rapport, where she feels at ease telling me every time she's done something, what happened, what didn't happen, what she's thinking of doing, how long it took to do something, and what her birth mother might say. The hardest part for me, as a mother, is that I don't want her to be hurt. The thought of her being rejected truly pains me."

Susan Burton also feared the possibility that Alexandra might be rejected. The private investigator they had hired found Alexandra's birth mother within the course of a weekend. "He asked me how he should proceed after he found her," Susan recalls. "I told him he had to call and ask her if she wanted to be approached and make 100 percent sure that she is certain she is the right woman we're looking for. I didn't want Alexandra having the door slammed in her face. We had discussed this possibility and about respecting her birth mother's privacy. We didn't know what she had done with the rest of her life. If she wasn't ready to be approached, no matter how hurtful that was, we would respect that. Luckily, for all of us, she was." According to Susan, losing her daughter was never a concern, but protecting her was of primary importance. "I was worried," she says, "that she would find something she couldn't deal with and that she might discover something she didn't like."

For some adoptive parents, it is a relief to seek answers that might explain or possibly alleviate an adoptee's disruptive behavior. Emily and Liam Murphy adopted their daughter Sarah when she was eight months old and never concealed from her the fact that she was adopted. Nevertheless, as soon as Sarah understood what it meant to be adopted, she became aggressively hostile. "She felt that she had been thrown away and rejected," recalls Emily. "She always had very low self-esteem. We tried many things to bolster her self-image, but when Sarah was seven or eight she decided to run away from home and go back where she came from." Sarah eventually came to understand why she was adopted, but she still did not accept it for years. During adolescence, she was riddled with self-doubt and engaged in a host of self-destructive activities. Emily says, "When she was fourteen she was giving us a lot of trouble about where she came from and always saying, 'You're not my parents.' When she got angry at us, she could be very cruel."

From fourteen to twenty-three, Sarah and her adoptive parents struggled to establish some harmony in their home. "We always told Sarah she wasn't thrown away," says Emily, "but that she was given away with great difficulty, and that it was a difficult decision for her birth mother. We tried to cast things in a positive light, but she always had this nagging insecurity." Finally, when Sarah reached her early twenties, she decided to search for her birth mother. Emily and Liam were supportive from the start, feeling it was necessary for her to search, and never felt threatened, although they did tell Sarah she had to be prepared for what she might find, even if it turned out not to be very pleasant for her. They said even if she found someone who wanted nothing to do with her or someone living in dire circumstances, they would always help her. "We made the search a positive goal in her life and were clear with her that it was her decision," remarks Liam. "She really did most of the work on her own and probably would have done it without our help. It would have made life much more difficult for everybody if we had made it difficult for Sarah. If we had been hostile toward the idea, we would have been the bad guys again in her mind."

Among the suggestions put forth by Roszia and Davis in the Dallas conference was the recommendation to adoptive parents to offer support but to realize that the responsibility of search and reunion belongs to the adoptee. Emily and Liam were clear that they would never stand in Sarah's way, but they also knew they could not search for her. "We wanted her to find out," says Emily, "but she had to take the responsibility, not us. We told her that whenever she was ready, we could send away for information from different organizations, but she had to take the first step. She watched *Oprah* and all the programs about adoptive parents and birth mothers and reunited people, but it took her a long time to take that step."

Susan Burton tried to take a backseat when it came to Alexandra's reunion, but there were a few instances where she felt it necessary to speak up. Alexandra has two half brothers who her birth mother wanted to bring to the reunion meeting. "I suggested," says Susan, "that the boys not be present at the first meeting because I felt she owed it to herself and Alexandra to meet alone. It turned out to be a good decision."

If the adoptee has involved the adoptive parents in the search and reunion, adoptive parents decide for themselves how much they need or want to be involved, and when. Some, like Katherine, acknowledge their adult child's need to search but then wait and see how things proceed. Others, like Bill, are eager to be in the midst of the reunion but hold back out of respect for their child's need to control the process. The other parents profiled in this chapter have found their own way of adjusting to and relating to the search and reunion, depending on their circumstances and the needs of their children. Once there is a reunion, the family enters yet another phase of their adoption journey.

After Contact Is Made

> If you have form'd a circle to go into,
> Go into it yourself and see how you
>   would do.
>
> William Blake

After an adoptee has made contact with a birth parent, the adoptive parent is often in limbo for a while, waiting to see what happens with the reunion —if it happens at all, or if so, how it works out. It is nerve-wracking for some, thrilling for others. For adoptive parents who had some internal reservations about the potential impact of reunion on the family, discovering that for the most part birth parents are not going to be a destructive force (as eventually Katherine realized about me) is a great relief. Fears of being replaced by another parent are gradually laid to rest, and adoptive parents prepare themselves to engage in new relationships with their children and their birth family.

In the beginning of a reunion, adoptive parents are not sure where they fit or how they should handle the situation. Most adoptees, like Andrew, choose to see their birth parents for the first time alone, but after Sarah Murphy and her birth mother made arrangements to meet, Emily and Liam thought it would be a good idea to drive her to the appointment. "I got all the baby pictures together to show her and to give her a sense of what Sarah's childhood had been like," Emily recalls, "and we bought her a couple dozen roses. I didn't know what we were going to find, but the last thing I worried about was losing my child. I thought this is going to make my life easier. If we had met Denise earlier, I suppose I might have felt more threatened. I also think it would not have been a good thing for Sarah to meet her before she was strong enough emotionally to handle it, as she is now."

The moment Sarah and Emily opened the door to the apartment, Emily was stunned to see that Sarah and her birth mother, Denise, looked exactly alike. Emily stayed for about an hour, making sure that her daughter would be all right, and then left. "At some point I felt it would be okay to leave her there so she and Denise could talk one-on-one and exchange a lot of thoughts and emotions without me there."

It did not take long for Sarah's birth and adoptive parents to become comfortable with each other. Liam remembers feeling like they were all related from the first time they met. About a month after the first meeting, the Murphys hosted Denise and her husband at their home. Emily presented Denise with an album of Sarah's life, from the adoption through to her high school graduation, so that she could have the history she had missed. At Christmas, Denise invited the Murphys over to meet the rest of her family. Emily says, "We all bonded instantly. We all had something in common through Sarah. Denise's father was there, and at one point he said to me, 'You know, I always said before I die, I hope to see my granddaughter.' That made me feel wonderful. I know he carried a lot of guilt, because he pushed his daughter to give Sarah up." Emily continues to feel close to Denise and her family, although they talk less frequently, now that Sarah has an apartment of her own.

Kimberly Nelson did not attend the first meeting between her daughter and her birth mother but was grateful that Janet and her husband came right over after the reunion to talk. "I couldn't believe how happy Janet looked. Her husband, who has always been very supportive of Janet and reassuring to me, told me that she and her birth mother look exactly alike. He said to Janet's birth mother, 'That's you when you were twenty-seven!' He said the meeting between them was wonderful and difficult, and that the women kept talking to each other, staring and not eating a thing."

Kimberly met Janet's birth mother a few months after the initial reunion, and they had an impromptu meeting at Kimberly's house:

> It was the best thing that could have happened. I knew the day would arrive when I would meet her, and I was still afraid that I was going to lose my daughter. When I met Janet's birth mother, we were really frank with each other and I was afraid I said things that might have really hurt her, but she dealt with them beautifully. I said, "You're the person I've been most afraid of meeting for twenty-seven years, and now I'm meeting you and no one has died and it's going to be okay." She was the person I'd feared so very much, running from her like a fugitive for twenty-seven years. I did things in the beginning of the adoption like

unlist my phone number because I was hiding from her. Now that we're
friends, I feel very differently, and I think she's wonderful.

It was painful for Kimberly when Janet spent her twenty-eighth birthday
with her birth mother, and again she felt she was losing her. "But then," she
recalls, "I realized how important it was for them and I kept thinking about
myself and my own birth mother, and wanting it for myself, knowing it
would never happen, and I just had to feel joy for them." Kimberly still feels
insecure and defensive at times, like when Janet invited both her mothers to
her annual Memorial Day picnic. She says, "I told Janet that I knew she
would always have a relationship with her birth mother, and I knew I
couldn't always say no when she wants to bring us together." Kimberly
decided she had to face these inclusive gatherings eventually, and much to
her delight, she had a terrific time.

Even the most supportive and grounded of adoptive parents can have
insecure moments. Susan Burton never doubted the importance of contact
between Alexandra and her birth mother, but when it was time to make the
prearranged phone call, her daughter did not want her mother at her side.
She says, "About thirty minutes later, I was shaking so much I said to
Alexandra's older sister that I couldn't stand it anymore and that I was
going upstairs to see how she was doing. Her sister wouldn't let me do that,
but went herself to check for me. She said, 'She has a smile on her face from
ear to ear, sitting Indian-style on her bed,' and she gave me the thumbs-up
sign. They talked for two hours!" Susan said the only bad moment she had
was when Alexandra came downstairs after the phone call and said that her
birth mother wanted to see the adoption papers. She says, "I guess I turned
white because Alexandra asked me if I had a problem with that. I said 'She
wants you back,' and Alexandra retorted, 'It's a little late for that.'"

When adoptive mother and daughter went out to the Midwest to meet
the birth family together, they enjoyed a warm reception. Susan thinks they
are lovely people, and she feels she established a good relationship with
Alexandra's birth mother. Later that summer they visited again. Susan says,
"I thought Alexandra needed a visit to process her feelings, not just a
reunion, which is so momentous." Susan has maintained an open mind
throughout the five years since Alexandra met her birth mother. As we have
seen, the relationship between birth mother and daughter is running into
some snags now, and Alexandra feels she needs to pull back for a while.
Susan says she thinks Alexandra's birth family is in a hurry to "ingest"

more of Alexandra than she is ready to give. She says, "You can't orchestrate feelings, you can't wave a magic wand and make instant daughter, instant mom, instant family. It takes time." She understands that relationships fluctuate, and that the present ambiguity her daughter feels is an inevitable part of the process, and she has the rare sensitivity and insight required to guide her daughter through the intricacies of a lifelong relationship with her birth family without letting anxiety or fear hinder her judgment:

> I'm now counseling Alexandra to realize that although she and Linda have a unique relationship, it is going to be subject to the dynamics of a changing relationship, and it doesn't always have to be perfect or horrific. It can be a mix of both. They don't have to adore each other, and they can certainly be annoyed at one another at times. I told Alexandra that personally, I was very grateful that her birth mother was not a dreadful person, that she was open and receptive to her, and that she had enough integrity to make it as comfortable as possible for us when we went out to visit. She's very open when she introduces Alexandra, and maybe Alexandra needs to keep her distance until she's more comfortable with her birth family again. I told her that I understood why all her birth relatives were begging for more of her, she's a terrific person.

Adoptive parents are delighted when discernible and positive changes in attitude and outlook develop as a result of a reunion. Susan Burton definitely sees a change for the better in her now "twenty-something" daughter. "I'm so glad for Alexandra because in subtle ways you can see that she is so much more centered now that she's met her birth mother. She is now more grounded and more comfortable with herself. She also knows more about her maternal family than most people I know."

Liam Murphy also feels the reunion has helped his daughter deal with her life more constructively. "Our relationship with Sarah hasn't changed much since the reunion," he says, "except that she's not as hostile as she was. That changed radically, a complete turnaround. I can see she needed to find her birth mother." Emily sees that "Sarah is a lot better. She's not all there yet, but she's taking her time putting her life in order, structuring it along the lines she wants it to go. We've seen tremendous strides in the last four years."

Kimberly Nelson found that her daughter changed tremendously since her reunion. "She is peaceful, not restless, happy beyond belief; she's complete and whole. Her life is in a perfect place right now, and I see her story as one of encouragement. It certainly was for me. Recently she told me that her reunion with her birth mother has now gone from the reunion stage to the relationship stage. Janet said she was always afraid that her birth mother would leave her again, but now she has received a letter from her vowing that she will always love her and never leave her. It's a beautiful thing."

When they are willing to open themselves to look into the biological connections of their children, adoptive parents find that they too have questions they need answered. For Emily Murphy, meeting her daughter's birth mother finally laid to rest the issue of why Sarah was so high-strung and nervous all the time. Her birth mother was exactly the same way. "When you put them together," she says, "there's no mistaking they're related. They talk very, very fast. Sarah's a little more rough-edged, but the genetics are definitely from Denise. Their reunion also made me realize how much she takes from me. She gets her approach to life from me, and I hope we have passed on our values to her, like the importance of family."

Going public with their story in a workshop sponsored by Spence-Chapin, called Finding Your Biological Roots, enabled the Murphys to explore on a new level what search and reunion meant to them as a family:

> We were really put through the ringer there, but Sarah had a good handle on it. At one point, somebody asked her what her relationship to Denise was. She said, "My mom is my mom, the woman who raised me. Denise is more like a big sister." That meant a lot to me. We really felt the panel offered closure for everyone. The place was jammed with triad members, and people were so thrilled by what we had to say. We felt really good that we had done it, but it was very emotionally draining. A lot of the audience was crying by the end.

A reception was held after the panel discussion, and Emily says Sarah and Denise snuck upstairs during the party to find the blue couch where Denise had sat in the last photograph she had of her and Sarah before she relinquished. "They never found the couch," Emily says, "but to them it really was closing the circle and was very therapeutic. A young adopted girl was there whose adoptive parents didn't know she had come. She really wanted to find her birth parents but didn't want to hurt her adoptive parents. Sarah didn't have to worry about that at all."

The people represented in this chapter have stories to tell that are generally positive. Their adult children have found birth mothers and extended families who have wanted to be found. Of course, many children go on to find birth fathers and presumably have equal or possibly better results. But we know, not all reunions have a fairy tale ending. Even those that are deemed positive are complicated. Adoptive parents are called upon to play a role in every reunion story. Some do it with reserve, others by openly embracing the birth family. In difficult situations, they have an opportunity to offer support and good counsel and to be there to uphold the family and provide safe haven.

Those parents whose children have faced rejection or whose search or reunion has been otherwise painful have the sadness of seeing their children suffer, which no parent wants, and they are naturally protective. When search and reunion meet with tragedy or disappointment, children of any age want to count on their parents being there to help them process their grief and find a way through the pain. Adoptive parents who do not let their own fear get in the way when their children first begin to search are best prepared to offer the support they need when they are in an emotional crisis.

As triad members across the country attempt to redefine their families, more and more are seeking answers that only those who have lived through search and reunion can offer. Triad members want information so they can settle urgent concerns and pressing questions, but acquiring knowledge is difficult when records are sealed and access limited. It is not surprising that adoptive parents initially found the appeal for open records hard to accept. According to the authors of *The Adoption Triangle,* however, "With the passing of time . . . we have found that many adoptive parents are feeling less threatened and realize that the adoptee's quest for genealogical information or an encounter with the birth parents is a personal need which cannot be accurately comprehended by a nonadopted person." When polled, the majority now appear to support their children's need to know, and many have testified before state legislatures in support of opening access to birth records.

Celebrating What We Share

Not what we give, but what we
    share—
For the gift without the giver is bare;
Who gives of himself his alms feeds
    three—
Himself, his hungering neighbor, and
    me.

James Russell Lowell

After emotions have settled and everyone has had a chance to reflect upon the reunion, adoptive and birth families can establish a middle ground that is safe and comfortable. Relationships between adoptive parents and their children resume their basic rhythm and very often grow closer. Often the children prefer to keep their relationship with birth parents separate from their adoptive family as a way of establishing comfortable boundaries for themselves. Depending on how the relationship develops between their children and their birth family, adoptive parents in some way accommodate birth families in their lives. For birth families, reunion with their birth children also settles into a pattern that is comfortable for them and their respective families. Essentially, families get back to living their lives, having made some adjustments and having extended to some extent the parameters of how they view themselves as a family.

Birth and adoptive mothers sometimes discover that they have a special connection. According to Betty Jean Lifton in *Journey of the Adopted Self,* some mothers feel a spiritual closeness for each other, having shared the most precious gift two people can. Both have unique emotions of motherhood that they can share with each other. My feelings for Katherine resonate perfectly with that sentiment. During our first meeting, Katherine commented on how she is more reserved than Bill, who she understood would be quick to embrace me. I told her even then that she was the "Mom" and our relationship would always be different. Regardless of how often we might meet, or what family occasions I attend, we are connected virtually umbilically as two women who share unconditional love for one son, each in our own way. That does not deprive Bill of any of his special and unique gifts as Andrew's father or place any limit on our potential for friendship. It simply honors the undeniable bond between birth mother and adoptive mother.

At the 1997 AAC Conference, birth mother Carol Schaefer and adoptive mother Nancy Verrier presented a talk that highlighted and reinforced the potential of parents working together. They focused on the powerful relationship between adoptive and birth mother and showed how positive it can be for two women to celebrate family and each other through their child.

Schaefer and Verrier also pointed out how the adoption community has managed to adapt to changing times and to absorb new ideas. Families that were once counseled to view their child's other parents as adversaries are now asked to redefine roles and to create a new paradigm through cooperation and mutual understanding. This is true for new adoptive parents who have agreed to an open adoption as well as for parents involved in a reunion. Once adoptive and birth parents begin to communicate, they find there was never a reason to live in fear of each other, and no longer any reason to fear the future.

When adoptive parents open their hearts to include their child's birth family, they are laying the groundwork for generations to come. They are also widening the scope of their child's support network and extending their family resources. Emily Murphy talks fondly of the relationship Sarah had with all her adoptive grandparents while they were alive. "Our parents are all gone now," she says, "so it's nice that Sarah has had the opportunity to bond with another set of grandparents who are really her blood relations. I'm also happy that Denise is younger than Liam or me. We were older than most parents when we adopted Sarah, and it's really nice that if anything should happen to us, she will have someone to turn to."

Emily and Liam have a perspective for their daughter that comes from their wholehearted desire to do what is best for Sarah. They, like Katherine and Bill, and the many other adoptive parents who look into their hearts and let love for their child override their fear are simply being the parents their children need them to be. Together, they are closing the circle that should be unbroken.

EPILOGUE

My Joy, My Grief, My Hope, My Love
Did All Within This Circle Move!

MY VENTURE INTO the world of adoption began the moment Andrew was conceived over thirty years ago. Our reunion in 1993 brought us full circle, back to the point of conception and eventual relinquishment, where our paths diverged. Since then we have embarked on another phase of our journey as we fill in the missing pieces of our lives and build bridges from our past to our present.

When I undertook to write this book, Andrew and I were just becoming acquainted. We had only discussed some of the bare facts of how I came to relinquish him and how each of us felt about what had happened. I had not yet met Katherine and Bill and had no certainty that we would ever develop any personal relationship. I now know that if we had not met, I would not have had a chance to hear from them directly how they came to adopt, how they experienced raising Andrew, and how they understood and grappled with his interest in knowing more about his birth family. Without knowing them, I could not completely appreciate in my heart the magnitude of their love for Andrew. In knowing them, I recognize them unequivocally as his parents.

In retrospect, I discern in myself a characteristically naïve optimism that allowed me to assume that I could write this book whether or not we would meet, and that whatever happened, I would faithfully incorporate the truth of our experience into the broader scheme of how families deal with adoption in their lives. I have come to realize, however, that without Andrew's and his parents' very important voices, this book would have fallen far short of my dream. The telling of our story with their participation has provided a point of entry into the heart of the adoption experience. It has also afforded us an exceptional opportunity to break through our own inhibitions and to engage in an honest dialogue that has become the foundation for our growing relationship.

Most recently, Andrew called me to offer his comments on the last chapters of the manuscript, and it struck me as I listened to him, how extraordinary it was that we were even having that conversation. Just a few years before, this would have been inconceivable. Now not only were we in touch, but Andrew was also offering me his very thoughtful and invaluable point of view about certain passages in my book. The very fact that we were absorbed in this process together brought home to me how far we had come and how my life has been touched by divine grace.

As I have moved beyond the experiences of my own family to explore adoption in a larger context, I have been deeply affected by the stories of the many people I have met in the process of writing this book. Each of our lives is filled with stories that shape our existence. In listening to one another's stories and in telling our own we enter into relationship with one another. Even when we are sharing stories of pain and loss, we are learning from one another, reaching for a common ground, a point of departure for something new to happen, perhaps even an epiphany of mutual love where fear dissipates and hearts open.

The stories people have shared with me have contributed to my understanding of how adoption continues to influence people's lives. I have learned from young birth parents how being able to choose the parents of their child and maintain some contact with the adoptive family has helped them feel better about their decision to relinquish, and how as a result they have a healthier self-image as they move forward in their lives. I have also learned from other birth parents like myself how search and reunion have helped heal the wounds incurred so many years ago. Adoptees have spoken of their fractured sense of self and underlying feeling of rootlessness that comes from not knowing their biological heritage. They have spoken, too, of their love for their adoptive parents and of how, for the most part, they have been happy in their adoptive homes. Search and reunion have helped them complete the picture of who they are. Adoptive parents have expressed their unconditional love for these children who come to them through adoption. Their accounts of their day-to-day lives reveal the joy they have of helping their children become the people they are meant to be. Despite their fears, these parents do their best to understand the extra charge they have to assist their children with their questions about adoption and their need to know more about their birth families.

Adoption practice has changed considerably since 1966 when I relinquished Andrew, and it continues to evolve. More and more agencies, independent attorneys, and adoption facilitators are offering the option of open adoption with full disclosure of identifying information and ongoing contact between birth and adoptive families. Once a woman and her partner make a properly considered decision to relinquish their baby, everything depends on the good faith agreement between them and the adoptive parents, and pre- and postadoption counseling can help them grow into their new "extended family" relationship. As the face of adoption changes, new questions are raised, and triad members are dealing with new layers of complexity in relationships that are more open, and therefore more complicated. With these changes comes a need for different approaches and new guidelines for adoption standards in policy and practice.

Parallel to this trend toward more open adoptions is a strong advocacy for unsealing records for adoptees in search of their birth families and for biological parents looking for their birth offspring. While the legislative debate rages, thousands of people are searching, finding, and living in reunion despite the closed records. With open adoption becoming more the norm, old laws are fast becoming obsolete.

The movement toward more openness has changed the way adoption is being practiced, but it has not significantly changed the number of healthy infants being placed for adoption in this country. For those unwilling to deal with the possibility of a birth mother changing her mind or a protracted wait for a perfect baby, there is the appealing option of international adoption. However, changing politics and the uncertain medical and emotional prognosis for some of these foreign-born children can make international adoption a risky business, and here, too, the number of available infants or young babies is limited.

There is no shortage, however, of young toddlers and older children, both domestic and international, waiting for adoption. As the emphasis shifts from finding babies for parents who want them to finding homes for children who need them, more attention must be given to outreach for families for these children with "special needs." As more children in foster care become freed for adoption, there will be a need for funding for health care and additional postadoption services to assist families who wish to adopt these children who may have suffered from neglect and abuse, or who may have been prenatally exposed to drugs or alcohol.

While paradigms are shifting in the world of adoption, new reproductive technologies are mushrooming. We have gone way beyond donor insemination and simple *in vitro* fertilization. The custom-made embryo makes it possible for people to choose both donor semen and egg and to preselect, as it were, the "pedigree" of their unborn child. Some ready-made embryos are also available and kept in stock, and further advances are expected. As reported recently in the *New York Times,* infertile foreigners whose countries have tougher restrictions on payment for egg donation or on the number of times a man can donate sperm are coming to America for these custom-made embryos. There is also a small but thriving mail-order business for frozen American sperm.

Most of the people using these advanced technologies plan to keep their infertility a secret from their families and from their children as well. Unlike parents of adopted children, they can more readily hide behind a pregnancy the fact that their child is not genetically related to at least one of its parents. They may express concern for unnecessarily confusing their children, but underlying that concern is a clear desire to be perceived as the sole parents, unencumbered by any link to the donors. Their fear of disclosure is reminiscent of the views of adoptive parents who were once told that it was not necessary for children to know they were adopted, or of prospective adoptive parents who have not been educated about the importance of disclosing the truth to their children.

We know, however, from the first generation of babies conceived through donor insemination that children inevitably do find out and do suffer the same sense of confusion about their identity. They long to learn more about their biological parent, as do adopted children who do not know their biological heritage. In adoption, there are more clear-cut ties to the birth family, especially for the birth mother, who has carried her baby to term and suffered the emotional trauma of relinquishment. The ties are obviously more tenuous emotionally for those who simply donate eggs or sperm, and children spawned from the union of these made-to-order embryos can be expected to have some difficulty understanding their connection to their genetic parents. We may not be able to change human nature and the natural desire people have to give birth to children, but as science advances, we would do well to heed the lessons learned from adoptive families. We would do well to remember to think about the children we are creating in this brave new world. Ironically, those of us involved with adoption can look to what is happening in reproductive science and take some measure of pride in how far we have come in understanding the issues of families that are not genetically related.

As we look toward the future of adoption, it is useful to take stock of where we are. In the summer of 1997, Princeton Survey Research Associates was commissioned by the Evan B. Donaldson Adoption Institute to conduct an in-depth survey on American public attitudes toward adoption and members of the adoption triad. Over 1,500 adults responded to a series of questions that asked them to indicate how they felt generally and specifically about various aspects of adoption. Surprisingly, it was learned that six in ten Americans have been touched in some way by adoption, either through direct personal experience or through friends and family. This number far exceeds the previous estimate of one in five and indicates a very broad experience with adoption in this country.

The great majority of those polled had a favorable view of adoption. However, the survey also showed that two-thirds of the people who indicated that they favored adoption do not unconditionally embrace it, and they break down further into groups of qualified and marginal supporters who have questions or doubts about its merits. Significantly, *only half consider adoption as good as having a biological child.* Overall, it seemed that less-educated Americans are more uncertain about adoption; men are less supportive; African-Americans are more skeptical than whites. Views of birth mothers and birth fathers also vary across educational, racial, and gender lines. Forty-two percent of Americans believe open adoption is seldom or never a good idea. Many expressed concern, as well, about the prospects for children adopted from other countries.

This survey is a solid first step in determining how adoption is viewed in America. Further studies can probe more deeply into the reasons behind people's attitudes. In the meantime, we can draw some conclusions about general public awareness and can better target campaigns for greater education and outreach. There is a continued need to inform people about the real experience of birth parents and adoptees, just as there is a need to convey that while choosing to adopt may be a second choice for most parents, raising adopted children is by no means second best. In addition, although open adoption is becoming more common, information about its benefits has not filtered through to the general public. With greater numbers of African-American children in need of homes, it appears from the survey as well as from adoption practice that more needs to be done to educate African-Americans to the value of formal adoption.

Public opinion and attitudes affect our perception of the world around us. The way we see things consequently affects our judgment and determines the choices we make. How society viewed single unwed women of my generation, for example, largely determined our "decision" to surrender our children. What people believe, however, is not always based on the most current or complete information. People are naturally afraid of what they do not know. The terms "open adoption" or "special needs" strike fear into the hearts of people who have little or no concept of what they really mean. The general public's views may also be based on inaccurate accounts of media-hyped stories that more often than not aggravate people's fears. As a result, prospective adoptive couples may have exaggerated fears of birth mothers reclaiming their children, or of foreign-born children's attachment problems. In the end, adopted children become the innocent victims of people's preconceived ideas of how things are or should be. Education is essential to improving public awareness of adoption and to fostering better understanding within the microcosm of the adoption community.

The misconceptions that exist in the general public also exist among triad members who have little contact with one another. Not only are we alienated from one another, but based on our own preconceived judgments, we have a tendency at times to vilify one another. We know from conflicts in the world at large that despite our differences—or our spiritual or ethical persuasion—there is a universal need for understanding, forgiveness, and reconciliation. Without it, the health and well-being of our families and community are compromised.

Recently, I have had the honor of becoming the first birth mother to be invited onto the board of directors of Spence-Chapin. It was exceptional for me that this agency where I had surrendered my baby would welcome me onto their board. In some ways I felt like the prodigal child come home. Like other adoption agencies, most board members are adoptive parents, and I have been keenly aware of my pioneering role. No doubt my fellow trustees have also had some private moments of discomfort about this alien in their midst. As time goes by, however, any strangeness has dissipated as we reach across boundaries and get to know one another. I feel secure in my sense of place and am confident in our mutual desire to help the agency develop its programs for all members of the triad.

Learning from one another helps dispel our fears. It brings us into community with one another and heals our wounds. In naming our truth, pain is transformed into the grace of understanding. Andrew and his parents have been my greatest teachers. The more I open myself to their feelings, the more my love for them deepens. Those of us involved in open adoption or reunion have an ongoing opportunity for forgiveness and reconciliation, but any of us can create a space for dialogue. Opening our hearts and minds allows us to break out of our traditional roles to close the circle of love that unites us.

BIBLIOGRAPHY

Books

Anderson, Carole J. *Thoughts to Consider for Newly Searching Adoptees*. Des Moines, Iowa: Concerned United Birthparents, Inc., 1996.

Arms, Suzanne. *Adoption: A Handful of Hope*. Berkeley, California: Celestial Arts, 1990.

Bartholet, Elizabeth. *Family Bonds: Adoption & the Politics of Parenting*. Boston: Houghton Mifflin Company, 1993.

Benson, Peter L., Ph.D., Sharma, Anu R., Ph.D., L.P., and Roehlkepartian, Eugene C. *Growing up Adopted: A Portrait of Adolescents & Their Parents*. Minneapolis: Search Institute, 1994.

Bloom, Suzanne. *A Family for Jamie: An Adoption Story*. New York: Clarkson N. Potter, Inc., 1991.

Bothun, Linda. *When Friends Ask about Adoption: Questions and Answer Guide for Non-Adoptive Parents and Other Caring Adults*. Chevy Chase, Maryland: Swan Publications, 1996.

Brodzinsky, Anne Braff. *The Mulberry Bird: Story of an Adoption*. Indianapolis, Indiana: Perspective Press, 1986.

Brodzinsky, David M., Ph.D., Schechter, Marshall D., M.D., and Robin Marantz Henig. *Being Adopted: The Lifelong Search for Self*. New York: Anchor Books, 1993.

Center for the Future of Children. *The Future of Children*, vol. 3, no. 1. Los Altos, California: The David and Lucile Packard Foundation, 1993.

Cohen, Mary Anne Manning. *Exile, A Journey: Poems about Losing a Child to Adoption*. Whippany, New Jersey: Self-Published, 1992.

Fisher, Florence. *The Search for Anna Fisher*. New York: Fawcett Crest Books, 1986.

Fowler, Deborah. *Loving Other People's Children*. London: Hodder & Stoughton, 1992.

Gediman, Judith S., and Brown, Linda P. *BirthBond: Reunion Between Birthparents & Adoptees—What Happens After*. Far Hills, New Jersey: New Horizon Press, 1991.

Green, Tim. *A Man and His Mother*. New York: Regan Books, 1997.

Gritter, James L., M.S.W. *The Spirit of Open Adoption*. Washington, D.C.: CWLA Press, 1997.

———, ed. *Adoption without Fear: Seventeen Couples Tell Their Emotion-Filled Experiences with Open Adoption*. San Antonio, Texas: Corona Publishing Company, 1989.

Howells, Dion, with Pritchard, Karen Wilson. *The Story of David: How We Created a Family through Open Adoption*. New York: Delacorte Press, 1997.

Johnston, Patricia Irwin. *Perspectives on a Grafted Tree: Thoughts for Those Touched by Adoption*. Indianapolis, Indiana: Perspectives Press, 1983.

Jones, Merry Bloch. *Birthmothers: Women Who Have Relinquished Babies for Adoption Tell Their Stories*. Chicago: Chicago Review Press, 1993.

Kirk, H. David. *Looking Back, Looking Forward: An Adoptive Father's Sociological Testament*. Indianapolis, Indiana: Perspectives Press, 1995.

Koh, Frances M. *Adopted from Asia: How It Feels to Grow up in America*. Minneapolis, Minnesota: EastWest Press, 1993.

Krementz, Jill. *How It Feels to Be Adopted*. New York: Alfred A. Knopf, 1994.

Lanier, Alicia, ed. *Hope: A Collection of Birthfamily Stories—Poems & Letters*. Dallas, Texas: Self-Published, 1993.

Lifton, Betty Jean. *Twice Born: Memoirs of an Adopted Daughter*. New York: St. Martin's Griffin, 1998.

———. *Lost and Found: The Adoption Experience*. New York: Perennial Library, HarperCollins, 1988.

———. *Journey of the Adopted Self: A Quest for Wholeness*. New York: Basic Books, 1994.

Lindsay, Jeanne Warren. *Open Adoption: A Caring Option*. Buena Park, California: Morning Glory Press, 1988.

Lindsay, Jeanne Warren, and Monserrat, Catherine. *Adoption Awareness: A Guide for Teachers, Counselors, Nurses and Caring Others*. Buena Park, California: Morning Glory Press, 1989.

Mason, Mary Martin. *Out of the Shadows: Birthfathers' Stories*. Edina, Minnesota: O.J. Howard Publishing, 1995.

Melina, Lois Ruskai. *Making Sense of Adoption*. New York: HarperPerennial, 1989.

———. *Raising Adopted Children: A Manual for Adoptive Parents*. New York: HarperPerennial, 1986.

Melina, Lois Ruskai, and Roszia, Sharon Kaplan. *The Open Adoption Experience*. New York: HarperPerennial, 1993.

Michelman, Stanley B., and Schneider, Meg, with Van Der Meer, Antonia. *The Private Adoption Handbook: The Complete Step-by-Step Guide to Independently Adopting a Baby*. New York: A Dell Trade Paperback, 1988.

Moorman, Margaret. *Waiting to Forget: A Mother Opens the Door to Her Secret Past*. New York: W.W. Norton & Company, 1996.

Partridge, Penny Callan. *Pandora's Hope: Poems and Prose about Being Adopted*. Amherst, Massachusetts: Self-Published, 1997.

————. *An Adoptee's Dreams*. Baltimore, Maryland: Gateway Press, Inc., 1995.

Paton, Jean M. *Orphan Voyage*. New York: Vintage, 1968.

Russell, Marlou, Ph.D. *Adoption Wisdom: A Guide to the Issues and Feelings of Adoption*. Santa Monica, California: Broken Branch Productions, 1996.

Schaefer, Carol. *The Other Mother: A Woman's Love for the Child She Gave up for Adoption*. New York: Soho Press, Inc., 1991.

Schooler, Jayne. *Searching for a Past: The Adopted Adult's Unique Process of Finding Identity*. Colorado Springs, Colorado: Pinon Press, 1995.

Severson, Randolph W., Ph.D. *Adoption: Philosophy and Experience*. Dallas, Texas: House of Tomorrow Publications, 1994.

————. *Dear Birthfather,*. Dallas, Texas: House of Tomorrow Productions, 1992.

————. *A Letter to Adoptive Parents on Open Adoption*. Dallas, Texas: Heart Words Center, 1991.

Silber, Kathleen, and Speedlin, Phylis. *Dear Birthmother: Thank You for Our Baby*. San Antonio, Texas: Corona Publishing Company, 1991.

Simon, Rita J., Alstein, Howard, and Melli, Marygold S. *The Case for Transracial Adoption*. Washington, D.C.: The American University Press, 1994.

Solinger, Rickie. *Wake up Little Susie: Single Pregnancy and Race Before Roe v. Wade*. New York: Routledge, 1992.

Sorosky, Arthur D., M.D., Baran, Annette, M.S.W., and Pannor, Reuben, M.S.W. *The Adoption Triangle: Sealed or Opened Records: How They Affect Adoptees, Birth Parents and Adoptive Parents*. San Antonio, Texas: Corona Publishing Company, 1989.

Stiffler, LaVonne Harper. *Synchronicity & Reunion: The Genetic Connection of Adoptees & Birthparents*. Hobe Sound, Florida: FEA Publishing, 1992.

Strauss, Jean A. S. *Birthright: The Guide to Search and Reunion for Adoptee, Birthparents, and Adoptive Parents*. New York: Penguin Books, 1994.

Verrier, Nancy Newton. *The Primal Wound: Understanding the Adopted Child*. Baltimore, Maryland: Gateway Press, Inc., 1996.

Waldron, Jan L. *Giving Away Simone*. New York: Times Books, 1995.

Walker, Alice. *Anything We Love Can Be Saved*. New York: Random House, 1997.

Watkins, Mary, and Fisher, Susan. *Talking with Young Children about Adoption*. New Haven: Yale University Press, 1993.

Wolff, Jana. *Secret Thoughts of an Adoptive Mother*. Kansas City, Missouri: Andrews and McMeel, 1997.

Papers, Articles, Conferences & Essays

Axness, Marcy Wineman. "Many Hands: An Adoptee's Healing Journey." *Jewel Among Jewels: Adoption News*. Summer, 1997.

————. "Everything Old Is New Again." *Origins*. Spring, 1997.

————. "Second Rejection: The Pain *After* Reunion." *CUB Communicator*. September, 1995.

————. "Ownership Needs—Children's Needs." *Roots & Wings*. Vol. 7, no. 2, Fall, 1995.

————. "A Mother's Call to Healing." *Whole Life Times*. July, 1995.

————. "Painful Lessons." *Roots & Wings*. July/August/September, 1994.

————. "A Post-Reunion Journey." *AdoptNet*. Fall, 1993.

———. "In Defense of the Primal Wound." *Adopt: Assistance Information Support.* 1993 (email: axness@MCI2000.com for transcript)

Babb, L. Anne, Ph.D. "Adoptees in Search in the United States." *The Decree*, the publication of the American Adoption Congress. 1996.

———. "Victory in Tennessee!: Judge Upholds Adoption Reform Law—Plaintiffs File Appeal." *Decree*. Vol. 13, no. 3, Fall, 1996.

Berry, Karin D. "Adoption, Race & Red Tape." *Emerge*. April, 1995.

Bredes, Amy. "Preparation before Contact." *Pacer Newsletter: Post Adoption Center for Education and Research*. Winter, 1996.

Brosnan, Rev. Thomas F. "Spiritual Transformation" (syllabus description). From the Sixth Biennial Conference on Open Adoption in Traverse City, Michigan. May, 1997.

Casey, Kathryn. "The Case of Baby L." *Ladies' Home Journal*. August, 1995.

Coffey, Rebecca. "From Home to Classroom." *Creative Classroom*. January/February, 1996.

Cohen, Mary Anne Manning, and Lifton, Betty Jean. Workshop entitled "What Adoptees and Birth Mothers Wish They Could Tell Each Other," presented to the American Adoption Congress, 1997.

Colberg, Michael. Workshop entitled "Open Adoption: What Is It and What It Is Not?," presented to the American Adoption Congress, 1997.

Compiled from the Associated Press and Gannett and Knight-Ridder news service. "Adoption Agency to Protest Film." *Times-Union* (Rochester, New York). October 26, 1995.

Craig, Conna. "What I Need Is a Mom." *Policy Review*. Summer, 1995.

Davis, Dee, and Roszia, Sharon Kaplan. Workshop entitled "Search and Reunion: The Emotional Unfolding," presented to the American Adoption Congress, 1997.

Dawson, Connie, Ph.D., LPC. "So 'Deal with It.'" *Jewel Among Jewels: Adoption News*. Fall, 1996.

———. "Are Relinquishment and Adoption Really Different?" *Jewel Among Jewels: Adoption News*. Spring, 1996.

DelVecchio, Rick. "Better Times for Adoption Searches." *San Francisco Chronicle*. November 17, 1996.

Demuth, Carol. Workshop entitled "Courageous Blessing: Adoptive Parents and Search," presented to the American Adoption Congress, 1997.

Eldridge, Sherrie. "The Invisible Race." *Jewel Among Jewels: Adoption News*. Spring, 1996.

Elsasser, Michael. "For Daddy and Poppy, A 'Fantastic' Decision," *Newsday*. November 3, 1995.

Escalante, Shelley. "'Bastards' Unite." *Saint Louis Obispo "New Times" Magazine*. March 27, 1997.

Frank, Elaine, M.S.W. (edited by Gloria Hochman). "Adoption and the Stages of Development." *National Adoption Information Clearinghouse*. 1990.

Garfinkel, Renee, Ph.D. "The Family Myth." *The Philadelphia Inquirer*. August 20, 1995.

Golombok, Susan, and Tasker, Fiona. "Do Parents Influence the Sexual Orientation of Their Children? Findings from a Longitudinal Study of Lesbian Families," *Developmental Psychology*. Vol. 32, no. 1, 1996.

Greenman, Frederick F. "A-742 and S-287: Access-to-Birth-Certificate-Bills." *To the Members of the New Jersey Legislature.* February 20, 1997.

Grimm, Shea. "Why Contact Vetoes Are Not an Acceptable Compromise." *Bastard Quarterly.* Vol. 1, issue 1, Spring, 1997.

Gritter, Jim. "Honoring the Pain." *Jewel Among Jewels: Adoption News.* Spring, 1997.

Gundersen, Edna. "Joni Mitchell Meets Long-Lost Daughter." *USA Today.* Friday, April 4, 1997.

Hochman, Gloria, and Huston, Anna. "Open Adoption." *National Adoption Information Clearinghouse.* September, 1994.

Hsu, Grace. "Why Do So Few Unmarried Women Make Adoption Plans?" *From Internet.* January 31, 1996.

Ingram, Laura. "Reg Day a Big Success in Bay Area." *Pacer Newsletter.* Winter, 1996.

Kadetsky, Elizabeth. "Mother and Child Reunions." *Self.* December, 1996.

Kaufmann, Carol. "Is Adoption the Answer to Abortion?" *George.* April, 1997.

Lavan, Rosemary Metzler. "Parenthood's Price." *Daily News.* April 21, 1996.

Lifton, Betty Jean. From a lecture entitled "Further Travels in the Ghost Kingdom," presented to the American Adoption Congress, 1997.

———. Workshop entitled "On the Journey: The Adoptee's Quest," presented to the American Adoption Congress, 1996.

Mason, Mary Martin. "Bringing Birthfathers into the Adoption Loop." *Roots & Wings.* October/November/December, 1995.

McMorrow, Margaret, and Hughes, Ann. Workshop entitled "Rocky Road or Smooth Sailing: Paths to Healing in Reunion," presented to the American Adoption Congress, 1996.

Melina, Lois R. "Adoptees Look to Birth Fathers for Identity, Claiming, and Responsibility for Decisions." *Adopted Child.* Vol. 16, no. 6, June, 1997.

———. "A Look at Open Adoption for Prospective Adopting Parents." *Open Adoption: National Federation for Open Adoption Education.* Vol. 1, no. 4, Summer, 1996.

———. "Talking with Children about Adoption." *OURS.* March/April, 1991.

———. "Teachers Need to Be More Sensitive to Adoption Issues." *Adopted Child.* Vol. 9, no. 8, August, 1990.

———. "New Studies Show Support for Open Records." *Adopted Child.* Vol. 5, no. 8, August, 1986.

———, ed. "The Best of 'Adopted Child': Research on Adoption Issues." Lois Melina, Publisher. 1997.

Moore, Kristin A., Ph.D. "Nonmarital Childbearing in the United States." *Report to Congress on Out-of-Wedlock Childbearing.* Department of Health and Human Services, September, 1995.

Napoli, Lisa. "International Adoption Network: Families Forged, Families Reunited." *The New York Times.* July 21, 1996.

Nast, Jane. "End the Secrecy and Lies." *USA Today.* Friday, April 14, 1997.

Norris, Betsie. "History and a Future in the Making: Tennessee." *Decree.* Vol. 13, no. 4, Winter, 1996.

Pavao, Joyce Maguire, Ed.D., LCSW, LMFT. Workshop entitled "Adoption and the Sense of Self," presented to the American Adoption Congress, 1997.

——. "Thoughts of Adoption by an Adoptee by the Sea . . ." *Decree*. Summer, 1997.

Pear, Robert. "House Passes Bill to Encourage Adoption of Abused Children." *New York Times*. May 1, 1997.

Plum, Damsel. "From Primal Wallow to Purposeful Work: Do Your P.I.E.C.E." *Bastard Quarterly*. Vol. 1, issue 1, Spring 1997.

Potok, Mark. "Adoption Groups Building Families Via the Internet." *USA Today*. March 18, 1996.

Romanchik, Brenda. "Involving Birthfathers in Open Adoptions." *Open Adoption: Birthparent*. Issue 8, Spring, 1996.

——. "Talking to Others about Adoption." *Open Adoption: Birthparent*. Winter, 1995.

——. "Your Role as a Birthparent." *Open Adoption: Birthparent*. Summer, 1994.

Roszia, Sharon Kaplan. "Siblings Transformed by Open Adoption" (syllabus description). From the Sixth Biennial Conference on Open Adoption in Traverse City, Michigan. May, 1997.

Roszia, Sharon Kaplan, and Deborah Silverstein. Workshop entitled "The Seven Core Issues of Adoptees," presented to the American Adoption Congress, 1988.

Rubin, Jody Melissa. "College Essay." Appeared on America Online on March 21, 1997. Copyright 1995 by Jody Melissa Rubin.

Saunders, Bayard. "Birthfathers Come of Age." *Open Adoption: Birthparent*. Issue 8, Spring, 1996.

Sebraski, John. Workshop on issues surrounding being adopted, presented at the 22nd NACAC conference. Training tape no. 51.

Severson, Randolph W., Ph.D. "An Open Letter to Adoption Funding Sources." *Origins*. Winter, 1996.

Smith, Debra G., ACSW. "Searching for Birth Relatives." *National Adoption Information Clearinghouse*. 1995.

——. "The Impact of Adoption on Birth Parents." *National Adoption Information Clearinghouse*. 1995.

——. "Answers to Children's Questions about Adoption." *National Adoption Information Clearinghouse*. 1994.

——. "Adoption and School Issues." *National Adoption Information Clearinghouse*. 1993.

Sonne, John C., M.D. "An Open Letter to the Pro-Life Community." *Decree*. Vol. 13, no. 3, Fall, 1996.

Stiffler, LaVonne H. "Adoption's Impact on Birthmothers: 'Can a Mother Forget Her Child?'" *Journal of Psychology and Christianity*. Vol. 10, no. 3, 1991.

Swarns, Rachel L. "Backlog Slows City Payments for Adoptees." *New York Times*. September 25, 1997.

"To a New Home: Twenty Years Later, Vietnam's Babylift Orphans Come of Age." *People*. May 1, 1995.

Wasserman, Joanne. "Should Families Be Color-Blind?" *Daily News*. June 23, 1996.

Watson, Ken, Ph.D. "What Adoption Is and What It Isn't." *Decree*. Vol. 14, no. 2, Summer, 1997.

Wolfe, Marjorie. "The Truth About Birthmothers." *Parentguide*. January, 1996.

"Woody's Biggest Gamble." *London Daily Telegraph*. October, 1995.

ORGANIZATIONS AND RESOURCES

Adopted Child Newsletter
P.O. Box 9362
Moscow, Idaho 83843
208-882-1794
208-883-8035
http://www.moscow.com/resources/
adoption/adoption.html

**Adoptees' Liberty Movement
Association (ALMA)**
P.O. Box 727
Radio City Station
New York, New York 10101-0727
212-581-1568

Adoption Network Cleveland
291 East 222 Street, Room 229
Euclid, Ohio 44123
216-261-1511
216-261-1164

Adoptive Families of America
(advocacy organization for adoptive
families; also publishes monthly
magazine)
2309 Como Avenue
St. Paul, Minnesota 55108
800-372-3300
612-645-0055

American Adoption Congress (AAC)
1000 Connecticut Avenue, NW
Suite 9
Washington, DC 20036
800-274-OPEN
202-483-3399
http://pages.prodigy.com//adoptreform/
aacorg.htm

Bastard Nation
12865 NE 85th Street
Suite 179
Kirkland, Washington 98033
Phone: 206-883-7293
Fax: 415-680-2420
Website: http://www.bastards.org/
E-mail: sheag@oz.net

Center for Family Connections
350 Cambridge Street
Cambridge, Massachusetts 02141
617-547-0909
617-497-5952
E-mail: kinnect@aol.com

Concerned United Birthparents (CUB)
2000 Walker Street
Des Moines, Iowa 50317
515-263-9538

**Council on Equal Rights in Adoption
(CERA)**
401 East 74th Street, Suite 17D
New York, New York 10021
212-988-0110

**The Evan B. Donaldson Adoption
Institute**
120 Wall Street. 20th floor
New York, New York 10005
212-269-5080
E-mail: geninfo@adoptioninstitute.org
http://www.adoptioninstitute.org

International Soundex Reunion Registry (ISRR)
(Soundex)
P.O. Box 2312
Carson City, Nevada 89701-2312
(Include self-addressed stamped envelope)
702-882-7755

Kinship Center
(agency referrals and counseling services)
30 Ragsdale Drive, Suite 210
Monterey, California 93940
408-649-3033
http://www.adopting.org/kinship center.org

National Adoption Information Clearinghouse (NAIC)
P.O. Box 1182
Washington, D.C. 20013-1182
Phone: 703-352-3488
Fax: 703-385-3206
E-mail: naic@calib.com
Internet: http://www.calib.com/naic

National Organization for Birthfathers and Adoption Reform (NOBAR)
Contact: Jon Ryan
P.O. Box 50
Punta Gorda, Florida 33951
941-637-7477

The North American Council on Adoptable Children
(provides information for families with children with special needs)
970 Raymond Avenue, Suite 106
St. Paul, Minnesota 55114-1149
Phone: 612-644-3036
Fax: 612-644-9848
E-mail: nacac@aol.com

Orphan Voyage
2141 Road 2300
Cedaredge, Colorado 81413
303-856-3937

R-Squared Press
contact: Brenda Romanchik
Open Adoption Birthparent Newsletter
721 Hawthorne Avenue
Royal Oak, Michigan 48067
Phone/Fax: 248-543-0997
E-mail: brenr@oeonline.com

Spence-Chapin Services to Families and Children
6 East 94th Street
New York, New York 10128
212-369-0300
212-722-0675
http://www.spence-chapin.org

Tapestry Books
(catalogue)
P.O. Box 359
Ringoes, New Jersey 08551-0359
800-765-2367

U.S. Government Agencies
Immigration and Naturalization Service (INS)
U.S. Department of Justice
425 I Street NW
Washington, D.C. 30536
202-514-2000

The National Archives
Washington, D.C. 20408
202-501-5402

Social Security Administration
6401 Security Boulevard
Baltimore, Maryland 21235
410-965-8882

INDEX

PERMISSIONS LIST

Grateful acknowledgment is made to the following for permission to reprint previously published material: